T0296017

Marxian Economics

Marxian Economics

An Introduction

David F. Ruccio

polity

First published in 2022 by Polity Press

Polity Press
65 Bridge Street
Cambridge CB2 1UR, UK

Polity Press
101 Station Landing
Suite 300
Medford, MA 02155, USA

ISBN-13: 978-1-5095-4797-5
ISBN-13: 978-1-5095-4798-2 (pb)

A catalogue record for this book is available from the British Library.

Library of Congress Control Number: 2021953230

Typeset in 11 on 13pt Swift
by Fakenham Prepress Solutions, Fakenham, Norfolk NR21 8NL
Printed and bound in Great Britain by CPI Group (UK) Ltd, Croydon

For further information on Polity, visit our website:
politybooks.com

Contents

Figures

About the Author

David F. Ruccio is Professor of Economics Emeritus at the University of Notre Dame, where he won college and university teaching awards. As a student, he studied economics at Bowdoin College (including a year at the Universidad Nacional del Centro, in Peru), and the University of Massachusetts Amherst. As a teacher, he taught many courses at both the undergraduate and graduate levels, including Introduction to Microeconomics, Economics for Noneconomists, Mathematics for Economists, Commodities: The Making of Market Society, and Marxian Economic Theory. He also spends his winters volunteering for Vermont Adaptive, teaching downhill skiing to people with various physical, cognitive, behavioral, and developmental disabilities.

Professor Ruccio is a prolific writer and a regular participant in academic and policy debates. His work has been published in scholarly journals, such as *World Development* and the *Cambridge Journal of Economics*, and in more popular forums, especially on his blog, *Occasional Links & Commentary on Economics, Culture, and Society*. He has published six books, the most recent of which is *Development and Globalization: A Marxian Class Analysis*.

In addition to teaching, research, and writing, Professor Ruccio has been a frequent speaker in interdisciplinary programs and conferences around the world and has been interviewed by a wide range of national and international media. He was one of the cofounders of the journal *Rethinking Marxism*, served as its editor for 12 years (from 1997 to 2009), and continues as a member of the international advisory board.

Preface

During my time as both a student and a professor, the course that excited me most was Marxian economics. In college, I had the opportunity to coteach a course on Marx's *Capital* with one of my professors, David Vail. Later, in graduate school, at the University of Massachusetts Amherst, I had the pleasure of learning about new developments in Marxian theory from two of the greatest Marxian economists of the twentieth century: Stephen Resnick and Richard Wolff. And then, during almost four decades of teaching my own courses at the University of Notre Dame, I was challenged to prepare engaging lectures and to answer the questions students had about the basic concepts and contemporary relevance of Marxian economics.

It is no exaggeration to say that, at each stage, Marxian economics changed my life. I grew up in a time when politics and economics were often discussed – at the dinner table, among my North American friends, and during my time in Latin America (as an exchange student in Brazil). But I often found myself expressing doubts about whether the common sense at the time was actually sensible. The Vietnam War, poverty and civil rights in the United States, underdevelopment in Latin America, the despoiling of the natural environment around the world – what were the causes and how might we think about alternatives? The Marxian approach to economics helped me to make sense of these events, because it broke the logjam created by mainstream economics and opened up a whole range of other analyses and possible solutions. It encouraged me to ask new questions about history, class, capitalism, and much else.

Over time, Marxian economics became even more interesting for me. I went from reading articles and books *about* Marxian economic theory to actually studying the original texts. I learned about the rich Marxian tradition as well as new interpretations of Marxian economic and social theory. I engaged in scholarly debates about Marxism and discussed many of the finer points with colleagues and friends. And, since I taught both mainstream economics and Marxian economics for almost four decades, I developed a better sense of how different they truly are – in everything, from abstract theory through empirical analysis to concrete policies.

Perhaps most importantly, I accumulated a wealth of knowledge not only about the questions mainstream economists couldn't answer, but also the untold damage mainstream economic theory and capitalism, the economic and social system celebrated by mainstream economists, have wrought in the world. Marxian economics was one of the nonmainstream or heterodox approaches I was able to turn to.

As I explain in more detail during the course of this book, Marxian theory plays a fascinating role in economics. Not only does it provide an alternative way of thinking about and doing economics; in a more general sense, Marxian economics demonstrates that mainstream economics is not the way capitalism works but only one story about what is going on in the world. And there are many other stories, including the one pioneered by Karl Marx (along with his good friend and frequent coauthor Friedrich Engels) and further elaborated and enriched by generations of Marxian economists.

Since Marxian economics represents a critique of and an alternative to mainstream economics, much of the book is set up as a dialogue between the two radically different approaches to economics – their dissimilar theories of capitalism, their contrasting ethical presumptions and promises, and their divergent consequences for the economy and wider society.

As it was passed on to me by my professors, and as I have explained to generations of my own students, the exciting thing about studying Marxian economics in this manner is readers get a "twofer": you will learn Marxian economics *and* mainstream economics at the same time. Then, in the best tradition of education, your world will have become more, not less, complicated. That's because, after reading this book, you'll have to figure out which of the approaches you want to use to make sense of your lives and the larger world we live in.

Acknowledgments

Marxian Economics: An Introduction presents an approach to teaching economics, including the Marxian critique of political economy, that I developed during almost four decades at the University of Notre Dame. To the thousands of students, both undergraduate and graduate, whose suggestions, criticisms, and challenging questions have guided me, I owe special thanks.

I am indebted to Dwight Billings, who read every word of the first draft, and then offered a series of helpful comments and suggestions – along with a great deal of much-appreciated encouragement during the long process of imagining and writing this book. I also want to thank Jack Amariglio, Antonio Callari, and Peter Schneider for their generous advice on specific sections and chapters. Finally, since the first three chapters initially took form as public posts on my blog, I want to express my gratitude to the following (many of them known to me only by their screen names): antireifer, Magpie, Jose, Lucas, mjlovas, Ikonoclast, Robert Locke, Ken Zimmerman, James Webber, Jonathan Hoskins, Greg Hannsgen, and Tom Hickey.

I am grateful to Polity Press's George Owers for his initial invitation to write this book, Julia Davies for her prompt responses to my many queries, and to the many other workers involved in the processing, production, and marketing of the manuscript. The anonymous reviewers of both the book proposal and the draft manuscript offered reassuring words, pointed concerns, and useful advice.

Last but not least, Lisa Markowitz was there for me every step of the way, with love, support, and understanding, even as working on the book got in the way of more pleasurable ways of spending our time together.

Glossary

This is a list of concepts that are specific to Marxian economics, along with brief definitions as the concepts are used in this book. (Other technical or unfamiliar concepts used in this book are defined either in the text or in footnotes.)

ABSOLUTE SURPLUS-VALUE. An increase in the rate of exploitation by increasing the length of the workday, while keeping the portion representing necessary labor constant. It is based on the formal subsumption of labor, that is, the expropriation of the direct producers outside of production.

ABSTRACT. The starting point for analysis, to which new determinations are added, leading to a concrete outcome or conclusion. The movement from (relatively) abstract to (relatively) concrete takes place entirely within the realm of theory.

ABSTRACT LABOR. Human labor viewed as a homogeneous mass of labor, by analytically separating it from the concrete characteristics of the labor performed. This is accomplished, economically, when different kinds of labor are made commensurable through the exchange of commodities.

ACCUMULATION OF CAPITAL. The use of a portion of surplus-value to purchase additional means of production and raw materials (using constant capital) and labor power (using variable capital), resulting in expanded reproduction.

ALIENATION. The process, specific to capitalism, whereby the products of human labor are separated from the direct producers and represent an alien force, standing against them and used to reproduce capitalist exploitation.

ANARCHY OF PRODUCTION. The result of the social division of labor, private property, and markets, in which the outcomes are often volatile and chaotic.

CAPITAL. An economic and social relationship whereby capitalists are able to deploy money to obtain more money, by appropriating the surplus-value created by workers. It is not, as in mainstream economics, a thing that is considered productive and is rewarded with profits.

CAPITALISM. An economic and social system defined by private property and markets (as it is in mainstream economics) and, in addition, the appropriation and distribution of surplus labor in the form of surplus-value (which is missing from mainstream economics).

CAPITALISTS. A group of class positions defined by deploying money as capital to capture more money. They include "industrial capitalists," "monopoly capitalists," "financial capitalists," and "merchant capitalists."

CLASS. The process whereby surplus labor is produced, appropriated, distributed, and received.

CLASS STRUGGLE. An attempt to change the quantitative and/or qualitative dimensions of a class process.

COMMODITY. A product of human labor that is bought and sold on a market. It is characterized by a use-value, exchange-value, and value. Commodities can be produced through a variety of class processes. Thus, there are capitalist commodities, communist commodities, feudal commodities, slave commodities, and so on.

COMMODITY FETISHISM. The subject or identity of those who engage in commodity exchange, which is the result of historical and social forces. It is opposed to *homo economicus*, the view on the part of mainstream economists that commodity exchange corresponds to an essential and universal (transhistorical and transcultural) human nature.

COMMUNISM. An economic and social system in which exploitation has been eliminated and the "commune," constituted by or representing the direct producers, appropriates and distributes surplus labor.

COMPETITION. A particular social interaction among capitalist enterprises to capture extra surplus-value, which involves an increase in productivity and results in a decrease in commodity values and exchange-values and a tendency for the rate of profit to fall.

CONCRETE. The outcome of an analysis, in which the knowledge produced includes more determinations than in the initial, abstract starting point. The movement from (relatively) abstract to (relatively) concrete takes place entirely within the realm of theory.

CONCRETE LABOR. Human labor when analyzed in terms of its concrete characteristics, as the source of different use-values (e.g., the concrete labor of teachers and carpenters is the source of education and chairs).

CONJUNCTURE. The central concept of Marxian analyses of capitalist crises and other economic and social events, which denotes the contradictory forces at play at a moment in time.

CONSTANT CAPITAL. The value of the raw materials and means of production that, combined with labor power, are used to produce capitalist commodities.

CONTRADICTION. A term for how movement and change emerge from the way different economic and social forces constitute, through distinct pushes and pulls, any process or event.

CRISIS. The ever-present possibility that capitalist commodity exchange is disrupted, thereby leading to changes within that system or the transition to another system. A common distinction is between a crisis *in* capitalism (when disruptions are resolved through capitalist solutions) and a crisis *of* capitalism (when the entire system is called into question).

CRITIQUE. Marx's project, first announced in his letter to Arnold Ruge (1843), which calls for a "*ruthless criticism* of all that exists, ruthless both in the sense of not being afraid of the results it arrives at and in the sense of being just as little afraid of conflict with the powers that be."

CRITIQUE OF POLITICAL ECONOMY. The Marxian critique of mainstream economic theory and of capitalism, the economic and social system celebrated by mainstream economists.

DEVELOPMENT. Changes in the class structure of society. It is not, as in mainstream economics, the smaller or larger sum total of commodities exchanged in the form of gross domestic product.

ENTRY POINT. A starting point for economic and social analysis. Class is used as one of the analytical entry points, but is not considered to be the causal determinant of everything else, in Marxian economics.

ETHICS. The premise and promise, within either an economic system or an economic theory, of justice. The ethics of mainstream economics is "just deserts," that everyone gets what they deserve under capitalism; the ethics of Marxian economics calls for the elimination of capitalist exploitation.

EXCHANGE-VALUE. The amount of socially necessary abstract labor for which a commodity exchanges in a market.

EXPLOITATION. The appropriation of surplus labor by one class from another. Capitalist exploitation is the appropriation of surplus labor in the form of surplus-value by capitalists from workers. The rate of capitalist exploitation is the ratio of surplus-value to variable capital.

FEUDALISM. An economic and social system defined by the appropriation and distribution of surplus labor in the form of rent (in kind, labor, or money) by feudal lords from serfs.

FINANCE CAPITAL. The group of capitalists who lend money to industrial capitalists and receive a distribution of surplus-value in the form of interest payments.

FORMAL SUBSUMPTION OF LABOR. Defined in contrast to the real subsumption of labor. Formal subsumption occurs when capitalists take over the labor and production processes, after the expropriation of the direct producers outside production, without changing technology. It is therefore a condition, not a consequence, of the Industrial Revolution.

HEGEMONY. A concept developed by Italian Marxist Antonio Gramsci, through which he analyzes the foundation of a ruling-class (such as the capitalist class) as being created through both force and consent.

INDUSTRIAL CAPITALISTS. Capitalists who engage in exploitation, by extracting labor from labor power and appropriating surplus labor in the form of surplus-value. Capitalists use money to purchase commodities, to produce new commodities that contain surplus-value, and to sell those commodities to realize profits.

LABOR. The work that is performed to produce commodities. The extraction of labor from labor power is the key to capitalist exploitation.

LABOR POWER. The ability to expend mental and manual energy to produce commodities, which itself takes the form of a commodity within capitalism. Capitalists purchase labor power in the realm of exchange, and then extract labor from labor power during the course of production. The owners of labor power exchange their ability to work for a wage and then purchase commodities to reproduce their social existence as laborers.

MARKET. The economic and social institution whereby the products of human labor take the form of commodities.

MARKET-PRICE. The price of a commodity as determined by fluctuations of supply and demand, which may be above, below, or equal to the commodity's exchange-value.

MEANS OF PRODUCTION. The buildings and machinery that, combined with raw materials and labor power, make capitalist production possible.

MERCHANT CAPITAL. Capitalists who purchase commodities from industrial capitalists at less than their value, sell those commodities at their value, and receive a distribution of surplus-value in the form of discounts.

MONEY. The universal equivalent, which can be used in exchange for any and all commodities in a system of generalized commodity exchange. It is the only commodity whose use-value is equal to its value. It serves as unit of account, means of payment, store of value, and debt. The use of money serves to both expand and disrupt capitalist commodity exchange.

MONEY-PRICE. The exchange-value of a commodity when converted into its price via the value of money.

MONOPOLY CAPITAL. Capitalists who, in addition to being "industrial capitalists," exercise market power and receive a distribution of the surplus-value appropriated by other "industrial capitalists" in the form of rents.

NECESSARY LABOR. The amount of labor necessary to reproduce the social existence of the direct producers. In capitalism, necessary labor is equal to the value of labor power.

PLANNING. The administration of the production and circulation of the products of human labor outside of markets. Capitalist planning (within corporations and countries, especially during wars) can be distinguished from socialist planning (which socialist and communist governments have attempted to use alongside or in place of markets).

PRICE OF PRODUCTION. The form exchange-value takes when capital is mobile between industries and the rate of profit is equalized across the economy.

PRIMITIVE ACCUMULATION OF CAPITAL. The historic emergence of the conditions of existence of capitalism (and thus of the accumulation of capital) where capitalism doesn't yet exist.

PRODUCTIVE LABOR. Labor that is productive of surplus-value, which means that labor power is exchanged against the variable part of capital.

PROFITS. The source of profits is surplus-value, the capitalist form of unpaid or surplus labor.

REAL SUBSUMPTION OF LABOR. Defined in contrast to the formal subsumption of labor. Real subsumption occurs when capitalists take over the labor and production processes through the expropriation of the direct producers inside production, by making workers appendages of the machines. It therefore coincides with the series of Industrial Revolutions.

RELATIVE SURPLUS-VALUE. An increase in the rate of exploitation by decreasing the portion of the workday representing necessary labor and increasing the portion that is surplus labor. It is based on the real subsumption of labor, that is, the expropriation of the direct producers within production.

REPRODUCTION. The securing of the conditions of existence of capitalism. Simple reproduction refers to the securing of those conditions of existence at the same level (when surplus-value is consumed, not invested); expanded reproduction involves reproduction on a larger scale (when surplus-value is used for the accumulation of capital).

SLAVERY. The extraction of surplus labor by slaveowners from slaves, in a system in which the workers are owned as human chattel.

SOCIAL DIVISION OF LABOR. The distribution of production among different producers, which is both a condition and consequence of markets, leading to the anarchy of production. It denotes the interdependence of producers in a system characterized by commodity production.

SOCIALISM. An economic and social system in which economic and social changes are made to create a transition from capitalism to communism.

SOCIALLY NECESSARY. The modifier attached to value and exchange-value, according to which the amount of abstract labor is not dictated by a technical minimum but instead considers the entire range of economic and social determinants (from technologies and types of markets to advertising and government regulations). It is therefore the amount of abstract labor that is "recognized" by society.

SURPLUS. The sum total of surplus labor at the level of society as a whole (and therefore the difference between the net total output and consumption).

SURPLUS LABOR. The amount of labor performed by workers which is the difference between total labor and necessary labor. In capitalism, surplus labor is unpaid labor and is equal to surplus-value.

SURPLUS-VALUE. The form of surplus labor in capitalism.

TECHNICAL DIVISION OF LABOR. The distribution of different jobs or activities within individual enterprises, which is both a condition and consequence of the despotism exercised by capitalists within those enterprises.

TRANSITION. The movement from the social predominance of one class process to another (such as the transition from feudalism to capitalism and from capitalism to communism). Transition is neither inevitable (there is no necessary plan or path of economic and social change) nor unitary (the social predominance of one class process, such as capitalism, does not mean that other class processes do not also exist within such a society).

UNEQUAL EXCHANGE. The exchange of unequal amounts of abstract labor embodied in commodities.

UNPRODUCTIVE LABOR. Labor that is not productive of surplus-value, which means that labor power is not exchanged against the variable part of capital; instead, it is often exchanged against a portion of surplus-value. This does not mean that unproductive labor is unimportant, both because unproductive laborers may be, and often are, exploited and because unproductive labor often creates the conditions for exploitation.

USE-VALUE. The social usefulness of a commodity, which is realized in the act of consumption.

VALUE. The amount of socially necessary abstract labor that is embodied in the commodity during the course of production.

VALUE OF LABOR POWER. The value of the elements of the wage bundle of sellers of labor power, which has a "historical and moral element" and thus represents workers' customary standard of living.

VARIABLE CAPITAL. The portion of capital capitalists use to purchase labor power that, combined with the elements of constant capital, is used to produce capitalist commodities.

WORKING-CLASS. The owners of labor power, who are forced to have the freedom to sell their ability to work to their employers. Members of the working-class perform both necessary and surplus labor.

References

The two principal sets of writings of Karl Marx (and Friedrich Engels) referred to in this book are *The Marx-Engels Reader*, edited by Robert C. Tucker, and the three volumes of *Capital*.

I give parenthetical page references to both sources throughout this book. To keep things simple, I have used the following conventions: specific pages in the Marx-Engels reader are ME, x (so, ME, 143–5 refers to pages 143 to 145 of the reader); pages in each of the three volumes of *Capital* are Ky, x (so, KI, 163–77 refers to pages 163 to 177 of volume 1 of *Capital*, KII to volume 2, and KIII to volume 3).

I have chosen the more recent (second) edition of the Tucker reader (published in 1978 by W.W. Norton & Company in New York). It is the one with the red, not blue, cover.

As for *Capital*, all references are to the latest edition, published by Penguin Books in association with New Left Review. Volume 1 was translated by Ben Fowkes, the appendix to volume 1 by Rodney Livingstone, and the other two volumes by David Fernbach. (A new English-translation of *Capital* is currently being prepared by Paul Reitter and Paul North.) There is also an earlier English-language translation of *Capital*, by Samuel Moore and Edward Aveling, which was published in 1909 in Chicago by Charles H. Kerr & Company (and is commonly referred to as the Kerr edition). I prefer the more recent published translation because, while not perfect, it does a better job rendering the original German manuscript into contemporary English. Therefore, all page references to *Capital* in this book are to the Penguin edition.

Interested readers can also consult the *Marx/Engels Collected Works*, which runs to 50 volumes and is the largest existing collection of English translations of many of the works of Marx and Engels. They were published between 1975 and 2004 by Progress Publishers (in Moscow), in association with Lawrence and Wishart (in London) and International Publishers (in New York).

All other references in this book are included in footnotes or listed, under the heading Suggested Readings, at the end of each chapter.

Variables

Because I have illustrated some of the arguments in the text with diagrams and equations, here is a list of relevant variables, divided into two sections: Marxian economics and mainstream economics.

Marxian economics
AL = abstract labor
c = constant capital
C = commodity (C_i is commodity i)
CL = concrete labor
Δ = change
DL = dead labor
e = exchange-value per unit use-value of commodities
EV = exchange-value (EV_i is the exchange-value of commodity i)
GR = ground rent
h = number of hours worked
K = value of total capital (where $K = c + v$)
l = number of workers
L = value of labor
LL = living labor
M = value of money
MOP = value of means of production
NL = necessary labor
NP = necessary product
P = production
PL = paid labor
PoP = price of production
π = capitalist profits (and $\hat{\pi}$ = profits of enterprise)
P_{lp} = price of labor power
q = number of use-values (e.g., in the wage bundle)
ρ = rate of profit
RM = value of raw materials
s = surplus-value
SL = surplus labor

SP = surplus product
UL = unpaid labor
UV = use-value (UV_i is the use-value of commodity *i*)
V = value of labor power
v = variable capital
W = the value of capitalist commodities

Mainstream economics
AD = aggregate demand
AS = aggregate supply
GDP = gross domestic product, which is the total monetary or market value of all the finished goods and services produced within a country's borders in a specific time period (e.g., a year).
MU = marginal utility (MU_i is the marginal utility of commodity *i*)
p = price of commodity (p_i is the price of commodity *i*)
P = price level
q = quantity of commodity (q_i is the quantity of commodity *i*)
Y = level of output for the economy as a whole (and Y^{FE} is the level of output at full employment)
v = velocity of money

PART I

RELEVANCE AND SOURCES

Chapter 1

MARXIAN ECONOMICS TODAY

As you open this textbook, you may be wondering, why should I study Marxian economics?

In the United States and in many other countries, Marxian theory, including Marxian economics, is a controversial topic. That's certainly been true for the past few decades, when the topic was all but taboo. But beginning with the crash of 2007–8 – the Second Great Depression or what some have called the Great Recession – the climate has dramatically changed. More and more people, especially young people, have become interested both in Marxian criticisms of mainstream economics and in possible alternatives to capitalism.

Here's Nouriel Roubini, professor of economics at New York University's Stern School of Business and the chairperson of Roubini Global Economics, an economic consultancy firm: "So Karl Marx, it seems, was partly right in arguing that globalization, financial intermediation run amok, and redistribution of income and wealth from labor to capital could lead capitalism to self-destruct."[1]

And then, from the other side of the Atlantic, there's George Magnus, Senior Economic Adviser to the UBS Investment Bank: "Policy makers struggling to understand the barrage of financial panics, protests and other ills afflicting the world would do well to study the works of a long-dead economist: Karl Marx. The sooner they recognize we are facing a once-in-a-lifetime crisis of capitalism, the better equipped they will be to manage a way out of it."[2]

Many of us were surprised, even those of us who have spent decades studying and teaching Marxian economics. I did so at the University of Notre Dame for almost four decades.

---

[1] Nouriel Roubini, "Is Capitalism Doomed?" *Project Syndicate*, August 15, 2011. https://www.project-syndicate.org/commentary/is-capitalism-doomed?

[2] George Magnus, "Give Karl Marx a Chance to Save the World Economy." *Bloomberg Opinion*, August 29, 2011. https://www.bloomberg.com/opinion/articles/2011-08-29/give-marx-a-chance-to-save-the-world-economy-commentary-by-george-magnus.

Living and working in the United States, we had just been through a 30-year period in which Marx and Marxian ideas had been attacked and marginalized, in the discipline of economics and in the wider society. Marx was declared either dangerous or irrelevant (or, often, both).

Capitalism was humming along (with, of course, the usual ups and downs) until ... the crash of 2008, when the world economy was brought to the brink of collapse. And Marx, almost in the blink of an eye, was relevant again.

To be honest, it wasn't that Marxists could take all, or even much of, the credit (or, for that matter, blame). It was actually the spectacular failure of mainstream economics that led to this dramatic change.

Mainstream economists were caught completely unawares. For all their claims to hard science and accurate forecasting, they failed to predict the crash. Even more, they didn't consider a crash to be even a remote possibility. The chance of a crisis starting with the housing and banking sectors didn't even exist in their theoretical framework.

And, once the crash happened, mainstream economists didn't really have much to offer. The policies that stemmed from their models suggested letting the banks sort out the problems on their own, without any kind of government supervision or intervention. Until, of course, the panic that set in with the failure of Lehman Brothers, which brought first the American economy and then the world economy to the brink of collapse.

The kinds of problems building up for decades simply didn't figure prominently in mainstream economic models and empirical analyses. They paid scant attention to the kinds of problems many others were increasingly worried about, such as:

- the deregulation of banks and the spectacular growth of the financial sector within the US and world economies
- the housing bubble that was supported by subprime bank loans, and then sliced and diced into collateralized debt obligations and other financial derivatives
- the outsourcing of jobs and the decline of labor unions, which if they paid attention at all were seen as freeing up national and global markets.

The result of these and other changes in the US economy created, for the first time in American history, a growing gap between productivity and workers' wages. According to the data illustrated in figure 1.1, productivity and wages grew at roughly the same rate during the immediate post-World War II period. But, from the late 1970s onward, that changed: while productivity continued to grow (increasing by more than 70 percent), wages increased by much less (only 17.2 percent).

The other result was an increasingly unequal distribution of income, reminiscent of the period just before the first Great Depression, when (as can be seen in figure 1.2) the share of income captured by the richest

The gap between productivity and a typical worker's compensation has increased dramatically since 1979

Productivity growth and hourly compensation growth, 1948–2020

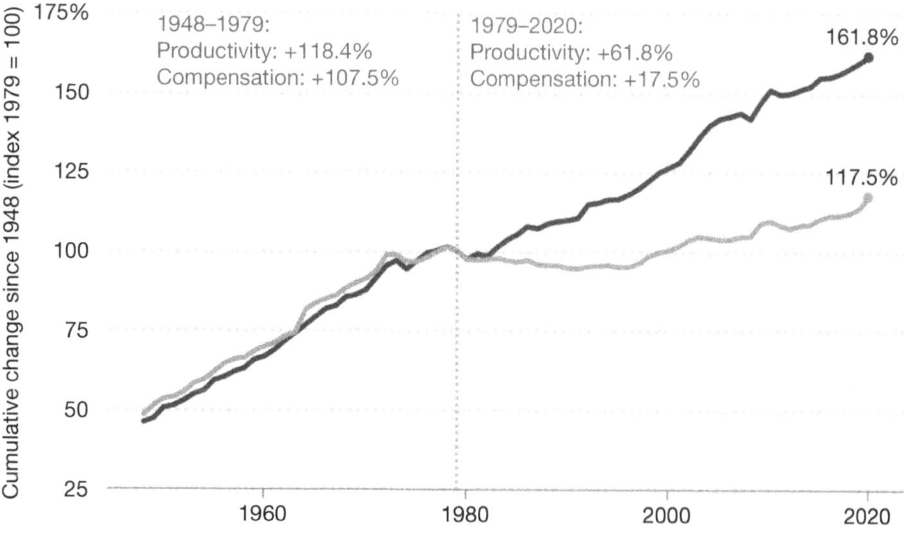

Notes: Data are for compensation (wages and benefits) of production/ nonsupervisory workers in the private sector and net productivity of the total economy. "Net productivity" is the growth of output of goods and services less depreciation per hour worked.

Source: EPI analysis of unpublished Total Economy Productivity data from Bureau of Labor Statistics (BLS) Labor Productivity and Costs program, wage data from the BLS Current Employment Statistics, BLS Employment Cost Trends, BLS Consumer Price Index, and Bureau of Economic Analysis National Income and Product Accounts.

Figure 1.1 Productivity and hourly compensation growth, 1948–2020
Source: Economic Policy Institute

10 percent of Americans (the dotted line) approached 50 percent of total income, and that of the bottom half of the population (the dashed line) hovered in the low teens.

Mainstream economists – both neoclassical and Keynesian economists, microeconomists as well as macroeconomists – either ignored these issues or explained them away as the necessary conditions for and outcomes of economic growth under capitalism.

The financial sector needed no oversight or regulation, because of the idea of efficient markets, which meant that participants had all the relevant information, and the risks faced by bankers and investors were already contained in market prices and interest rates. As for inequality, it was

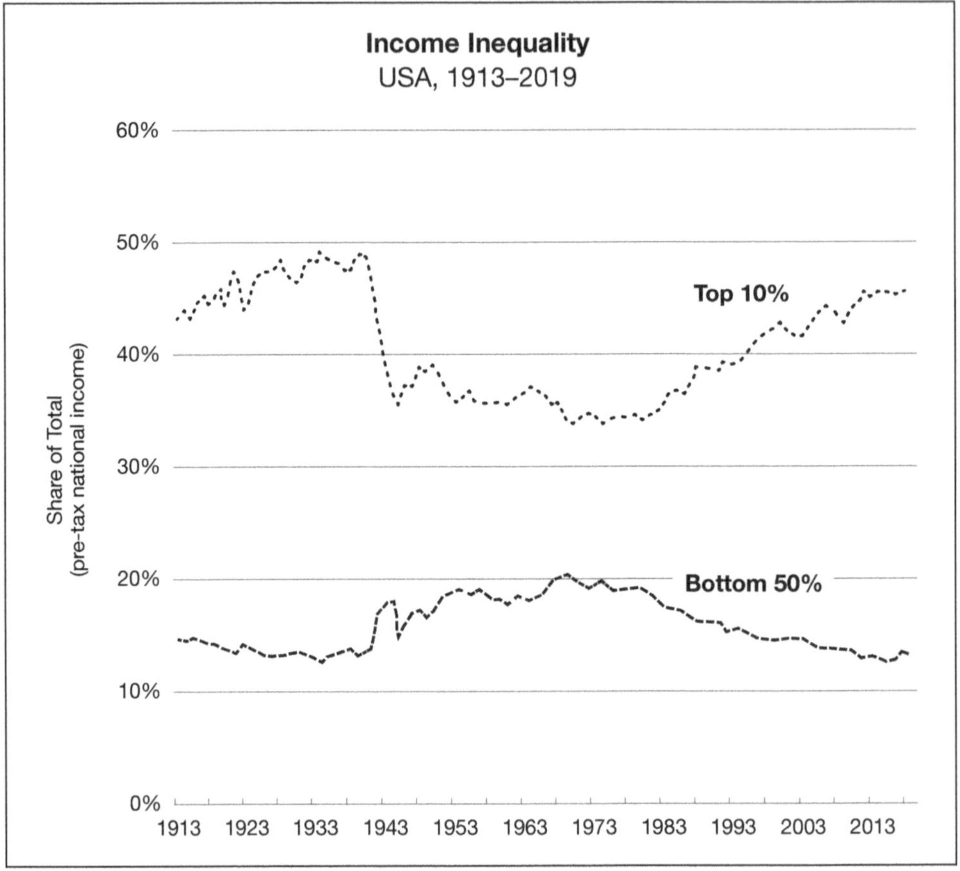

Figure 1.2 Income inequality in the United States
Source: World Inequality Database

either catalyst for growth or, if seen as a problem, it was the inevitable result of technology and globalization, which could be handled by encouraging workers to acquire better skills and more education to compete in the labor market. Moreover, both economic history and the history of economic thought – the history of capitalism and the history of thinking about capitalism – had disappeared as relevant areas of training for mainstream economists. As a result, not only had they never read any Marx; they'd never read Adam Smith, John Maynard Keynes, or Hyman Minsky.[3]

[3] Hyman Minsky was a professor of economics at Washington University. He is best known for his thesis of "financial instability," according to which bank lending passes through three distinct stages over the course of the business cycle: the Hedge (when banks and borrowers are cautious and loans are made in modest amounts), the Speculative (when borrowers are more confident but can only afford to repay the interest on loans), and the Ponzi stage (when the previous crisis is a distant memory and borrowers are unable to pay either the interest or the principal, presuming instead that asset prices will continue

Then things changed, especially as the problems cited above never really disappeared, even as stock markets entered another boom period. Marxian criticisms of both mainstream economic theory and capitalism became appropriate topics of discussion and debate again.

Reading Marx

While references to Marxian economics have increased in recent years, there is no indication commentators have actually read the works of Karl Marx. Perhaps they remember reading the *Communist Manifesto* at some point in their education but not Marx's magnum opus *Capital*. And they certainly have not read the scholarly work on Marxian theory. Perhaps they were afraid to or didn't know how to, or were just too caught up in their own theories and models. But the fact remains, the time is ripe for a new reading of Marx's *Capital*.

If they did such a reading, what would they find?

They would encounter something quite different from what they – and perhaps you, reading this book – expect. For example, they would not discover a set of predictions about when or how the crises of capitalism would inevitably occur. Nor would they find a blueprint for socialism or communism. In fact, many of the ideas that are regularly attributed to Marx or considered as defining characteristics of Marxian economics simply aren't there.

What readers *would* find is a critique of political economy, in two senses: a critique of mainstream economic theory; and a critique of capitalism, the economic system celebrated by mainstream economists. That's what Marx came up with after spending all those hours reading the classical political economists and the factory reports in the British Museum. In fact, Christopher Hitchens relates the story of a retiree who had worked in the British Museum's reading room during the Victorian period:

> Asked if he could remember a certain Karl Marx, the wheezing old pensioner at first came up empty. But when primed with different prompts about the once-diligent attendee (monopolizing the same seat number, always there between opening and closing time, heavily bearded, suffering from carbuncles, tending to lunch in the Museum Tavern, very much interested in works on political economy), he let the fount of memory be unsealed. "Oh Mr. Marx, yes, to be sure. Gave us a lot of work 'e did, with all 'is calls for books and papers".[4]

---

to rise). The "Minsky moment" is when the whole house of cards comes tumbling down, as borrowers rush to sell assets, thus causing an even larger fall in their prices. Minsky's writings were mostly ignored within mainstream economics, and only discovered (mostly not by mainstream economists, but in the press) after the crash of 2008.

[4] "The Revenge of Karl Marx," *The Atlantic*, April 2009. https://www.theatlantic.com/magazine/archive/2009/04/the-revenge-of-karl-marx/307317/

The critiques Marx developed during the course of working his way through all those books and papers are what generations of Marxian economists have been discussing, debating, and further developing ever since.

Five Themes

When all is said and done, Marxian economics is organized around five key ideas: critique, history, society, theories, and class. These are themes readers will encounter many times over the course of this book.

- CRITIQUE. *Capital* (and the many other economic texts Marx wrote) are less a fully worked-out theory of capitalism than a critique of the ideas – the concepts, methods, and models – that are central to mainstream economics. In other words, Marx carefully studied the works of the most influential classical economists, such as Adam Smith and David Ricardo. He used them as his starting-point but then ended up in a very different place, challenging much of what was taken then as the "common sense" within economics. Following his example, readers may find themselves questioning some of the key ideas within contemporary mainstream economics while reading this book.
- HISTORY. Much of mainstream economics is based on models of a world that never really changes. Marxian economics is different; it is focused on history – both the history of economic systems and the history of economic ideas – that change over time. Thus, for example, within Marxian economics, capitalism has a history: it didn't always exist; once it came into existence, it has continued to change; and, at least in principle, capitalism can come to an end, replaced by a fundamentally different way of organizing economic and social life.
- SOCIETY. Marx's approach was always about an economy *within* society, both affecting and being affected by everything else – social rules, political power, cultural norms, and much else. Therefore, different societies (and, for that matter, different parts of specific societies) have different ways of arranging economic life, now as in the past. This means they have radically different ways of allocating labor, organizing production, exchanging goods and services, distributing incomes, and so on.
- THEORIES. Not only are there different economies and societies; there are also different economic theories. Marxian economics is one, mainstream economics is another. (And there are many other theories or approaches readers may have encountered or heard about: radical, Post Keynesian, feminist, postcolonial, green, and the list goes on.) Moreover, economic theories are not the same as economic systems. For example, Marxian and mainstream economists have different theories – they tell different stories, they arrive at different conclusions – about the same economic

system. So, as readers will see over the course of this book, the Marxian theory of capitalism is very different from the mainstream theory of capitalism.

- CLASS. One of the particular interests or entry points of Marx and Marxian economists is class, the specific way workers (e.g., wage-laborers under capitalism or serfs within feudalism) perform more labor than they receive to sustain their lives. The rest, the extra or surplus labor, is appropriated and controlled by another, much smaller group (e.g., the class of capitalists or feudal lords). Marx created a special name for this: class exploitation.

  Different societies have different class structures, which have been transformed historically and continue to change today – without, however, getting rid of that crucial element, class exploitation. Marx was therefore critical of both the mainstream economic theories that deny the existence of exploitation as well as the economic systems in which the class of workers who perform the surplus labor are excluded from making decisions about the surplus they create.

Readers can therefore see how there would be, from the very beginning, an animated debate between mainstream and Marxian economists.

A Tale of Two Capitalisms

Marxian economists recognize, just like mainstream economists, that capitalism has revolutionized the world in recent decades, continuing, and in some cases accelerating, long-term trends. For example, the world has experienced spectacular growth in the amount and kinds of goods and services available to consumers. Everything, it seems, can be purchased either in small retail shops, big-box stores, or increasingly online. Every year, more and more of the goods and services we consume are being produced for and purchased in markets.

What this means is that the wealth of nations has climbed sharply. Thus, technically, real gross domestic product per capita has risen since 1970 in countries as diverse as the United States (where it has more than doubled), Japan (more than tripled), China (risen almost ten-fold), and Botswana (where it has increased by a factor of more than 22) (see figure 1.3).[5]

[5] Gross domestic product (or GDP) is the total monetary or market value of all the finished goods and services produced within a country's borders during a specific time period (e.g., a year). It is used by mainstream economists to measure the size of a country's economy and its growth rate. Gross domestic product per capita is the total value of those goods and services divided by a country's population. Thus, for example, while in 2019 the GDP of the United States was about one and a half times that of China, its per capita GDP was more than six times as large (because of the differences in population size between

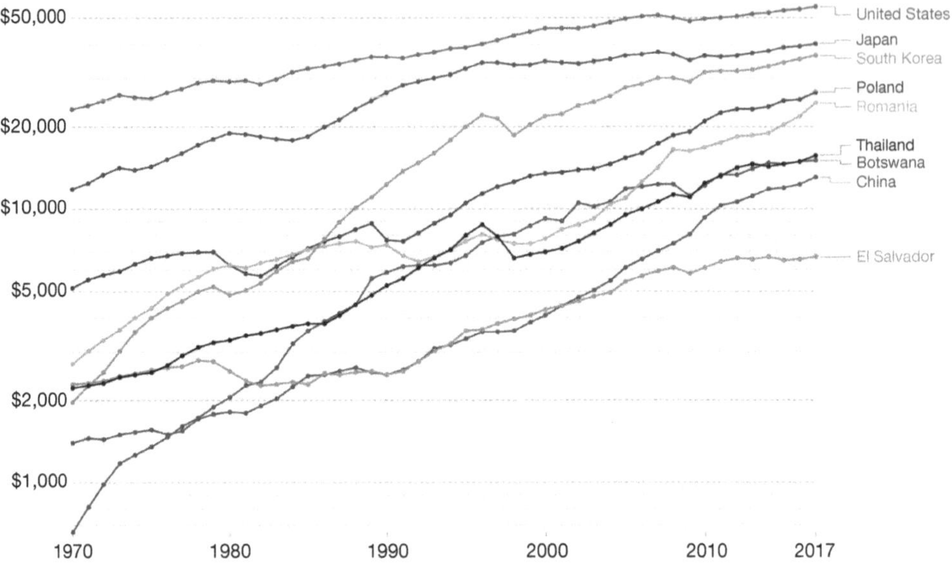

Figure 1.3 Real gross domestic product per capita, 1970–2017

Source: Feenstra et al. (2015) Penn World Table 9.1. OurWorldInData.org/econonomic-growth/CC BY

International trade has also soared during the same period. Goods and services that are produced in once-remote corners of the world find their way to customers in other regions. Both physical commodities – such as smart phones, automobiles, and fruits and vegetables – and services – like banking, insurance, and communications – are being traded on an increasing basis between residents of different national economies. To put some numbers on it, merchandise trade grew from US$322.7 billion in 1970 to US$17.22 trillion in 2020. And exports of services have become a larger and larger share of total exports – for the world as a whole (now 23.5 percent, up from 15 percent) and especially for certain countries (such as the United Kingdom, where services account for about 45 percent of all exports, and the Bahamas, where almost all exports are services).[6]

the two countries). Real GDP per capita is adjusted for price changes and is therefore net of any inflation. However measured, all that the GDP numbers reveal is that the value of goods and services in a country is growing. They don't tell us anything about who gets what, that is, how the incomes generated during the course of producing those commodities are distributed – or, for that matter, what the pattern of ownership of the wealth generated during the course of economic growth looks like.

[6] The World Trade Organization has a wealth of trade statistics on its website (https://www.wto.org/index.htm).

The world's cities are the hubs of all that commerce and transportation. It should come as no surprise that the urbanization of the global population has also expanded rapidly in recent decades, from about one third to now over half. In 2018, 1.7 billion people – 23 per cent of the world's population – lived in a city with at least 1 million inhabitants. And while only a small minority currently reside in cities with more than 10 million inhabitants, by 2030 a projected 752 million people will live in so-called megacities, many of them located in the Global South.[7]

We are all also aware that, during recent decades, many new technologies have been invented – for producing and distributing goods and services as well as in consuming them. Think of robotics, artificial intelligence, and digital media. And, with them, new industries and giant firms have been formed and taken off. Consider the so-called Big Four technology companies: Amazon, Google, Apple, and Facebook. They were only founded in the last few decades but, as they have continued to grow, they have become inextricably intertwined with the strategies of millions of companies and the lives of billions of people around the world.

The profits of those tech companies have, to no one's amazement, skyrocketed. And their owners are all billionaires. When the first *Forbes World Billionaires List* was published in 1987, it included only 140 billionaires. Today, they number 2,825 and their combined wealth is about US$9.4 trillion. That works out to be about US$3,300,000,000 per billionaire. Their wealth certainly represents one of the great success stories of capitalism in recent decades.[8]

Finally, capitalism has grown in more countries and expanded into more parts of more countries' economies and societies over the course of the past 40 years. Both large nations and small ones (from Russia, India, and China to El Salvador, Algeria, and Vietnam) are more capitalist than ever before. As we look around the world, we can see that the economies of rural areas have also been increasingly transformed by and connected to capitalist ways of producing and exchanging goods and services. Global value chains have incorporated and fundamentally altered the lives of millions and millions of workers around the world. Meanwhile, areas of the economy that had formerly been outside of capitalism – for example, goods and services provided by households and governments – can now be bought and sold on markets and are the source of profits for a growing number of companies.

But, unlike mainstream economists, Marxists recognize that capitalism's extraordinary successes in recent decades have also come with tremendous economic and social costs.

---

[7] See, for example, the United Nations' *World Urbanization Prospects: The 2018 Revision* (available online at https://population.un.org/wup/Publications/Files/WUP2018-Report.pdf).

[8] The *Forbes World's Billionaires List* is available online (at https://www.forbes.com/billionaires/) and is regularly updated.

All that new wealth of nations? From a Marxian perspective, it has been produced by workers who receive in wages and salaries only a portion of the total value they have created. The rest, the surplus, has been captured in corporate profits and handed over to those at the top of the economic pyramid. So, it should come as no surprise that the distribution of income has become increasingly unequal over time – both within countries and for the world economy as a whole.

According to the latest *World Inequality Report*, income inequality has increased in nearly all countries, especially in the United States, China, India, and Russia. In other countries (e.g., in the Middle East, sub-Saharan Africa, and Brazil), income inequality has been relatively stable but remains at extremely high – some would say, obscene – levels.[9]

At a global level, inequality has also worsened. Thus, for example, the top 1 percent of the richest individuals in the world has captured more than twice as much of the growth in income as the bottom 50 percent since 1980. Basically, the share of income going to the bottom half has mostly stagnated (at around 9 percent), while the share captured by the top 1 percent has risen dramatically (from around 16 percent to more than 20 percent).

And it is no accident. Inequality has increased precisely because the surplus labor performed by workers, in both rich and poor countries, has not been kept by them but has gone to a small group who stand at the top of the national and world economies.

So, we really are talking about a tale of two capitalisms: one that is celebrated by mainstream economists, but only benefits those in the top 1 or 10 percent; and another that is recognized by Marxian economists, who emphasize the idea that the growing wealth of nations and increasing inequality are characteristics of the same economic system.

But that's not the end of the story. All that capitalist growth has been anything but steady. The two most severe economic downturns since the Great Depression of the 1930s have happened in the new millennium: the Second Great Depression (after the crash of 2007–8) and the Pandemic Depression (with the outbreak and spread of the novel coronavirus). In both cases, hundreds of millions of workers around the world were laid off or had their pay cut. Many of them were already struggling to get by, with stagnant wages and precarious jobs, even before economic conditions took a turn for the worse. And then those same workers had to look up and see one part of the economy recovering – for example, the profits of their employers and shares in the stock market that fueled the wealth of the

[9] The *World Inequality Report* is compiled by the World Inequality Lab and is available, along with a wealth of data on individual countries, on the website of the World Inequality Database (https://wid.world/).

billionaires – while the one in which they earned their livelihoods barely improved, and in many cases became even more difficult.

Meanwhile, those stunning global cities and urban centers, the likes of which the world has never seen, also include vast slums and informal settlements – parking lots for the working poor. According to the United Nations, over 1 billion people now live in dense neighborhoods with limited and unreliable access to basic services like water, sanitation, and electricity.[10] Many don't have bank accounts, basic employment contracts, or insurance. Their incomes and workplaces are not on any government agency's radar.

They are not so much left out as, just like their counterparts in the poor neighborhoods of rich countries, incorporated into capitalism on a profoundly unequal basis. They are forced to compete with one another for substandard housing and low-paying jobs while suffering from much higher rates of crime and environmental pollution than those who live in the wealthy neighborhoods. In countries like the United States and the United Kingdom (and many others), a disproportionate number are ethnic and racial minorities and recent immigrants.

The working poor in both urban and rural areas are also the ones most affected by the climate crisis. A product of capitalism's growth, not only in recent decades, but since its inception, global warming has created a world that is crossing temperature barriers which, within a decade, threaten ecosystem collapse, ocean acidification, mass desertification, and coastal areas being flooded into uninhabitability.

Meanwhile, the democratic principles, practices, and institutions that people have traditionally relied on to make their voices heard are being challenged by political elites and movements that are fueled by and taking advantage of the resentments created by decades of capitalist growth. The irony, of course, is many of them call for more, not less, unbridled capitalism as the way forward.

Clearly, the other side of the coin of capitalism's tremendous successes has been its spectacular failures.

It should come as no surprise that there's more interest these days in both criticisms of and alternatives to capitalism. According to the Edelman Trust Barometer 2020 (a survey conducted during 2019, the results of which are illustrated in figure 1.4), 48 percent of respondents said that capitalism was failing them and 56 percent that "capitalism as it exists today does more harm than good in the world."[11] Marxian economics is one of the key sources for both: for ways of analyzing capitalism that

[10] The data about the world's cities are from the Statistics Division of the Department of Economic and Social Affairs of the United Nations (available online at https://unstats.un.org/sdgs/report/2019/goal-11/).

[11] The survey is available online at https://www.edelman.com/trust/2020-trust-barometer.

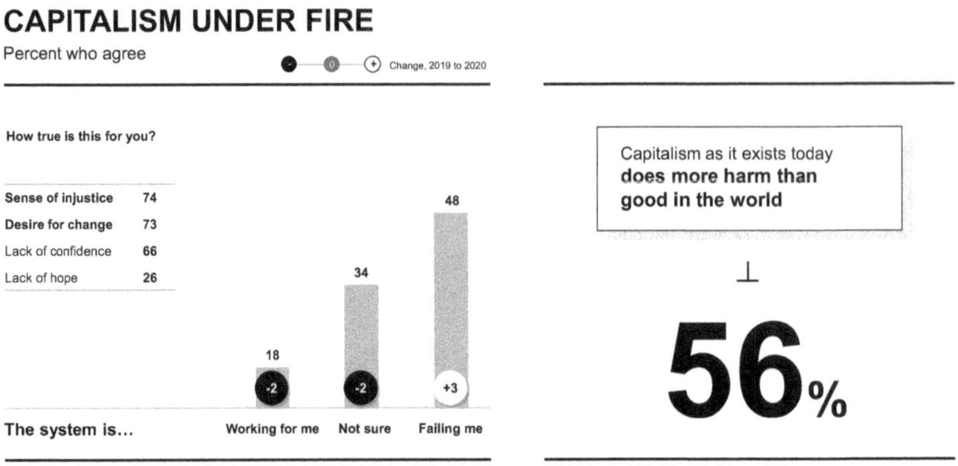

CAPITALISM UNDER FIRE

Percent who agree

Change, 2019 to 2020

How true is this for you?

Sense of injustice	74
Desire for change	73
Lack of confidence	66
Lack of hope	26

The system is...

Working for me	Not sure	Failing me
18 (-2)	34 (-2)	48 (+3)

Capitalism as it exists today **does more harm than good in the world**

56%

Figure 1.4 Capitalism does more harm than good

Source: 2020 Edelman Trust Barometer Global Report

point to these and other failures not as accidents, but as intrinsic to the way capitalism operates as a system; and for ideas about how to imagine and create other institutions, fundamentally different ways of organizing economic and social life.

Young people, especially, have become interested in the tradition of Marxian economics. They are trying to pay for their schooling, find decent jobs, and start rewarding careers but they are increasingly dissatisfied with the effects of the economic system they are inheriting. Mainstream economics seems to offer less and less to them, especially since it has mostly celebrated and offered policies to strengthen that same economic system.

For them, Marxian economics offers a real alternative – in terms of both criticizing capitalism and helping them to imagine changes to the current economic system that can deliver on the longstanding promises of freedom, fairness, and justice.

Beyond the Mainstream

This is certainly not the first time people have looked beyond mainstream economics. There is a long history of criticisms of both mainstream economic theory and capitalism from the very beginning, although they typically don't appear in traditional economics textbooks. Those texts are generally written with the presumption there's only one economic theory and one economic system. The existence of Marxian economics opens up the debate, creating space for both multiple ways of thinking about economics and a variety of different economic systems.

Criticisms of Mainstream Economic Theory

In the history of economic thought, criticisms of the mainstream approach were formulated early on.

The first group of mainstream economists – Adam Smith, David Ricardo, and others (such as Jean-Baptiste Say, Thomas Robert Malthus, and John Stuart Mill) – developed classical political economy in the late-eighteenth and early-nineteenth centuries, when the new economic system we now call capitalism was just getting off the ground. They developed, as we will see in chapter 2, a labor theory of value to analyze the value of commodities, the goods and services that were bought and sold on markets. They then utilized that theory of value to argue that capitalism, based on increasing productivity and free international trade, would lead to the growth of industry, higher productivity, and an increase in the wealth of nations.

Almost immediately, that mainstream approach to economics was debated and challenged. The early critics of classical political economy included a wide variety of writers, especially in the United Kingdom and Western Europe, from William Godwin (an opponent of private property, which he regarded as the primary cause of the poverty and calamitous state of the lower classes of the population), Thomas Carlyle (an English Romantic who expressed his opposition to the market system, because it rewarded "salesmanship" and not hard work), and John Barton (a British Quaker who argued that the introduction of labor-saving machinery would permanently displace workers who would not be absorbed by other branches of the economy) to Jean Charles Léonard de Sismondi (a Swiss historian who viewed capitalism as being detrimental to the interests of the poor and particularly prone to crisis brought about by an insufficient general demand for goods), Thomas Hodgskin (one of the so-called Ricardian socialists, a critic of capitalism and a defender of early trade unions), and William Thompson (who characterized as exploitation the appropriation of the lion's share of "surplus value," a term he coined, by the capitalist owners of the tools of production).

In the middle of the nineteenth century, Marx (along with his friend and frequent collaborator Friedrich Engels) became a close student of classical political economy, developing his now-famous critique. During the course of his writings, he expressed both great admiration for and trenchant opposition to the methods and conclusions of the classical political economists. Over the course of this book, we will examine in some detail the ways Marx, Engels, and later Marxian economists both built on and broke from classical political economy.

But the debate about early mainstream economics didn't stop there. In the late 1800s, a new school of economic thought – neoclassical economics – was created, which represented both an extension of and a break from classical political economy, although in a manner quite different from that of Marx. The early neoclassicals – such as William Stanley Jevons, Carl Menger, and Léon Walras – rejected the classicals' labor theory of value, in favor of consumer utility. At the same time, they accepted the classicals' celebration of capitalism's rising productivity, free markets, and international trade. Hence, both the "neo" and the "classical" of their name.

The neoclassical economists' basic argument was that, if all markets are allowed to operate freely, all consumers will maximize utility, all firms will maximize profits, and the economy as a whole will reach full employment. The "invisible hand" became the central thesis of the new mainstream microeconomics, and enjoyed growing adherence and influence until the Great Depression of the 1930s, when in the United States and elsewhere capitalist economies crashed and the unemployment rate soared to over 25 percent. Not surprisingly, the neoclassical orthodoxy was challenged at the time by many economists, including John Maynard Keynes. Keynes's idea was that, because of fundamental uncertainty, especially on the part of investors, it was highly unlikely that free-market capitalist economies would ever operate at full employment. The need for the "visible hand" of government monetary and especially fiscal policy to achieve full employment became the basis of mainstream macroeconomics.

Attempts to combine neoclassical microeconomics and Keynesian macroeconomics – the invisible hand of markets and the visible hand of government intervention – have defined mainstream economics ever since. That's why, today, in most departments, mainstream economics is still taught in two separate courses, neoclassical microeconomics and Keynesian macroeconomics. Very few of those courses, however, include references to other approaches, including Marxian economics.

Criticisms of Capitalism

Just as mainstream economic theory has been challenged from the very beginning, so has capitalism, the economic and social system praised by mainstream economists.

Perhaps the most famous early mass movement against capitalism was directed by the Luddites, a radical faction of English textile workers who in the early-nineteenth century attacked mills and destroyed textile machinery as a form of protest against low pay and harsh working conditions. While the name has come to be associated with anyone opposed to the use of new technologies, the participants in the actual historical movement objected to machinery only because it was introduced to speed up production and to change the balance of power in favor of employers and against workers.

Later, when workers could form labor unions – against a great deal of opposition, often violent, from their employers and the governments that backed those employers – they developed new strategies to challenge their subordinate role and adverse treatment within capitalism. They often demanded higher pay, more secure employment, additional benefits, and even a say in how the enterprises in which they worked were managed. Depending on the situation, they set up picket lines, went on strike, occupied their workplaces, and organized unemployed workers. In many cases, even though the workers were mainly concerning with meeting their daily needs, attempting to create a better life for themselves and their families, their activities were viewed as attacks on capitalism itself.

This was certainly the case during the first Great Depression, when the campaign to win union recognition was accompanied by the greatest wave of strikes in US history. Early on, widespread unemployment had caused union membership to dip precipitously – to 2 million, down from a high of 5 million 13 years earlier. But then, starting in 1933, with favorable legislation and dynamic organizing drives (especially the Wagner Act and the creation of the Congress of Industrial Organizations), the smoldering coals of worker discontent turned into flames, leading to an unprecedented growth in union membership. Particularly effective was the use of the sit-down strike, in which workers occupied the factories.

While many of the movements that have challenged capitalism have emerged from, been based on, or allied with workers and labor unions, others have not. Readers may recognize the names of some of the early utopian socialists and utopian experiments: Charles Fourier, Henri de Saint-Simon, Robert Owen, and Henry George. Beginning in the nineteenth century, in the United States and around the world, groups of individuals (often, but not always, influenced by various strands of socialist thinking) formed "intentional communities" and cooperative societies. The Shakers (in the United States) and Mondragón (in Spain) are perhaps the best known.

And the list of critics of capitalism – both individuals and movements – goes on. It includes a wide variety of left-wing populist, socialist, and communist political parties (some of which have come to power, either through democratic elections or armed revolutions). A fundamental questioning of the capitalist system has also emerged from and influenced many other individuals, groups, and traditions, from Civil Rights leaders (such as Martin Luther King, Jr. and Malcolm X, in the United States) and religious groups (e.g., the Catholic liberation theologians in Latin America) to anti-colonial independence movements (Angola and Mozambique are cases in point) and transnational protests (like Occupy Wall Street).

What can we conclude from this brief survey? From the very beginning, both mainstream economic thought and capitalism have brought forth their critical others.

Why Study Marxian Economics?

One of the best reasons for studying Marxian economics is to understand all those criticisms – the criticisms of mainstream economic theory and the criticisms of capitalism. Students of economics (and, really, all citizens in the world today) need to have an understanding of the origins and implications of those criticisms.

Marx certainly took those criticisms seriously. As he carried out his in-depth study of both the mainstream economic theory and the capitalist system of his day, his work was influenced by the criticisms that had been developed before he even directed his attention to economics. In turn, Marx's critique of political economy has influenced generations of economists, students, and activists. While certainly not the only critical theory that can be found in and around the discipline of economics, Marxian economics has served as a touchstone for many of those theories, not to mention public debates about both economics and capitalism the world over. Understanding both the broad outlines and the specific steps of Marxian economics is therefore crucial to making sense of those debates.

Consider a contemporary example (depicted in figure 1.5). On 26 February 2019, US Democratic congresswoman Alexandria Ocasio-Cortez responded on Twitter to an attack on her idea of a living wage by Donald Trump's daughter and presidential advisor Ivanka Trump, explaining that "A living wage isn't a gift, it's a right. Workers are often paid far less than the value they create." While there's no evidence that Ocasio-Cortez ever studied Marxian economics (or, for that matter, considers herself a Marxist), certainly the idea that within capitalism workers are often paid

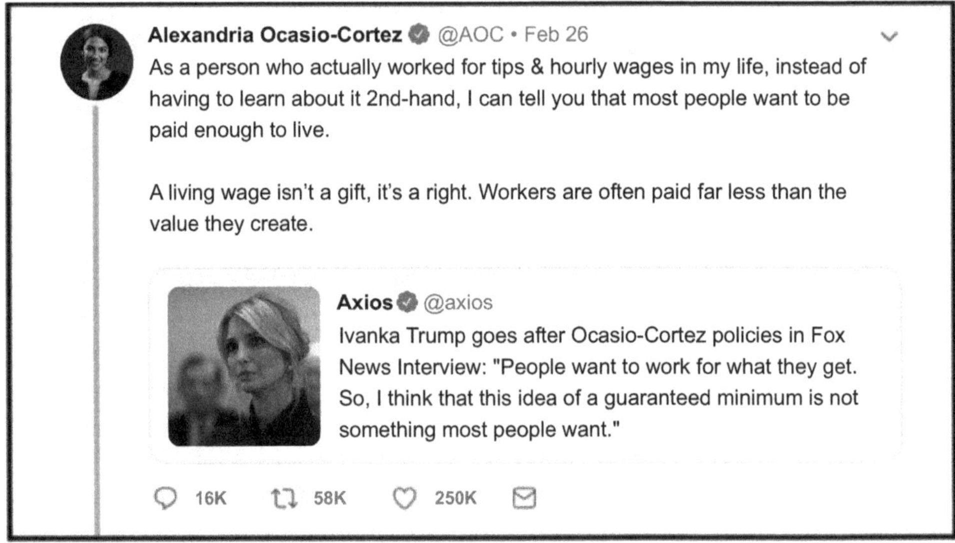

Figure 1.5 Alexandria Ocasio-Cortez on a living wage

less than the value they produce resonates with Marxian criticisms of both mainstream economic theory and capitalism.

Mainstream economists, as any student of contemporary mainstream microeconomics is aware, generally presume that workers' wages are equal to their marginal contributions to production. (The same is true, as we will see in the next chapter, of capitalists' profits and landlords' rents.) Everyone within a market system, mainstream economists argue (after a great deal of theoretical work, involving lots of equations and graphs), gets what they deserve. Therefore, since capitalism delivers "just deserts," it should be considered fair.

Not so quick, says Ocasio-Cortez, just like Marx more than a century before her. If workers are paid less than the value they create, then they are "exploited" – that is, they produce a surplus that goes not to them (in their wages), but to their employers (as profits). And while Marxian economists argue a living wage wouldn't by itself eliminate that exploitation, it would certainly lessen it and improve workers' standard of living.

Much the same holds for alternatives to capitalism. They often take their name from some version of socialism (and sometimes communism). That's why Ocasio-Cortez calls herself a "democratic socialist." It is also why so many people these days, especially young people, have positive views of socialism – even more so than capitalism. That represents a dramatic break both from mainstream economists and from their Cold War-era parents and grandparents.

Many ideas and policies that were once labeled (and then quickly dismissed) as "Marxist" or "socialist" are now accepted parts of the contemporary economic and social landscape. Progressive income taxes, a social security system for retirees, public healthcare and health insurance, minimum wages, labor unions for workers in private industry and public services – all were at one time derided as "dangerous" Marxist ideas, and now they form part of the common sense of how we think about economic and social policy. Much the same kind of change may be taking place right now – for example, with calls for a Green New Deal and the recognition of links between the inequalities and violence of contemporary capitalism and the history of slavery and structural racism.

Marxian Economics Today

In short, this is a fascinating time to be studying Marxian economics. It is a way of learning some of the main criticisms of mainstream economic theory and of capitalism. It also serves to lift the intellectual taboos and discover other ways of thinking about and organizing economic and social life. In a more general sense, studying Marxian economics is a path to learn what it means to be an intellectual. Within modernity, intellectuals are necessarily critical thinkers. Whether professors in colleges and universities or people who work in research units of enterprises or government offices, or really anyone who has to think and make decisions on or off the job, as intellectuals, they have to follow ideas wherever they might go. This means not being afraid of the conclusions they reach or of speaking truth to power.

That tradition of critical thinking is in fact what animated the work of Marx (along with Engels). He didn't have a predetermined path. Instead, he worked his way through existing economic theory, carefully and critically engaging the process whereby mainstream economists produced their extreme conclusions. He then started from the same general premises they did – in a sense, offering mainstream economists their strongest possible case – and showed how it was simply impossible for capitalism to fulfill its stated promises. For example, capitalism holds up "just deserts" as an ideal – everybody gets what they deserve – but it actually means that most people are forced to surrender the surplus they create to their employers, who are allowed to either keep it (and do with it what they want) or distribute it to still others (such as the tiny group at the top that manages the way those enterprises operate). Capitalism also pledges stable growth and full employment but then, precisely because of that private control over profits, regularly delivers boom-and-bust cycles and throws millions out of work. Marx, following his critical procedure, arrived at quite different conclusions – conclusions that were at odds with those of both mainstream economics and capitalism itself. And then he kept going – with more reading and more thinking and more political activity. He established some initial ideas, threads that were then picked up and extended by other Marxian economists, right on down to the present.

We will see over the course of this book how his work has affected not just economics, but many other academic disciplines, from sociology and anthropology through political science and cultural studies to philosophy and biology. In fact, one of the most famous and influential historians of the nineteenth century, whose books are read by thousands of college and university students around the world every year, is the British Marxist Eric Hobsbawm (who died in 2012, at the age of 95).[12]

Is Marxian Economics Still Relevant?

It is an obvious question for those of us living now, in the twenty-first century. Is Marxian economics still relevant? After all, Marx wrote *Capital*

[12] Hobsbawm's best-known works include *Primitive Rebels* and a trilogy about what he called the "long nineteenth century": *The Age of Revolution: Europe 1789–1848*, *The Age of Capital: 1848–1875*, and *The Age of Empire: 1875–1914*.

in the middle of the nineteenth century, when both capitalism and mainstream economics were quite different from what they are today.

Back in the mid-1800s, capitalism was a relatively new way of organizing economic and social life; having emerged first in Great Britain, it still encompassed just a small part of the world. As Marx looked around him, he saw both the tremendous progress and the horrendous conditions created by the Industrial Revolution: steam power, gigantic factories, growing cities, and increased production. The small group of successful industrial capitalists, merchants, and bankers at the top of the economic pyramid managed to accumulate great wealth. However, the men, women, and children who spent long hours huddled in urban centers and working in those new factories experienced squalor, malnutrition, and low wages.

The world today is, of course, quite different. We take for granted many of the ideas that were once considered radically new, such as the abolition of slavery and the spread of democracy. Other ideas, which were barely even imagined at the time, are today considered novel: demands for a guaranteed income and the extension of democracy beyond political elections to the places where people work.

As for capitalism, in some parts of the world, it would be immediately recognizable by nineteenth-century observers. Giant steel mills, workers denied the right to form labor unions, polluted living environments, minds and bodies damaged by demanding and dangerous jobs. Elsewhere, capitalism has changed in many ways, both large and small. Cutting-edge technologies in the twenty-first century include robotics, extended reality, and artificial intelligence. Production of many goods and services is dispersed among enterprises around the world instead of being concentrated in single factories. A much larger share of production and of the world's population – although, as we will see, certainly not all – has become part of capitalism.

And yet ... The gap between a small group at the top and everyone else is increasing. Workers still labor much longer, even utilizing much more productive technologies, than many had predicted.[13] Inadequate housing, food insecurity, and abject poverty remain the condition of many in the world today – to which we need to add the dangers created by the looming climate crisis.

Throughout this book, we will therefore have to ask: is the kind of critique of capitalism that Marx pioneered more than 150 years ago

[13] Back in 1930, Keynes famously predicted (in "Economic Possibilities for Our Grandchildren," pp. 321–34, in his *Essays in Persuasion* [New York: Palgrave Macmillan, 2010]) that over the next 100 years (and therefore for his contemporaries' grandchildren) the amount of wealth produced would make it possible for people to devote less and less time to work – such that a 15-hour workweek would become standard. The problem, Keynes thus presumed, would not be to provide adequate living standards and work for people, but instead to find ways of filling the growing number of hours of nonwork.

relevant, at least in broad outlines, to contemporary economies? And, following on from that: in what ways have Marxian economists changed and extended their theory to account for the many transformations the world has undergone since the mid-1800s?

Much the same question holds for the Marxian critique of mainstream economics: in what ways might Marx's original critique of classical political economy, the mainstream economics of his day, be relevant to contemporary mainstream – neoclassical and Keynesian – economics?

As will see in the next chapter, Smith and the other classical political economists made five major claims about capitalism, which Marx in his own writings then confronted and criticized. They are, in no particular order, the following:

1. Capitalism produces more wealth, and thus higher levels of economic development.
2. Capitalism is characterized by stable growth.
3. Everybody gets what they deserve within capitalism.
4. Capitalists are heroes.
5. Capitalism represents the end of history.

We have already touched on the first three in previous sections of this chapter, and in subsequent chapters we will return to them in some detail. For example, capitalism produces more wealth but, Marx argues, it only does so on the basis of class exploitation. Capitalism is inherently unstable because of the use of money and the private appropriation and distribution of the surplus. And, even if commodities are bought and sold at their values, capitalism is based on a fundamental class injustice, whereby the producers of the surplus are excluded from participating in decisions about that surplus.

What about the other two claims? Capitalists are celebrated but only if they accumulate more capital and thus create the conditions for more wealth and more employment for others. If they don't, and that is often the case, then there's nothing heroic about their activities at all. As for capitalism representing the end of history – the problem is, it still rests on class exploitation, not unlike feudalism, slavery, and other societies in which workers produce, but do not participate in appropriating, the surplus. That still leaves open the possibility of creating an economy without that class injustice.

Those, in short, are Marx's main criticisms of classical political economy.

Contemporary mainstream economists, as is turns out, also make all five of those claims. They don't do so in exactly the same manner as the classicals but they stand by them nonetheless.

1. Capitalism produces more wealth, and thus higher levels of economic development – which is now measured in terms of gross domestic product and gross domestic product per capita.

2. Capitalism is characterized by stable growth – and the possibility of internally generated crises is not even included in contemporary mainstream models.
3. Everybody gets what they deserve within capitalism – especially when, in the modern view, all "factors of production" receive their marginal contributions to production.
4. Capitalists are heroes – to which modern mainstream economists add that everyone is a capitalist, since we all have to decide how to accumulate and rationally utilize our "human capital."
5. Capitalism is fundamentally superior to previous ways of organizing economic and social life, such as feudalism and slavery – and to any recent alternative, such as socialism or communism.

Although the language and methods of mainstream economics have changed since Marx's time, many of Marx's criticisms do seem to carry over to contemporary mainstream economics. We will see, in the remainder of the book, just exactly how that works.

This Book

The other eight chapters of this book are designed to flesh out and explore in much more detail, with clear explanations and plenty of concrete examples, the issues raised in this chapter.

Chapter 2: Marxian versus Mainstream Economics

The aim of the second chapter is to explain how the Marxian critique of political economy has, from the very beginning, been a two-fold critique: a critique of mainstream economic theory and of capitalism, the economic system analyzed and celebrated by mainstream economists. I discuss the key differences between Marxian and mainstream approaches to economic analysis, both in Marx's time (so, classical political economy) and now (in neoclassical and Keynesian economics).

Chapter 3: Origins of the Marxian Critique of Political Economy

I do not presume readers will have any background in Marxian economic and social theory. Therefore, in this chapter, we will examine where Marx's critique of political economy came from – in British political economy, French socialism, German philosophy, and the development of capitalism itself – and how his ideas changed and developed in some of the key texts of the "early" Marxian tradition, prior to his writing of *Capital*.

Chapter 4: Commodities and Money

In this chapter, I present the material contained in the first three chapters of volume 1 of *Capital*, perhaps the most difficult and misinterpreted section of that book. Marx begins with the commodity, proceeds to discuss such topics as use-value, exchange-value, and value, presents the problem of "commodity fetishism," and then introduces money. In the most general sense, Marx starts with the common sense of both mainstream economics and capitalism and shows how strange it truly is.

Chapter 5: Surplus-Value and Exploitation

The goal of this chapter is to explain how Marx, starting with the presumption of equal exchange, ends up showing how capitalism is based on surplus-value and class exploitation. Along the way, he makes a key distinction between labor and labor power, develops a theory of the value of capitalist commodities, and then shows how capitalist employers are able to extract more surplus-value from their workers.

Chapter 6: Profits, Wages, and Distribution of the Surplus

According to Marx, once surplus-value is extracted from workers, it is then distributed to others for various uses: the "accumulation of capital," the salaries of corporate executives, the financial sector, and so on. The analysis of these distributions forms the origin of the Marxian theory of capitalist economic growth and the treatment of the role of instability and crises within capitalist economies, as well as the Marxian critique of the capitalist distribution of income.

Chapter 7: Applications of Marxian Economics

How have Marxist concepts been applied to major trends, debates, and events in recent decades? In this chapter, we examine the ways Marxian economists have developed their own approach to a wide variety of different topics. The selections in this chapter include the following: capitalist crises, the class structure of capitalism, class consciousness and class struggle, patriarchy, racial capitalism, the existence of forms of organization and social organization other than capitalism, globalization, and the climate crises created by global warming.

Chapter 8: Debates in and around Marxian Economics

Marxian economic theory has, of course, been discussed and debated from the very beginning – by both Marxian and mainstream economists. In this chapter, I present some of the key criticisms of Marxian economics by mainstream economists, focusing in particular on their rejection of the labor theory of value. I also explain some of the principal debates among different schools of thought within the Marxian tradition on changes within capitalism (such as monopolistic finance capital and imperialism), attempts to construct a socialist economy, and the problems of underdevelopment in the Global South. Finally, we will see how the Marxian critique of political economy has drawn on ideas from both outside economics (e.g., in philosophy, anthropology, and geography) and inside economics (in the realm of ethics and other economics theories, such as rent-seeking behavior and Modern Monetary Theory). These debates demonstrate that Marxian economics is not a settled theory or dogma but, instead, an ongoing tradition of critical thinking.

Chapter 9: Transitions to and from Capitalism

Much to the surprise of many students, Marx (and his frequent collaborator Engels) never presented a blueprint of socialism or communism, either in *Capital* or anywhere else. However, Marxian economics is based on a clear understanding that capitalism has both a historical beginning and a possible end. In this concluding chapter, I discuss how Marx and later generations of Marxian economists have analyzed both the transition to capitalism (e.g., from feudalism in Western Europe), the transition to noncapitalism (in the contemporary world), the successes and failures of countries where socialism or communism has been tried, and how the Marxian critique of political economy creates a utopian moment in economic debates today.

Before We Dive In

As I explained above, this book is not written with a presumption that readers have any kind of background in, or serious engagement with, Marxian economic and social theory. Much the same holds for mainstream economic theory. Perhaps some readers will have learned some Marx or mainstream economics in the course of their studies or discussions of economic issues in the mass media but, if not, everything they need to understand Marxian economics is presented in this book.

Here are some other issues I'd like readers to keep in mind as you work your way through this book.

As is often the case in theoretical debates, the same words often have different meanings. So, for example, the way Marx defines and uses such concepts as markets, value, labor, and capital are quite different from what they mean in mainstream economics or even everyday life. To help you make sense of those differences, I have included a glossary of terms at the beginning of the book that you can turn to as you work your way through the remaining chapters. In part II of the book (chapters 4–6), all concepts will be carefully defined, while using as little jargon as possible. I have also added a couple of technical appendices for readers who want to follow up on the discussion in the main text.

Marxian economics, like all economic theories, is subject to different interpretations – by both Marxian and non-Marxian economists. I offer one such interpretation in this book. However, so that readers have a thorough sense of the past and ongoing debates, I also include references (throughout the text and in footnotes) to other ways of thinking about the concepts, methods, and conclusions of the Marxian critique of political economy.

Since we are dealing with economics, some specialized expressions and visual illustrations are indispensable. That's because basic assumptions, even ethical claims, are often buried in the technical apparatus. I have kept them to a minimum but readers should be prepared for some graphs, the occasional statistical chart, a few equations, and a bit of algebra. I will therefore pass on the best piece of advice I received as a student: when something doesn't make sense immediately, don't jump over it but be prepared to work it out with paper and pencil.

The context for Marx's critique of political economy, written in the middle of the nineteenth century, is unfamiliar to many of us in the twenty-first century. How many of us today have read Adam Smith or Hegel, after all? The necessary background is covered below, in chapters 2 and 3.

While Marx's name has long been linked with communism, readers won't find any kind of blueprint or detailed plan of a communist society in Marx's writings. Nor does any general – valid for all times and places – economic and political program follow from his work. That's a topic we return to in chapter 9, together with a discussion of real-world cases of socialist economic organization.

This book is prepared as a stand-alone introduction to Marxian economics. No other texts are necessary to understand the material in this book. However, I have added references (to specific works and chapters) in the event readers want to use this book as a companion text, as they read *Capital* and other writings by Marx, as well as a list of suggested readings at the end of each chapter.

Finally, while the book is primarily aimed at students in economics (both undergraduate and postgraduate), it will also be relevant for and accessible to students and scholars in other disciplines – such as sociology, anthropology, geography, history, and cultural studies. My fervent hope is it will also be useful to people who are not currently involved in the academy, because in my view a clear, concise, and accessible introduction to Marxian economics is relevant to their work and lives.

Suggested Readings

Brian Bailey, *The Luddite Rebellion* (New York: New York University Press, 1998).
John Barton, *Observations on the Circumstances which Influence the Condition of the Labouring Classes of Society* (London: John and Arthur Arch, 1817).
Thomas Carlyle, *Past and Present*, intro. Chris Ramon Vanden Bossche (Berkeley: University of California Press, 2006 [1843]).
William Godwin, *An Enquiry Concerning Political Justice*, ed. and intro. Mark Philp (Oxford: Oxford University Press, 2013 [1793]).
Thomas Hodgskin, *Popular Political Economy: Four Lectures Delivered at the London Mechanics' Institution* (Edinburgh: Charles and William Tait, 1827).
Hyman Minsky, *Can "It" Happen Again? Essays on Instability and Finance* (New York: Routledge, 2016).
Isaac Ilych Rubin, *A History of Economic Thought*, trans and ed. Donald Fitzer (London: Ink Links, 1979 [1929]).
Joseph Anthony Rulli, *The Chicago Haymarket Affair: A Guide to a Labor Rights Milestone* (Charleston: History Press, 2016).
Jean Charles Léonard de Sismondi, *Political Economy and the Philosophy of Government* (London: John Chapman, 1847).
Hadas Their, *A People's Guide to Capitalism: An Introduction to Marxist Economics* (Chicago: Haymarket Books, 2020).
William Thompson, *An Inquiry into the Principles of the Distribution of Wealth Most Conducive to Human Happiness, Applied to the Newly Proposed System of Voluntary Equality of Wealth* (London: Longman, Hurst, Rees, Orme, Brown, and Green, 1824).

Chapter 2

MARXIAN VERSUS MAINSTREAM ECONOMICS

In the previous chapter, we saw that Marxian economics represents a two-fold critique: a critique of mainstream economic theory and a critique of capitalism, the economic and social system lauded by mainstream economists. In this chapter, we focus on the first part of that critique, the critique of the ideas that have been developed, utilized, and disseminated by mainstream economists.

Today, mainstream economics is the approach that predominates within colleges and universities in the United States and around the world, as well as within many government agencies, private think tanks, and mainstream media (including newspapers, television broadcasts, and websites). It is certainly not the only approach, and may perhaps not even be the numerically most prevalent. But, in terms of importance (e.g., according to the best-selling economics textbooks, many government policies, professors in elite colleges and universities, and the bulk of research funding), mainstream economics is dominant.

It is also important to note that what is considered mainstream economics has changed over time. When Marx developed his critique, the mainstream approach was what is commonly referred to as classical political economy, associated with the writings of Adam Smith, David Ricardo, and others. In our time, mainstream economics is different, consisting of an ever-shifting combination of neoclassical theories and Keynesian theories. Basically, mainstream economics today is what students typically learn in standard courses on microeconomics (stemming from neoclassical economics) and macroeconomics (based on Keynesian economics).[1]

---

[1] While in Marx's time there was no clear distinction between microeconomics and macroeconomics, that is now the convention within mainstream economics. Microeconomics generally refers to the study of the interaction of households and firms within individual markets for goods and services and factors of production (such as labor, capital, and land), while macroeconomics represents the study of the economy as a whole (in terms of aggregates, such as employment, growth, and inflation).

Economic Theories and Systems

Before we move on to look at the key differences between Marxian economics and mainstream economics, it is important to stop for a moment to clear up a common confusion: economic theories are *not* the same as economic systems. There is no such thing as a Marxist economy – or, for that matter, a classical, neoclassical, or Keynesian economy. Rather, these economic theories represent different ways of understanding – analyzing, telling a story about, or representing – a capitalist economy. There's a Marxian theory of capitalism, as against a classical theory of capitalism, a neoclassical theory of capitalism, and a Keynesian theory of capitalism. Each represents a different way of seeing or making sense of capitalism. In fact, economists from these different schools of thought often use different names for capitalism: while Marxian economists insist on using capitalism to describe the predominant economic system in the world today, mainstream economists often use other terms, such as "market system" or "mixed economy" or sometimes just "the economy." All are supposedly referring to the same thing out there in the real world but, of course, what they see and how they analyze it depend on the theory they are using.

The relation between economic theories and economic systems is even more dynamic. The various economic theories of capitalism have emerged, developed, and changed over time as capitalism itself has changed. And, in turn, they have effects back on capitalism. Both mainstream economics and its Marxian critique first appeared – and then fluctuated in influence, were debated and questioned, gave rise to new concepts and methods, and so on – as capitalism first came into existence and then changed over time. For example, after the crash of 2007–8, mainstream economics was widely questioned. Its theories and policies were responsible, at least in part, for creating the conditions that led to the crash; it failed to include even the possibility of such a crash in its models; and because, once the crash occurred, it had little to offer in the way of effective remedies. Precisely because mainstream economics did not adequately address such pressing issues as capitalist instability, the role of finance, growing inequality, and much else, professors, students, activists, and pundits stepped forward to question its theories and policies. Not surprisingly, that period also saw the resurgence of interest in theories that could be used to criticize mainstream economic theory and capitalism. Many people, inside and outside the academy, went back to ideas, including those associated with the Marxian critique of political economy, to make sense of what was going on.

But the relation between economic theories and economic systems doesn't go in only one direction. The ideas of different schools of thought within economics also have an impact on the economic systems they are designed to analyze. This is what is often called the "performativity" of economics.[2] The ideas that are produced and disseminated by professional economists (as well as noneconomists, inside and outside the academy) often lead to changes in capitalism itself. This is particularly true, as neoclassical economist Milton Friedman famously wrote, in times of crisis.

> Only a crisis – actual or perceived – produces real change. When that crisis occurs, the actions that are taken depend on the ideas that are lying around. That, I believe, is our basic function: to develop alternatives to existing policies, to keep them alive and available until the politically impossible becomes politically inevitable.[3]

Economic theories are not just out there, as a matter of academic curiosity and endeavor (or, sometimes for students, a necessary evil to be learned and repeated on an exam). They often lead to changes in capitalism, especially if they influence the way people think about their role in capitalism and attract the attention of influential economic and social groups who run capitalism's key institutions. In fact, economic theories are designed to do exactly that. When, for example, mainstream economists argue that free markets are the best solution to various economic and social problems – whether budget deficits or poverty or unemployment – they are saying that the world should have more of such markets. And, when market autonomy expands, mainstream economics has performed its role.

The Marxian critique of mainstream economics also has a performative dimension – with one key difference: Mainstream economists want to create a world of which their theory is a better representation, with more rational decision-making, more markets, more growth and employment, and so on. Marxian economists want to do exactly the opposite. They want to contribute to the project of eliminating and moving beyond capitalism and, when that happens, Marxian economics will no longer have a reason to exist.

The performativity of the Marxian critique of political economy is precisely to be its own grave-digger.

---

[2] Economic performativity, an idea that can be traced back to the work of Michel Callon ("What Does it Mean to Say that Economics is Performative?" in *Do Economists Make Markets? On the Performativity of Economics*, ed. Donald MacKenzie, Fabian Muniesa and Lucia Siu, pp. 311–57 [Princeton, NJ: Princeton University Press, 2008]), means that economists are not just outside observers, but actually produce the economies they analyze.

[3] *Capitalism and Freedom*, 40th anniversary edition (Chicago: University of Chicago Press, 2002), p. xiv.

Mainstream Economics Today

Readers these days will be more familiar with contemporary mainstream economics than with the mainstream economics of Marx's day. So, we should start there – with a look at the predominant approach that is taught in academic courses, applied in government policymaking, and used in media stories about economic ideas and events. Today, what we refer to as mainstream economics is a combination of neoclassical economics and Keynesian economics, a framework of analysis that encompasses both microeconomics and macroeconomics. Mainstream economics also extends far beyond those areas, to include a wide variety of specific topics, from labor markets through economic growth to international trade. In this chapter, we will look at the basic building blocks of mainstream economic theory, as well as the key criticisms from the perspective of Marxian economic theory. In later chapters, we will turn to some of the principal extensions of the theory and the various ways they have been challenged by Marxian economists.

Neoclassical Economics

Neoclassical economic theory came first, having emerged simultaneously in the writings of three economists in three different countries: William Stanley Jevons in England; the French-born Léon Walras in Switzerland; and Carl Menger in Austria. Capitalism had already produced and been subsequently transformed by the First Industrial Revolution (the birth of capitalist industry lasting, according to Eric Hobsbawm, from the 1780s to the 1840s) and was on the cusp of launching the Second Industrial Revolution (the revolutionizing of capitalist industry, which took place from 1870 to the beginning of World War I), in Europe and the United States. Separately, but roughly at the same time, Jevons, Walras, and Menger were the major contributors to what we now call the Marginalist Revolution in economics. They aimed to create a theory of economic value that mimicked the scientific protocols of nineteenth-century physics.

You may recall the paradox of diamonds and water? The idea is that diamonds are not as useful as water but they tend to fetch a much higher price on markets. Why is that? Neoclassical economists argued that the classical political economists couldn't solve the paradox. That's because they failed to understand that it is not the total usefulness but the extra or marginal utility gained from consuming an object that matters in determining the prices of commodities. Overall, water is much more abundant and useful than diamonds. But the larger marginal utility of less-abundant diamonds – the extra pleasure from the last unit consumed – compared to that of water is what explains its higher price.

There, in a nutshell, we can see the foundations of what has become neoclassical economic theory – a theory of economic value based on scarcity, utility, and decisions at the margin (along with the corresponding mathematics, calculus). The result is both an analysis and a celebration of capitalism, an economic system based on private property, free markets, and rational self-interested decisions.

Without going into unnecessary detail, let's see how neoclassical economic theory works.

The usual starting point is the supply-and-demand conception of markets. Neoclassical economists assume that there are markets for all goods and services – not only butter and banking services, but also the "factors of production," labor, capital, and land. Each has a corresponding set of supply (S) and demand (*D*) curves and an equilibrium price (P^*) and quantity (Q^*), where the quantity supplied is equal to the quantity demanded, as in figure 2.1.

But that's only the beginning of the story. In order for the model to work, each of the supply and demand curves has to be traced back to their ultimate determinants. In neoclassical economics, the given or exogenous determinants of supply and demand reside in nature – mostly human nature, but also physical nature. Thus, for example, the demand for goods and services is determined by human preferences (along with consumers' incomes). Those preferences are assumed to be given, from outside the economy, and to behave in predictable ways (as in the marginal utilities of the diamond–water paradox).

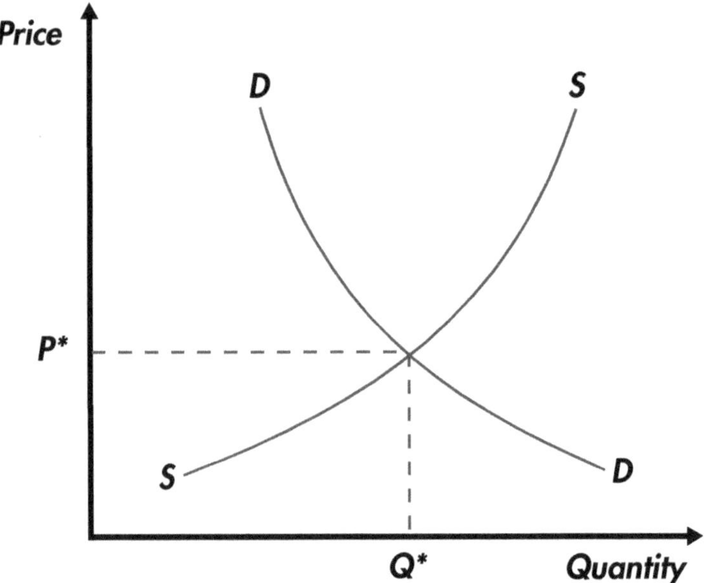

Figure 2.1 Market demand, supply, and equilibrium

Individual households are assumed to maximize utility, by making rational, self-interested decisions in choosing between different bundles of commodities in the "celestial supermarket." When they make their purchases at the market equilibrium, the prices can be shown to correspond to those given preferences or utilities.[4] Household incomes, meanwhile, derive from the sum of wages, profits, and rents they obtain when they sell labor, capital, and land to the firms that are producing the goods and services they purchase. These "factor" incomes are determined, like all other commodities, by supply and demand in markets. Households are assumed to make utility-maximizing choices in selling their services to firms. The result is that consumer incomes can also be said to correspond to nature – human nature in terms of individual preferences, along with the physical nature of land. And the more labor, capital, and land households choose to sell, the higher their incomes, and the more commodities they can purchase.

Firms, for their part, demand labor, capital, and land according to their marginal productivities, in order to maximize profits.[5] And they make factor payments to households, who use those incomes to purchase the goods and services produced by the firms, thus completing the circular flow of expenditures and incomes, both sales and purchases, that characterize the neoclassical conception of a capitalist economy.

The final neoclassical assumption is perfect competition, such that all consumers and firms are said to be "price-takers." They don't set prices but, instead, take the prices as given when they make their utility-maximizing and profit-maximizing decisions as households and firms in the markets for goods and services as well as in markets for factors of production.[6]

The neoclassical conclusion of this story is that not only is each market in equilibrium, the economy as a whole reaches an equilibrium. What this means is that the economy-wide or general equilibrium represents a perfect balance between the limited means of available resources and the unlimited desires of consumers. Production is at its maximum and full employment is achieved. Moreover, nothing is left over in the circular flow of the economy (as illustrated in figure 2.2): the sum of expenditures by

[4] Technically, the ratio of prices (p_1/p_2) is equal to the ratio of marginal utilities (MU_1/MU_2), where the subscripts 1 and 2 represent two different commodities.

[5] Firms are assumed to demand amounts of labor, land, and capital to the point where the extra revenue brought in by the last unit purchased is equal to the market-determined factor payment. Thus, for example, firms, in order to maximize profits, hire labor to the point where the marginal revenue product of labor is equal to the equilibrium wage rate. The same holds for capital (equal to the equilibrium price of or return on capital) and land (equal to the equilibrium rental rate).

[6] An obvious question immediately arises: if everyone is assumed to be a perfectly competitive price-taker, then who sets the prices of goods and services in capitalist markets? The neoclassical answer is the "auctioneer." That's the name given to the fictional entity that calls out different sets of prices, adjusting them up and down, until all markets are in equilibrium.

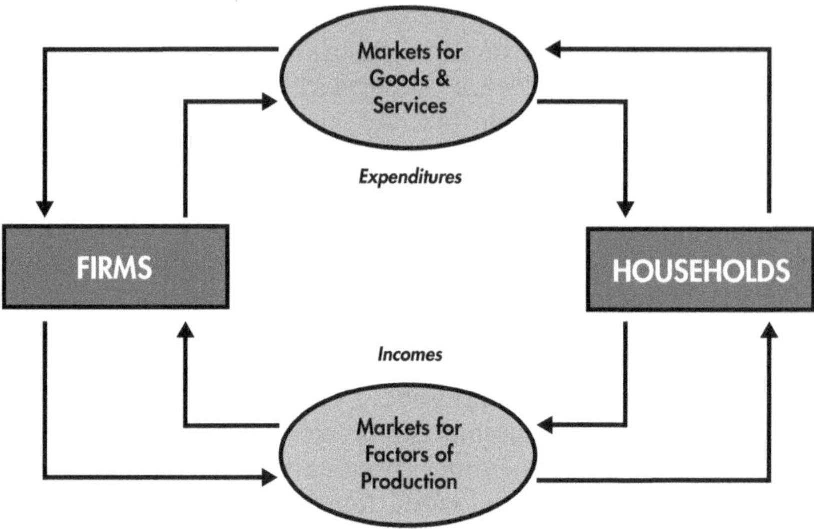

Figure 2.2 Circular flow

households for the goods and services produced by firms (the expenditures in the markets for goods and services, in the upper loop) is exactly equal to the total of incomes paid by firms to households for factor services (the incomes generated in the markets for factors of production, in the lower loop). In other words, there is no remainder, nothing in the way of a surplus. Finally, neoclassical economists argue, the set of equilibrium prices in both sets of markets – goods and services as well as factors of production – represent the preferences of households. That is, they correspond to human nature.

Ethics

As will be evident to readers, those are very powerful conclusions! Starting with atomistic individuals, directed only by their own self-interest, along with private property and markets, neoclassical economists conclude that the economy as a whole reaches a position where no one can be made better off without making someone else worse off.[7]

But neoclassical economics is not only a theory about the efficiency of capitalism or the way it solves the problem of scarcity or, for that matter, a proof that equilibrium market prices exist and correspond to human nature. Implicit within neoclassical economics, as in all economic theories, is also a particular theory of ethics or economic justice.

[7] This is known as Pareto efficiency, named after the Italian sociologist and economist Vilfredo Pareto, who succeeded Walras to the chair of Political Economy at the University of Lausanne in Switzerland.

The first key ethical claim made by neoclassical economists is that everyone is equal. Households may have vastly different amounts of income or wealth (because of their different utility-maximizing decisions to sell labor, capital, and land to firms) but they are considered to be fundamentally equal. That's because they are all assumed to be price-takers and, as if by an "invisible hand," they are led to make decisions such that their individual utilities are the same as those of everyone else.[8]

According to neoclassical economists, capitalism is also characterized by "just deserts" – the idea that everyone gets what they deserve. This is shown in two ways. First, consumers purchase commodities at prices that are equal to their preferences. Second, the incomes households use to purchase goods and services are the sum of the wages, profits, and rents they receive for selling factor services to firms. And those factors – labor, capital, and land – are remunerated according to their marginal contributions to production.[9] What that means is that households receive incomes and firms pay for factor services according to their contributions to production. So, in both product markets and factor markets, everyone within capitalism – households as well as enterprises – receives the appropriate reward for their decisions and actions.

From the perspective of neoclassical economics, then, capitalism promotes both equality and fairness. That's true even if there is considerable inequality among households – in terms of either income or wealth. Such inequalities are due to the different decisions households make, as well as their different initial endowments, which are considered to be determined outside the market. Therefore, according to neoclassical economists, capitalism, even if it delivers dramatically unequal levels of remuneration to households (and allows individuals to accumulate even more unequal amounts of wealth), as long as they correspond to the decisions and abilities of individual households, still delivers economic justice.

There is one final ethical principle that is prominent within neoclassical economics, which is the notion of freedom. It stems from a more Austrian interpretation of neoclassical theory (in a line that runs from Menger through such economists as Ludwig von Mises and Friedrich von Hayek to Milton Friedman). Dispensing with some of the arguments above (such as general equilibrium and economy-wide efficiency), mainstream Austrian economists emphasize the freedom that capitalism grants to individuals

[8] The way this works is, the ratio of prices (p_1/p_2) is equal to the ratio of marginal utilities of each and every individual $(MU_1/MU_2)^A \ldots (MU_1/MU_2)^Z$, where the subscripts 1 and 2 represent two different commodities and the superscripts A through Z represent the individuals.

[9] In more technical terms, the real wage rate is equal to the marginal physical product of labor, that is, the extra contribution to production by the last unit of labor hired; the real profit rate is equal to the marginal product of capital; and the real rental rate is equal to the marginal product of land.

– whether households or firms – to decide on their appropriate actions. They alone (and not, for example, governments or other non-market authority) have the knowledge of their particular circumstances and, to the extent they are free to choose what is best for themselves within markets, capitalism is said to be just.

Keynesian Economics

Once it was created as a new theory of capitalism, neoclassical economics expanded its influence – in its original countries as well as elsewhere.[10] It was also challenged. Within mainstream economics, the most far-reaching critique occurred during the Great Depression of the 1930s, when, against one of the main conclusions of neoclassical economists – that capitalism would always tend toward full employment – millions of workers were thrown out of their jobs and the rate of unemployment soared to over 25 percent.

British economist John Maynard Keynes is the most famous of those critics. He challenged two major features of government policy at that time, measures that had come straight out of neoclassical economics: first, that a decrease in wages would restore full employment, and, second, that government budget deficits should be avoided at all costs. Instead, Keynes argued, lowering wages would merely lead to less spending, and therefore more unemployment; and budget deficits during economic downturns were actually a good thing, as they were a way for governments to stimulate private spending in order to move capitalist economies back toward full employment.

In 1936, Keynes wrote and published his magnum opus, *The General Theory of Employment, Interest and Money*, which provided the theoretical basis for his attacks on austerity measures and his alternative program of government deficit spending.

One way to see the impact of Keynes's theoretical innovation is to use the contemporary model of aggregate supply and aggregate demand (as in figure 2.3).[11] Basically, neoclassical economists conclude that a capitalist

---

[10] The second generation of neoclassical economists included the following: in England, Philip Wicksteed, Francis Edgeworth, and Alfred Marshall; in Switzerland, Pareto; and, in Austria, Eugen von Böhm-Bawerk and Friedrich von Wieser. Neoclassical economics also found fertile ground in the United States early on, in the work of John Bates Clark, Fred M. Taylor, and Frank William Taussig. Later, especially after World War II, with the continued rise of both neoclassical economics and US hegemony, the theories, methods, and policies developed by neoclassical economists spread across the globe.

[11] While Keynes introduced the concepts of aggregate supply and demand in chapter 3 of the *General Theory*, a model based on aggregate supply and demand as a way of representing and teaching mainstream macroeconomics wasn't common until the 1990s. Today, it is ubiquitous. The problem is, in many textbooks, aggregate supply/aggregate demand

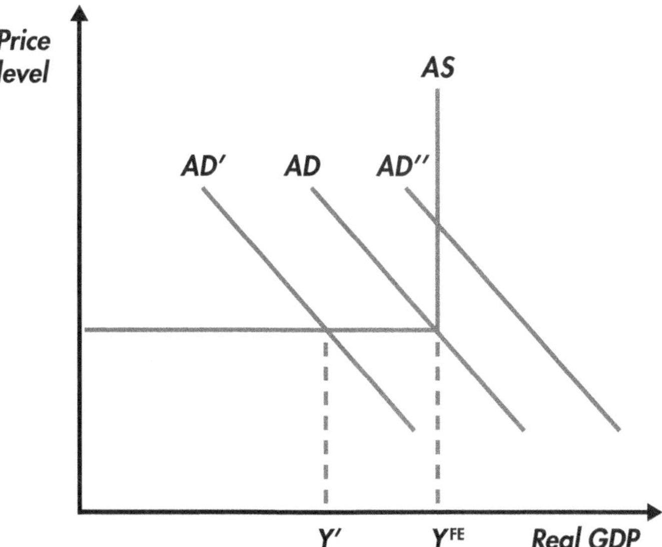

Figure 2.3 Aggregate demand and supply

economy will always be at full employment (at a level of output Y^{FE}, where Y is inflation-adjusted national output, measured in terms of *GDP*, and FE is full employment) at the intersection of downward-sloping aggregate demand (*AD*) and perfectly vertical aggregate supply (*AS*) curves. Therefore, any attempt to raise aggregate demand (e.g., to *AD″*), will only raise prices (an increase in the price level, on the vertical axis) and leave the level of output (and therefore employment) unchanged.[12]

Keynes, in contrast, argued that, during economic downturns, aggregate demand would decline (e.g., to *AD′*) and, with a perfectly elastic aggregate supply curve at less than full employment (the horizontal section of *AS*), output would fall to less than full employment (*Y′*). Moreover, he argued, there were no automatic mechanisms within capitalism to restore full employment. Without the visible hand of government intervention – for example, a level of government spending that was greater than its revenues – the economy would operate at a level of output below full

analysis has had the effect of misleading students into thinking that the analysis of the aggregate economy is essentially the equivalent of the equilibrium analysis of individual markets. While we need not go into detail here, it is worth noting that the underpinnings of aggregate supply and aggregate demand have nothing to do with the way market supply and demand are determined, such as in the section above on neoclassical economics.

[12] Therefore, the only way to raise output and employment in the neoclassical version of the macroeconomic model is to increase (push out to the right) the vertical aggregate supply curve. That can only happen if the exogenous determinants of aggregate supply change – for example, through an increase in labor, capital, and land or an improvement in technology. That's why the neoclassical approach to macroeconomics is often referred to as "supply-side economics."

employment. Finally, Keynes argued, aggregate demand could be increased without provoking inflation (again, a general increase in the price level), an idea that economists and politicians opposed to deficit spending argued then and continue to claim today.

How did Keynes arrive at conclusions that ran so much against the neoclassical grain? Keynes did not reject all aspects of neoclassical economics – neither its theory of income distribution nor its celebration of capitalism. But he did criticize some key assumptions, especially the idea that capitalism should be analyzed starting from individual decisions based on utility-maximization and complete knowledge. Instead, Keynes placed a great deal of importance on mass psychology and the limits to rational decision-making in the form of uncertainty.

Mass psychology and uncertainty are particularly important when it comes to capitalists' investment decisions, which are an important component of aggregate demand. For Keynes, working-class households can be expected to use for consumption a large and relatively stable share of their income (what is often referred to as the consumption function). Investors, however, engage in a much more volatile set of decisions, and that's because in many instances they don't have complete information about the future. They simply cannot know.

Given their uncertainty, how can capitalists make investment decisions? Much to the chagrin of other mainstream economists, then as now, Keynes argued in the *General Theory* that investors are guided by "animal spirits" – an urge to act that cannot be understood in terms of quantitative benefits and probabilities. If capitalists can't make rational decisions, and are propelled instead by their "animal spirits," what guide can they follow? Keynes turned to mass psychology, a kind of herd mentality, according to which capitalists look at what other capitalists are doing and follow suit. This makes investment demand, the other key component of aggregate demand, quite volatile – and can often (as during and after the stock market crash of 1929) initiate a downward spiral. Capitalists stop investing, thereby decreasing production and destroying investor confidence, which leads to even less investment and production, in a kind of capitalist freefall. Moreover, since private decisions in markets only worsen the initial downturn, there is no mechanism within capitalism to turn things around. The invisible hand simply fails.

That's why Keynes argued – first in letters to government leaders, including the US president Franklin Delano Roosevelt, and then in the *General Theory* – that the only thing that would save capitalism would be for the government to step in with aggressive fiscal policy (deficit spending) and an accommodating monetary policy (such as expanding the supply of money and lowering interest rates), to raise aggregate demand (from AD′ back toward AD, in figure 2.3). In other words, the solution Keynes proposed was the visible hand of government intervention.

Limits of Mainstream Economics Today

Keynes's criticisms of neoclassical economics set off a wide-ranging debate that came to define the terms of – and, ultimately, the limits of – debate within mainstream economics.

On one side are neoclassical economists, who invoke the invisible hand and argue that markets are the best way to efficiently allocate scarce resources. On the other side are Keynesian economists, who argue instead for the visible hand of government intervention to move markets toward full employment.

That tension, between the theories and policies of neoclassical and Keynesian economics, is the reason why in most colleges and universities the principles of economics are taught in two separate courses: microeconomics and macroeconomics. Moreover, the tension between the two schools of thought plays out within every area of economics, including (but certainly not limited to) microeconomics and macroeconomics. We see much the same debate in international trade and finance, labor economics, economic development, public policy, and so on.

One way of understanding the differences between the two approaches is to think about them as conservative and liberal interpretations of mainstream economics – where I am using the appellations conservative and liberal in the political sense (especially as those terms are currently understood in the United States). Conservative mainstream economics tend to presume that the basic assumptions of neoclassical economics hold in contemporary capitalism, while liberal mainstream economists think they don't.

Let's consider two examples. First, within microeconomics, conservative mainstream economists (such as Milton Friedman) believe that individuals make rational decisions within perfectly competitive markets. Therefore, if markets exist, they should be allowed to operate without any regulations; and, if a market doesn't exist, it should be created. Liberal mainstream economists (e.g., Joseph Stiglitz), on the other hand, see both individual decisions and markets as being imperfect – because individuals have limited or asymmetric information, some firms have more market power than others, and so on. Therefore, they argue, individuals and markets need to be regulated and guided by government interventions toward the best possible outcome.

The second example is from macroeconomics. The view of conservative mainstream economists is that capitalism operates at or close to full employment (where, in figures 2.3 and 2.4, aggregate demand intersects the vertical portion of the aggregate supply curve), whereas liberal mainstream economists believe that unregulated markets often lead to considerable unemployment (where aggregate demand intersects the horizontal portion of the aggregate supply curve, at a level of output less

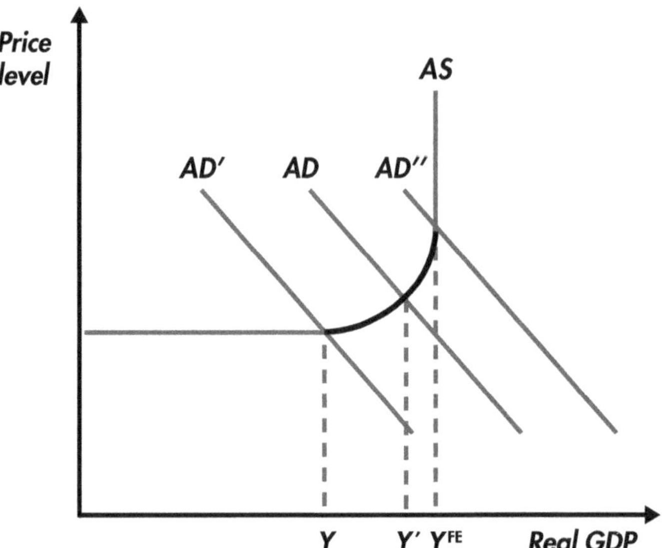

Figure 2.4 The middle view

than full employment).[13] In an attempt to reconcile the two competing views, many mainstream economists argue for a "middle position" – somewhere between the opposed neoclassical and Keynesian views. There (in the upward-sloping black portion of the aggregate supply curve in figure 2.4), mainstream economists find a tradeoff between increases in output and changes in the price level, that is, between inflation and unemployment.

The predominant view within mainstream economics tends to shift back and forth between the two poles. Sometimes, as in the years before the crash of 2007–8, mainstream economics moves closer to the neoclassical approach. That's when policies such as deregulation, privatization, the reduction of government deficits, welfare reform, and so on were all the rage, within both academic and political circles in many different countries. After the crash, when the neoclassical approach was widely believed to have failed, mainstream economics swung back in the other direction. That's why there were calls for more government intervention and fewer worries about budget deficits and the like. In the midst of the Pandemic Depression, much the same kind of debate between advocates of the two poles of mainstream economics took place. On one side, conservative

[13] As many contemporary Post Keynesian economists have noted, when neoclassical and Keynesian theories were combined in a single approach to economics (e.g., in the "neoclassical synthesis" in the decades following World War II), many of the critical aspects of Keynes's writings – including the notion of radical uncertainty and the idea that much stock market investment was merely speculation and added little to the productive capacity of the "real" economy – were downplayed or ignored altogether.

mainstream economists argued in favor of rescuing banks and corporations, such that an economic recovery would "trickle down" to workers and their households. Liberal mainstream economists, on the other hand, favored direct payments to workers who were furloughed or laid off – an idea that was attacked by their conservative counterparts, because such payments were seen as providing a "disincentive" for workers to return to their jobs. Every time capitalism enters into crisis, the same kind of debate breaks out between conservative and liberal, neoclassical and Keynesian, economists (and, of course, between the respective groups of pundits and politicians).

If mainstream economists are so divided between the two approaches, what in the end unites them into what I have been calling mainstream economics? Like all such labels, it is defined in part by what it includes, and also by what it excludes. Mainstream economics *includes* the idea that neoclassical and Keynesian approaches establish the limits within which theoretical and policy debates can and should take place. Together, they define what is in the "economic toolkit," and therefore what it means to "think like an economist." Moreover, the two groups of economists argue that capitalist markets are the way a modern economy can and should be organized. They may disagree about the relevant approach – for example, the "invisible hand" of free markets versus the "visible hand" of government intervention. But they all agree on the goal: to create the appropriate institutional environment so that capitalist markets work properly. They also share the view that the only way capitalism can operate away from its general equilibrium, full-employment potential is because of some external "shock." In other words, all economic downturns, such as recessions and depressions, are due to external causes, not because of anything internal to the normal workings of capitalism.

What the definition of mainstream economics *excludes* is any approach, such as Marxian economics, that is based on a theoretical approach that lies outside the theories, methods, and policies of neoclassical and Keynesian economics. For example, the idea of class exploitation is generally overlooked or ignored within mainstream economics. Similarly, imagining and creating ways of allocating resources other than through capitalist markets are pushed to or beyond the margins by mainstream economists.

Together, the inclusions and exclusions contained within the definition of mainstream economics serve to define what mainstream economists think and do in their theoretical practice as well as in the courses they teach and the policy advice they offer.

Classical Political Economy

Marxian economists have been quite critical of contemporary mainstream economics. As we saw in chapter 1, and will continue to explore in the remainder of this book, Marxian economists have challenged the general approach as well as the major theoretical conclusions and policies of both neoclassical and Keynesian economists.

What about Marx, who wrote his critique of political economy, let's remember, long before neoclassical and Keynesian economics even existed? Writing in the middle of the nineteenth century, Marx trained his critical eye on the mainstream economic theory of his day. He read Adam Smith's *Wealth of Nations* and David Ricardo's *Principles of Political Economy and Taxation*, as well as the writings of other classical political economists, such as Thomas Robert Malthus, Jean-Baptiste Say, and John Stuart Mill. His critique of political economy can rightly be seen as both an extension of and a break from the work of those late-eighteenth-century and early-nineteenth-century mainstream economists. In order to understand why and how Marx proceeded in the way he did, we need to have a basic understanding of classical political economy.

Before we begin, however, we have to recognize that Marx's interpretation of the classical economists was very different from the way they are referred to within contemporary mainstream economics. Today, within non-Marxian economics, the classicals are reduced to a few summary ideas. They include the following: a labor theory of value (which contemporary mainstream economists reject, in favor of utility), the invisible hand (which, as it turns out, Smith mentioned only three times in his writings, just once in the *Wealth of Nations*), and comparative advantage (but not the rest of Ricardo's theory, especially his theory of conflict over the distribution of income). We therefore need more background on these thinkers in order to make sense of Marx's critique.

Adam Smith

Let's start with Adam Smith, the so-called father of modern economics. The author of, first, the *Theory of Moral Sentiments* and, then, the *Wealth of Nations*, Smith asserted that people have a natural "propensity to truck, barter, and exchange one thing for another." In other words, according to Smith, the ability and willingness to participate in markets were natural, and not social and historical, aspects of all humanity. That's not unlike contemporary mainstream economists' insistence on presuming the existence of markets, and thus writing down supply and demand functions (or drawing them on a graph), without any further evidence or argumentation. They are presumed to be natural.

Smith then proceeds by showing that the division of labor (such as with his most famous example, of the pin factory) has two effects: First, it leads to increases in productivity, and therefore an increase in production. Second, the extension of the division of labor within factories propels a division of labor within capitalism as a whole, as firms specialize in the production of some goods, which they can then trade in markets with other producers. In turn, the expansion of markets leads to more division of labor and higher productivity, thus increasing the wealth of nations. The parallel with contemporary mainstream economics is quite evident, which is recognized in the "classical" portion of the name for neoclassical economic theory. Using GDP as their measure of the wealth of nations, contemporary mainstream economists admire capitalism because higher productivity results in more output, which is then traded on markets. This is the basis of contemporary mainstream economists' definition of development as an increase in GDP per capita, that is, more output per person in the population.

However, unlike contemporary mainstream economists, Smith analyzed the value of commodities in terms of the amount of labor it took to produce them. With increasing productivity, more goods and services could be produced and sold in markets, each containing less labor – and therefore available at lower prices to consumers. The nation's wealth would therefore grow, especially as the number of workers increased.

Still, Smith worried about whether capitalist growth would persist in an uninterrupted fashion. The division of a nation's production into "natural" rates of wages, profits, and rent to workers, capitalists, and landlords was not sufficient. What if, Smith asked, a large portion of capitalists' profits was used to hire more "unproductive" labor, that is, the labor of household servants and others that did not contribute to increasing productivity? Purchasing labor involved in what we now call conspicuous consumption represented, for Smith, a slowing of the accumulation of additional capital. Therefore, it created a problem, an undermining of the promise of capitalist growth.

Smith (in chapter 8 of Book I of *The Wealth of Nations*) also took note of the conflict between "masters" and "workmen," an issue that is missing entirely from contemporary mainstream economics:

> What are the common wages of labour, depends everywhere upon the contract usually made between those two parties, whose interests are by no means the same. The workmen desire to get as much, the masters to give as little as possible. The former are disposed to combine in order to raise, the latter in order to lower the wages of labour.
>
> It is not, however, difficult to foresee which of the two parties must, upon all ordinary occasions, have the advantage in the dispute, and force the other into a compliance with their terms. The masters, being fewer in number, can combine much more easily; and the law, besides, authorizes, or at least does not prohibit their combinations, while it prohibits those of the workmen. …
>
> We rarely hear, it has been said, of the combinations of masters, though frequently of those of workmen. But whoever imagines, upon this account, that masters rarely combine, is as ignorant of the world as of the subject. Masters are always and everywhere in a sort of tacit, but constant and uniform combination, not to raise the wages of labour above their actual rate.

David Ricardo

David Ricardo picked up where Smith left off. He extended the celebration of capitalist markets to international trade. His argument was that, if nations specialize in the production of commodities for which they have a relative (or comparative) advantage, and trade them for goods from other countries (his most famous example was British cloth for Portuguese wine), both countries benefit.[14] Their wealth increases.

That's the only reason Ricardo's work is cited by contemporary mainstream economists.[15] What they never mention is Ricardo's concern that conflicts over the distribution of income might slow capitalist growth. In particular, Ricardo was worried that, as capitalism developed, the profits received by capitalists would be squeezed from two directions: an increase in workers' wages and a rise in rent payments to landlords. Lower profits would mean less capital accumulation and slower growth – and, in the limit, capitalism would grind to a halt.

We can see how this might happen using figure 2.5. At a certain point (e.g., a level of population, *Pop*, which is the pool of workers), total output (the dark grey line) would be divided into workers' wages (the white rectangle), capitalists' profits (the light grey rectangle), and landlords' rents (the dark grey rectangle). It is easy to see that, at any point in time, if the wage rate paid to workers increased (which would mean an increase in the slope of the straight black line, wages), that would cut into profits (the vertical distance between the black and light grey lines would decrease). That's the major reason Ricardo supported free trade (and thus a repeal of the so-called Corn Laws): so that cheaper wheat could be imported from abroad (and thus cheaper bread made domestically), thereby lessening the upward pressure on workers' wage demands.

Even if the rate paid to workers remained the same over time (and thus the total amount of wages rose at a constant rate, with an increase in population), capitalists' profits would be squeezed from the other direction, by an increase in the rents paid to the class of landlords (the vertical distance between the light grey and dark grey lines). Basically, as agricultural production was moved to less and less fertile land, the rents on more productive land would rise, siphoning off a larger and larger portion of profits.

---

[14] According to the theory of comparative advantage, even if a country has an absolute advantage in the production of all goods (that is, it can produce all goods more cheaply than another country), both countries will benefit if they specialize in the production of goods for which each has a *relative* advantage (that is, goods that are relatively cheaper for them to produce) and trade them for the goods from the other country.

[15] The irony is that, while mainstream economists today reject the classical labor theory of value, the examples they use to demonstrate the gains from international trade are often calculated on the basis of labor costs.

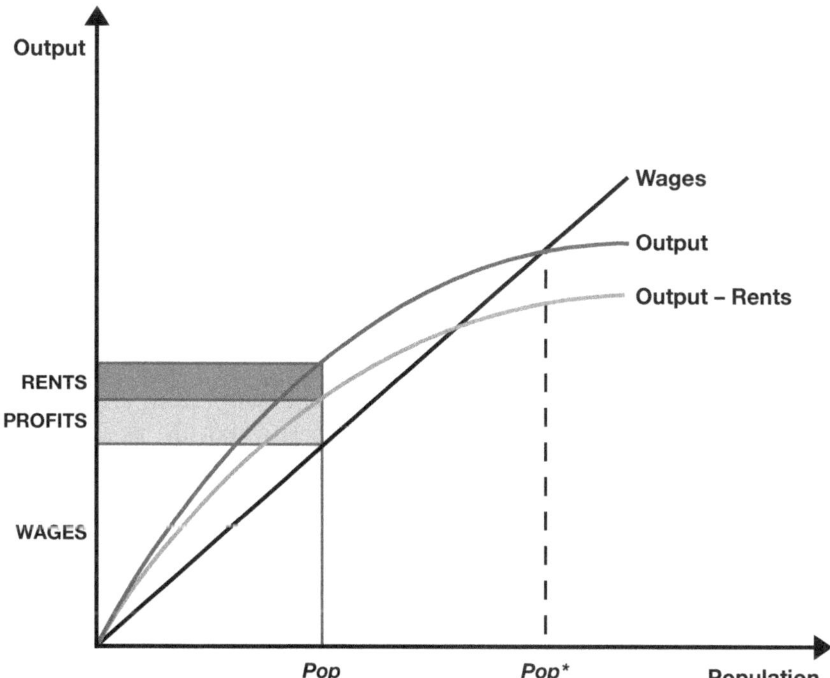

Figure 2.5 Ricardo: wages, profits, and rents

At a certain point (e.g., at a level of population *Pop**), the entire output would be divided between workers' wages and landlords' rents – and nothing would be left for capitalists' profits. As a result, capitalists would be forced to stop investing, and capitalist growth, the premise and promise of classical political economy, would cease.

Other Classicals

The Reverend Thomas Malthus was, if anything, more pessimistic than Ricardo. But he foresaw capitalism's problems coming from the natural fertility of the working masses. In his *Essay on the Principle of Population*, he argued that population would likely grow faster than the expansion in food production, especially in times of plenty. With such an increase in the supply of labor and a rise in the price of available food, workers' real wages would inevitably fall. The only solution was for capitalists to hire all the additional labor, and for workers' wages to be restored to their "natural" level.

If Malthus focused on the up-and-down cycles of population and wages, and both Smith and Ricardo the potential limits to capitalist growth, the French classical economist Jean-Baptiste Say emphasized the inherent stability of capitalism. Why? Say's argument was that the production of commodities causes incomes to be paid to suppliers of the labor, capital, and land used in producing these goods and services. And because the sale price of those commodities is the sum of wages, rents, and profit, the incomes generated during the course of producing commodities would be sufficient to purchase all the commodities brought to market. The result is what was later coined as Say's Law: "supply creates its own demand." As readers will immediately note, it is the precursor to the equality of the upper and lower loops of the circular flow diagram we saw above (figure 2.2) in the case of contemporary neoclassical economics.

Finally, it was John Stuart Mill who added utilitarianism to classical political economy. Extending the work of Jeremy Bentham, especially the "greatest-happiness principle" (which holds that one must always act so as to produce the most aggregate happiness in the world), Mill argued that the greatest happiness and the least pain could be achieved on the basis of free markets, competition, and private property – with the proviso that everyone should be afforded an equal opportunity, however unequal the actual results might turn out to be.[16]

Marx's Critique of Mainstream Economics

That, in a nutshell, is the mainstream economic theory Marx confronted while sitting in the British Museum in the middle of the nineteenth century. Marx both lauded the classical political economists for their efforts – especially Ricardo, who in his view "gave to classical political economy its final shape"[17] – and, at the same time, engaged in a "ruthless criticism" of their theory. In this sense, Marx took the classical political economists quite seriously.[18] Even as he broke from their work in a decisive manner, many of the themes of Marx's critique of political economy stem directly from the issues the classicals attempted to tackle. That's why the overview

[16] In fact, toward the end of his life (and as can be seen in later editions of his *Principles of Political Economy*), Mill came to espouse what we would now call liberal socialism: while continuing to defend individualism and personal liberty, Mill held that everyone, not just wealthy property owners, should be guaranteed the ability to lead good lives. Thus, for example, he endorsed worker cooperatives, argued that the state should help secure more equal economic opportunities for all, and took seriously the problem of gender inequality.

[17] *A Contribution to the Critique of Political Economy* (p. 51) was first published in 1859 and was originally issued as the first installment of a complete treatise of political economy. Later, Marx modified his plans and, eight years later, he published the first volume of *Capital*.

[18] This is in contrast to contemporary mainstream economists, whose reading of classical political economy – apart from Smith's *Wealth of Nations* – is generally dismissive. Paul Samuelson ("Economists and the History of Ideas," *American Economic Review*, 52, 1 [March 1962]), for example, considered Ricardo "the most overrated of economists" (p. 9). Thus, his view of Marx was even more contemptuous: "From the viewpoint of pure economic theory, Karl Marx can be regarded as a minor post-Ricardian" (p. 12).

provided in previous sections of this chapter is so crucial to understanding Marxian economics.

Still, the question remains, how does Marx's critique of the mainstream economics of his day transfer over to contemporary mainstream economists? As we will see, although neoclassical and Keynesian economists reject the labor theory of value and other elements of classical political economy, the basic assumptions, conclusions, and ethical implications of their approach are so similar to those of the classicals as to make it a relatively short step from Marx's critique of the mainstream economic theory of his day to that of our own.

Looking Ahead

Before proceeding to that theoretical encounter, in part II, we need to explore how the terms of Marx's critical engagement with classical political economy emerged over the course of his writings – before, in the mid-1860s, he sits down to write the three volumes of *Capital*. That's the task of the next chapter.

Suggested Readings

Maurice Dobb, *Theories of Value and Distribution since Adam Smith* (Cambridge: Cambridge University Press, 1973).

Robert L. Heilbroner, *The Worldly Philosophers: The Lives, Times, and Ideas of the Great Economic Thinkers*, 7th ed. (London: Touchstone, 1999).

Randall G. Holcombe, *Advanced Introduction to the Austrian* School (Northampton, MA: Edward Elgar, 2014).

Karl Marx, *A Contribution to the Critique of Political Economy*, trans. S. W. Ryazanskaya, ed. Maurice Dobb (Moscow: Progress Publishers, 1970 [1859]).

David Ricardo, *On the Principles of Political Economy and Taxation* (Cambridge: Cambridge University Press, 2015 [1817).

Robert Skidelsky, *Keynes: A Very Short Introduction* (Oxford: Oxford University Press, 2010).

Adam Smith, *The Wealth of Nations*, intro. Alan B. Krueger (New York: Bantam Dell, 2003).

Richard D. Wolff and Stephen A. Resnick, *Contending Economic Theories: Neoclassical, Keynesian, and Marxian* (Cambridge, MA: MIT Press, 2012).

Chapter 3

ORIGINS OF THE MARXIAN CRITIQUE OF POLITICAL ECONOMY

In the first two chapters, we looked at some of the major differences between Marxian economics and mainstream economics, both in Marx's time and in our own.

But where did Marx's critique of political economy come from? It certainly did not emerge in one fell swoop, as a ready-made critique of mainstream economics and of capitalism. And it wasn't produced in isolation, independent of the society within which it was first produced and then further elaborated. Quite the opposite: we can trace the development of Marx's critique through a variety of texts – many of them now quite famous, even if they are rarely mentioned or discussed within economics. There, we can see Marx's ideas developing and changing, until he began to work on his critique of political economy, finally presented in *Capital*.

Moreover, Marx's critical appraisal of both mainstream economic theory and capitalism was, like all theories or discourses, a product of its time – of the economic and social structures he lived in and keenly observed, as well as the ideas that were prevalent when he was writing. In turn, once they were produced, Marx's ideas participated in changing that same intellectual and social environment – as they continue to do, right up to the present.

In this chapter, we investigate some of the major influences on Marx's critique of political economy. These include Marx's intellectual heritage, especially the philosophy of G. W. F. Hegel and the politics of utopian socialism (in addition to classical political economy), as well as the larger economic and social environment of capitalism in the middle of the nineteenth century. Without having a basic sense of those moments, it is impossible to understand where Marx's critique came from and the form it eventually took.

The task is even more germane because those influences are so different from those of our own time, when you are reading this book. Capitalism has changed a great deal in the intervening period, and the ideas we take to be relevant today are quite different from those that influenced Marx's work. How many of us, for example, know about or read Hegel today? Instead, in recent decades, postmodernism and other ideas have exercised much more of an influence on contemporary interpretations of Marxian economics. Socialism, too, has been reimagined, moving away from the centralized Soviet model and toward new ways of involving workers and their communities in deciding what to do with the surplus. And, as we saw in the previous chapter, contemporary mainstream economics is not at all the same as the mainstream economic theory that was Marx's starting point.

Once we have accomplished that goal, we will turn our attention to some of Marx's most famous writings prior to *Capital*. These include such texts as the *Economic and Philosophic Manuscripts of 1844* and *The German Ideology*, as well as the copious notebooks, the *Grundrisse*, Marx kept as he first started delving into classical political economy.

For a Ruthless Criticism of Everything Existing

So, where to begin? Perhaps the best place is one of the letters Marx wrote to his friend Arnold Ruge.

Marx was 25, just two years beyond completing his doctorate in Philosophy at the University of Jena. He had recently married Jenny von Westphalen – but, seeing that working in his native Germany was becoming increasingly difficult, he was already planning to leave and move to France. Police reprisals had forced Marx to resign from *Rheinische Zeitung* (*Rhenish Newspaper*), which he edited. During that time, Marx corresponded with Ruge, and their eight-letter exchange was eventually published in the *Deutsch-Französische Jahrbücher (German-French Annals)*, which appeared in Paris in 1844.[1]

The most relevant piece of that correspondence is the letter Marx composed in September 1843, which eventually acquired the title "For a Ruthless Criticism of Everything Existing" (ME 12–15). With those words, Marx announced the task confronting him and the other "young Hegelians" at that moment: "a ruthless criticism of everything existing, ruthless in two senses: The criticism must not be afraid of its own conclusions, nor of conflict with the powers that be."

[1] The aim of this chapter is not to present the details of Marx's life. The focus here, as in the book as a whole, is on the development of Marx's ideas, especially those that are relevant to economics, as well as their conditions and consequences. For interested readers, the classic biography is Franz Mehring's *Karl Marx: The Story of His Life* (published in 1918). A recent film directed by Raoul Peck, *The Young Karl Marx* (2017), is an excellent historical drama about Marx and his relationship to Friedrich Engels. It also emphasizes, perhaps for the first time, the important role played by their respective wives, von Westphalen and Lizzie Burns.

In one sense, there is nothing remarkable about Marx's formulation of their task. It is part and parcel of modernity, the "tradition of no tradition," defined by self-criticism, openness to novelty, suspicion of authority, a questioning of the existing common sense, and much else. It is, in short, what modern intellectuals (professors, students, workers, and people in general) are supposed to do: follow ideas wherever they may go, without being afraid of their consequences, and, as we say these days, of "speaking truth to power." In another sense, Marx formulated his project of "ruthless criticism" in a novel fashion. He ties it to socialism and communism – and therefore a radical transformation of the world. He was, even at that young age, a radical thinker and activist.

However, he wrote,

> we shall confront the world not as doctrinaires with a new principle: "Here is the truth, bow down before it!" We develop new principles to the world out of its own principles. We do not say to the world: "Stop fighting; your struggle is of no account. We want to shout the true slogan of the struggle at you." We only show the world what it is fighting for, and consciousness is something that the world must acquire, like it or not.

Therefore, Marx explains, he does not believe in, nor is he in favor of, holding up any kind of "dogmatic flag," a single approach that merely needs to be learned and applied. The whole point was to define a project of "ruthless criticism of everything existing" – which, as we will see in the remainder of this chapter, passes through various stages on the way to composing the critique of political economy in *Capital*.

Hegel

It is difficult to fully understand the Marxian critique of political economy without some understanding of Hegel. No less an authority than the Russian revolutionary Vladimir Lenin wrote that "it is impossible completely to understand Marx's *Capital*, and especially its first chapter, without having thoroughly studied and understood the whole of Hegel's *Logic*."[2] Marx himself wrote "I therefore openly avowed myself the pupil of that mighty thinker, and even, here and there in the chapter on the theory of value, coquetted with the mode of expression peculiar to him."[3]

Those are the two major reasons for keeping Hegel in mind: because Marx, like many young German intellectuals in the 1830s and 1840s, started with Hegel; and because, many years later, Marx's critique of political economy was still influenced by his theoretical encounter with

[2] "Conspectus of Hegel's Book *The Science of Logic*," in *Collected Works*, vol. 38, ed. Stewart Smith, trans. by Clemens Dutt, p. 180 (London: Lawrence & Wishart, 1961).
[3] "Postface to the Second Edition" (KI, 102–3).

Hegel.[4] But, of course, that makes understanding the movement toward the Marxian critique of political economy a bit difficult for contemporary readers, who generally aren't familiar with Hegel's writings. So, in this section, I want to present a brief summary of Hegel's philosophy. Still, I caution readers, this should not be taken to be a presentation of all aspects of Hegel's thought. We only want to examine Hegel's philosophy to the extent that it aids our comprehension of Marx's theoretical journey and his later critique of political economy.

In his twenties, Marx, along with other young German intellectuals (including Ruge, Bruno Bauer, and Ludwig Feuerbach), formed a loose grouping called, variously, the Young Hegelians or the Left Hegelians. In their discussions and debates, these young thinkers sought both to draw on Hegel's philosophy and to radicalize it, aiming their attacks especially at religion and the German political system.[5] Later, they turned their radical critique on Hegel's philosophy itself.

What was it in Hegel's thought that was so influential for Marx and the other Young Hegelians? Two areas are particularly important: the theory of knowledge and, closely related, the philosophy of history.

On the first point, Hegel's view was that the two previous traditions – of René Descartes and Immanuel Kant – got it wrong. Descartes argued that it was impossible to know things as they appear to us (phenomena) but only things as they are in themselves (noumena). Experience was deceptive. Hence, his focus was on reason ("I think, therefore I am"), which alone can provide a certain foundation for knowledge about the world. Kant posited exactly the opposite – that it *was* possible to know things as they appear to us but not their essences, things as they are in themselves. Therefore, science was only capable of providing knowledge of the appearances of things, of empirical experiences and observations about nature; morality and religion operated in the unknowable realm of things in themselves.

---

[4] Even though many scholars insist on the idea that a basic understanding of Hegel is necessary for understanding Marx's theoretical journey, it is also possible to overstate the case. Marx's method is neither a straightforward application nor a simple reversal of the Hegelian dialectic. As we will see, by the time he began writing *Capital*, Marx had criticized and moved far beyond Hegel's philosophy.

[5] At the time (beginning in 1840), Germany was governed by a new king, Frederick William IV, who undermined his promise of a political opening by curtailing political freedom and religious tolerance. For the Young Hegelians, this was a real step backward in terms of following the rest of Europe (especially Britain and France) in modernizing political institutions and expanding the realm of freedom. It was key to their eventual break from Hegel, since, according to Hegel's philosophy, the Prussian state represented the fulfillment of history. The contemporary equivalent is Francis Fukuyama's famous book *The End of History and the Last Man* (New York: Macmillan, 1992), in which he argued that "not just ... the passing of a particular period of post-war history, but the end of history as such: That is, the end-point of mankind's ideological evolution and the universalization of Western liberal democracy as the final form of human government."

Hegel's great contribution was to solve the problem and affirm what both Descartes and Kant denied. For him, history is an unfolding of the mind (Absolute Spirit) coming to know itself as phenomenon, to the point of its full development, when it is aware of itself as it is, as noumenon. In other words, the consciousness of things as they appear to us leads to knowledge of the essence of things. At the end of the process, when the object has been fully "spiritualized" by successive cycles of consciousness's experience, consciousness will fully know the object and, at the same time, fully recognize that the object is none other than itself. That, for Hegel, marks the end of history.

How does this historical process work? How does the mind or Absolute Spirit pass through successive stages until it reaches full awareness? That's where the dialectic comes in. According to Hegel (especially in the *Phenomenology of Spirit*), human understanding passes through a movement that is characterized by an initial thesis (e.g., Being) that passes into its opposite (e.g., Nothingness), which entails a contradiction that is resolved by a third moment (e.g., Becoming), which is the positive result of that opposition.[6] For Hegel, this process of thesis-antithesis-synthesis (or, as it is sometimes referred to, abstract-negative-concrete) is both a logical process (the development of philosophical categories) and a chronological process (the development of society), which leads to greater understanding or universality (in both philosophy and in social institutions such as religion and politics), eventually leading to complete self-understanding – again, the end of history.

What Marx and the other Young Hegelians took from Hegel was a method and a language that allowed them to challenge tradition and the existing order: a focus on history, both of theories and society, and a stress on flux, change, contradiction, movement, process, and so forth. But they also turned their critical gaze on the more conservative dimensions of Hegel's philosophy. For example, Feuerbach (in *The Essence of Christianity*, published in 1841) argued that Hegel's Absolute Spirit was nothing more than the deceased spirit of theology, that is, it was still an inverted world consciousness. Instead, for Feuerbach, God was the outward projection of people's inward nature. People were "alienated" from their human essence in and through religion – because they cast all their human powers onto a deity, instead of assuming them as their own. The goal, then, was to change consciousness by becoming aware of that self-alienation, through critique.

Marx, in particular, considered Feuerbach's critique to be an important step beyond Hegel. Ultimately, however, he rejected the way Feuerbach formulated the problem (as individuals separated from their human

[6] The third moment serves to replace, but at the same time preserve aspects of, earlier moments – a process that Hegel refers to as *aufheben* (to sublate). Thus, Becoming sublates, both replacing and preserving, Being and Nothingness.

essence, outside of society) and settled his account with the eleven "Theses on Feuerbach" (ME, 143–5), the last of which has become the most famous: "The philosophers have only *interpreted* the world, in various ways; the point is to *change* it."

Utopian Socialism

The third major influence on Marx's critique of political economy (in addition to and combined with mainstream economics and Hegel's philosophy) was utopian socialism.

During the early to mid-nineteenth century, socialist ideas were sweeping across Western Europe – starting in France and Britain, and traveling from there to many other parts of the world. They provoked extensive discussions and debates, a wide variety of plans to ameliorate the ravages of capitalism and to replace it with something better, and not a few attempts to create a radically different economic and social order.

The modern idea of utopia can be traced back to the sixteenth century, to Thomas More's famous text of that name. But socialist versions of utopia came much later, in response to the frustrated promises of the French Revolution. The crises of the *Ancien Régime*, caused by obscene levels of economic and social inequality, provoked a demand for liberty, equality, and fraternity. But for all the upheaval in France – the breaking-up of the feudal order (including the stripping-away of the privileges of nobility and the breakup of large Church-owned estates) and the creation of radically new social and political institutions (such as the institution of universal suffrage and the abolition of slavery in the colonies) – the initial revolution and the subsequent restoration, which combined to enshrine individual rights and private property, actually served to clear the way for capitalism and thus to create new forms of inequality.

Socialist ideas sprung up in response, inspired by the combination of utopian promises and the failures in practice of the revolution. They served as a counterpoint to the other utopia being offered at that time, that of the classical political economists, which celebrated the emergence of capitalism. The utopian socialists, in contrast, were critical of capitalism and its negative effects on workers and the wider society. The most interesting and influential of this latter group were, in France, Henri de Saint-Simon and Charles Fourier, and, in Britain, Robert Owen.

Saint-Simon claimed that the needs of the industrial class, which he also referred to as the working-class, needed to be recognized and fulfilled to have an efficient economy and an effective society.[7] He argued, in conse-

[7] To be clear, Saint-Simon's definition of the working-class was not restricted to the contemporary meaning (according to which it consists of blue-collar workers or those

quence, that the direction of society should be in the hands of scientists and engineers (not the "idling class," who produce nothing but instead live off the labor of others), in order to allow for the rapid development of technology and industry (*Industry*, which appeared in 1816–17), and that the role of religion was to guide the community toward improving as quickly as possible the conditions of the poorest class (*The New Christianity*, published in 1825).

Fourier, for his part, presented a more radical critique of the existing order and a more ambitious plan for creating a new kind of economic and social organization. Not only did he attack poverty as one of the principal disorders of society (which could be solved by raising wages and providing a basic income for those who could not work); he argued that labor itself (indeed, all creative endeavors) could be transformed into pleasurable activities.[8] The primary mechanism for this would be the formation of "phalanxes" (based upon buildings called *phalanstères* or grand hotels) that would encourage the cooperation of different kinds of labor (based on jobs chosen according to the interests and desires of their members), which would both raise productivity and create social harmony.

In Britain, it was Robert Owen who became best known for attacking the deplorable conditions in which factory workers lived and labored – blaming the economic and social structure of capitalism, not the workers themselves. He then sought to change the system: first, in the New Lanark Mills in Scotland, which he owned and managed and where he improved working conditions as well as providing youth education and child care; and then on a much larger scale, as an avowed socialist. Owen advocated radical social reform (such as the formation of trade unions and the provision of free education for children) and proposed a model for the organization of self-sufficient cooperative communities to serve as the basis for a "new moral world."

During the first half of the nineteenth century, when Marx was developing and then extending into new areas his "ruthless criticism of everything existing," and beginning his lifelong collaboration with Engels,

---

without a college education), much less the Marxist notion (which will be analyzed in detail in part II), but included all people he considered to be engaged in productive work that contributed to society, such as industrialists, managers, scientists, and bankers, along with manual and skilled laborers.

[8] See especially *Le nouveau monde industriel et sociétaire, ou Invention du procédé d'industrie attrayante et naturelle distribuée en séries passionnées* ["The New Industrial World"], originally published in 1829. Fourier also criticized the repressive family structure, in which men treated their spouses as if they owned them and children had little freedom to express their deepest sentiments. He believed that humans should create more equitable relationships between the sexes and that equality could exist only if people were freed from the constraints of marriage. He thus advocated free love and the collective raising of children within the community.

these were the socialist ideas that were "in the air," discussed and debated by a wide variety of thinkers and activists.[9] They weren't just critical ideas and lofty plans. The utopian socialists and their followers also sought to go beyond writing books and giving speeches by creating communities based on their ideas. This was particularly true in the United States, where more than 30 Fourierist phalanxes were established in the 1840s (two of the most famous being Brook Farm, in Massachusetts, and the Wisconsin Phalanx, in Ceresco). Owen himself financed and founded the community of New Harmony, in Indiana, based on his principles (where the Working Men's Institute, Indiana's oldest continuously operating public library, still exists).[10]

Eventually, as we will see in chapter 9, Marx and Engels developed a critique of the ideas put forward by the utopian socialists. But they also expressed a great deal of admiration for these initial socialist thinkers, and were certainly influenced by them as they developed their own critique of both mainstream economic theory and capitalism.

Capitalism

As we have seen in previous sections, we have to understand three major theoretical and political currents – classical political economy, Hegel's philosophy, and utopian socialism – in order to understand the path Marx traversed in his writings prior to setting to work on *Capital*. We also have to keep in mind the larger context, the development of capitalism in the nineteenth century.

It was during the "age of capital," as the illustrious British historian Eric Hobsbawm aptly called it, that Marx formulated his critique of political economy. By the time he landed in London (in 1849, after leaving Germany and spending short periods first in Paris and then Brussels), where he would remain based for the rest of his life, England had become the epicenter of capitalism.

[9] Socialism also became, then as now, the pejorative epithet that was attributed to any criticisms and suggestions for economic and social change their opponents wanted to stop.

[10] Hundreds of other "intentional communities," many of them short-lived, proliferated during this time, especially in the United States (but also as far flung as Australia, where Herrnhut was founded in 1855). Only some of them were directly inspired by utopian socialism. The others often looked to spiritual leaders and religious principles of community for inspiration. In fact, the longest-lasting experiment with communism in the modern age was not, as is generally presumed, the Soviet Union (which lasted from 1922 to 1991), but the Shakers (from its first settlement at Watervliet, New York, in 1774 to when the leaders of the United Society of Believers in Canterbury Shaker Village, Maine voted to close the Shaker Covenant in 1957).

Today, we think of capitalism as encompassing the entire world.[11] That certainly was not the case in the first half of the nineteenth century, when most economic and social life around the globe was organized along decidedly noncapitalist lines. In England, however, by the end of the first Industrial Revolution, capitalism was well established, especially in the burgeoning cities of London, Liverpool, Manchester, and Birmingham. More and more, both consumer goods and producer goods (from textiles to machinery) were being produced in capitalist factories. In other words, they had become capitalist commodities, created by laborers who received a wage working for the capitalists who owned the mills and workshops.

Elsewhere, the transition to capitalism, while less advanced than in England, was also taking place and leaving its mark on the existing social order. For example, the conditions and consequences of capitalism were quite evident in France and Belgium, much more so than in Germany; while the United States, as it slid toward civil war, was also creating a hothouse for capitalist industry, especially in the northeast. In all those places, enormous fortunes (accumulated through local and global trade, owning large estates, lending money, putting slaves to work, and so on) were utilized to purchase the ability to labor of workers (many of them former feudal serfs, self-sufficient farmers, artisans, and slaves) as well as new machinery and technologies (from the power loom and cotton gin through steam power and iron-making to new modes of transportation, such as canals and railroads).

The age of capital was nothing less than a project for remaking the world, in every dimension. It was a revolution in industrial production that, as Engels wrote in his classic study of *The Condition of the Working Class in England*, was changing the whole of civil society – from the organization of work and production to politics and culture and the entire class structure. Then as now, the captains of industry and supporters of capitalism were confident about their project. They promised to create general prosperity and to universalize the bourgeois individual guided solely by self-interest and rational calculation. And, in many ways, it succeeded. The development of capitalism created gigantic factories, titanic temples of industrial production, and colossal cities, occupied by an escalating number of native and immigrant workers. Traditional ways of life and meaning were cast aside and new habits acquired, with an eye (at least among the middle and upper classes) to accumulate individual wealth and extol the virtues of free and expanding markets.

[11] That's certainly how mainstream economists and many others think of capitalism, as characterizing the entire economy in pretty much all places around the globe. As we will see in chapter 7, what they forget or overlook is that many parts of contemporary society, in rich and poor countries alike, include various forms of noncapitalism. Consider for the moment one prominent example: how many of our households, where of course a great deal of labor is performed on a daily basis, are based on a capitalist mode of production?

But, by the same token (and no different from today), the new capitalist order was itself fragile – subject to fits and starts and periodic downturns, and characterized by obscene levels of inequality and widespread misery. The bulk of the population experienced a decline in their living standards, with wages that didn't keep pace with the prices of necessary consumer goods, along with poor sanitation, inadequate housing, and precarious access to clean water. Moreover, their jobs and skills were threatened by the combination of technological change, embodied in the new factory machinery, and the more detailed divisions of labor that could be instituted once they were collected to work in one place. In many instances, workers became mere appendages of the machines they once managed. That meant more profits for their employers but, in relative terms, much less for them in the form of wages.

It should come as no surprise, then, that the capitalist project was contested wherever it took hold. We read in chapter 1 about the Luddites, the radical faction of English textile workers that attempted to destroy factory machinery as a form of protest. This period also saw the resurgence of other labor organizations, especially trade unions (such as Robert Owen's short-lived Grand National Consolidated Trades Union) and the demand for more democracy (a working-class suffrage movement led by the British Chartists) – which, in their growing influence, led to the repeal of laws that had made any sort of strike action illegal.

The development of capitalism led to even more widespread political upheavals, culminating in 1848, during what Hobsbawm refers to as the "springtime of the peoples." That year was filled with the specter of revolution across continental Europe (with the notable exceptions of England and Russia) and beyond. Government after government was overthrown and, in the end, over 50 countries – from Sweden to Colombia – were affected. The revolutions were informed by diverse ideologies, including various forms of liberal democracy and socialism, their banners carried by the new social classes created by capitalism, from members of the grand bourgeoisie, their intellectuals, and the middle classes to the masses of rural landless laborers, urban artisans, and industrial workers. In the end, while the revolutions eventually failed and the old regimes restored, starting in 1849 (Marx argued, in various speeches and newspaper articles, the revolutions were betrayed by many of the liberal intellectuals, who sought an accommodation with the monarchs and governments on their own terms), it was clear that all that was considered solid was melting into thin air.[12]

[12] This is a paraphrase from one of the most famous texts of 1848, *The Manifesto of the Communist Party*, which Marx and Engels were commissioned to write: "All that is solid melts into air, all that is holy is profaned, and man is at last compelled to face with sober senses his real conditions of life, and his relations with his kind" (ME, 476). We will return to a discussion of the *Communist Manifesto* in chapter 9.

It was in the maelstrom of this age of capital – of the widening and deepening of capitalism and of the revolutionary upheavals it provoked – that Marx pursued his "ruthless criticism of everything existing." In the next section, we look at some of his best-known texts of that period, before he wrote *Capital*.

Toward Marx's Critique of Political Economy

There is no necessary trajectory to Marx's writings, no reason his earlier writings had to lead to or culminate in *Capital*. However, as we look back from the vantage point of his critique of political economy, we can see the ways his thinking changed and how the elements of that critique eventually emerged.

In this section, we take a quick look at some of Marx's key texts prior to writing *Capital*: the *Economic and Philosophic Manuscripts of 1844*, the "Theses on Feuerbach," the *German Ideology*, the *Grundrisse*, and *A Contribution to the Critique of Political Economy*. Together, they give us a sense of how Marx's ideas developed and changed over time.

We will also see two themes emerge over the course of these texts: the role of critique and a focus on social context. First, Marx doesn't start (in these texts or, for that matter, in *Capital*) with a given approach or set of first principles. Instead, his method is to engage with ideas and problems that were "out there," in the intellectual and social worlds he inhabited, and to formulate a critique, thereby giving rise to new ways of raising issues, posing questions, and coming up with answers. Second, Marx's concern is always with social and historical specificity, as against looking for or finding what others consider to be given and universal. Thus, for example, Marx eschews any notion of a transhistorical or transcultural "human nature." Instead, in his view, different human natures are both the condition and consequence of particular social and historical circumstances. Much the same holds for his method of engaging economic issues.

Once Marx left Germany and found his way to Paris, he met Engels for the first time (thus initiating, following on their previous written correspondence, a life-long collaboration) and also began what he considered to be a "conscientious critical study of political economy," the mainstream economics of his day. The result was a series of three manuscripts (often referred to as the *Economic and Philosophic Manuscripts of 1844* or the *Paris Manuscripts*, which were written between April and August 1844 but only finally published, to considerable interest, in 1932). What readers will find in the manuscripts (ME, 66–125) is, having "proceeded from the premises of political economy" (meaning "its language and laws," the assumption of "private property, the separation of labor, capital and land, and of wages, profit of capital and rent of land," and so on), Marx arrives at conclusions and formulates new terms that run directly counter to those of Smith, Ricardo, and the other classical political economists. In particular, Marx argues, under capitalism, as workers become reduced to commodities, what they produce confronts them as "something alien." Therefore, their labor (using terms borrowed from Feuerbach's critique of Hegel) becomes "alienated" or "estranged."

> The *alienation* of the worker in his product means not only that his labour becomes an object, an *external* existence, but that it exists *outside him*, independently, as something alien to him, and that it becomes a power of its own confronting him; it means that the life which he has conferred on the object confronts him as something hostile and alien. (ME, 72)

Marx then demonstrates that the taken-for-granted assumptions of classical political economy – the existence of private property, wages, and so on – are themselves the products of estranged labor. Thus, the distinctions made by the mainstream economists of Marx's time – between profit and rent, between both and wages, and so on – are rooted not in the nature of things, but in particular social and historical circumstances. They are, in other words, peculiar to capitalism. Marx also argues that mainstream economics, despite its "worldly appearance," is actually "the most moral of all the sciences," because it exhorts workers to consume less and save more, thereby celebrating the "*ascetic* but *productive* slave" (ME, 95–6).

As we saw in the section on Hegel, Marx then (in 1845) developed a critique of Feuerbach. Over the course of his eleven short theses (ME, 143–5), Marx rejects the idea of a single anthropology (the "essence of man" or human nature) and focuses, instead, on the ensemble of "social relations," the "historical process," and "social humanity." The result is social practice, that is, the goal of not just interpreting the world, but of changing it.

The next year, Marx coauthored with Engels a long set of manuscripts (like the 1844 manuscripts, only published in 1932), *The German Ideology* (ME, 146–200), in which they challenge the one-sided criticisms of Hegel by Bruno Bauer, other Young Hegelians, and the post-Hegelian philosopher Max Stirner. There, in their attack on German philosophy for having become obsessed with religion (and therefore with self-consciousness or the realm of ideas), Marx and Engels announce for the first time what they call the "materialist conception of history," with an alternative starting-point: "real individuals, their activity and the material conditions under which they live, both those which they find already existing and those produced by their activity" (ME, 149). This focus on social production means Marx and Engels can transform consciousness itself into a "social product," which develops historically and changes according to particular forms of society or social relationships. They also announce what, at least at this stage, they mean by "communism": "not a *state of affairs* which is to be established, an *ideal* to which reality [will] have to adjust itself. We call communism the *real* movement which abolishes the present state of things. The conditions of this movement result from the premises now in existence" (ME, 162).

Later, once Marx had settled in London, he spent much of his time in the British Museum (a national public museum, which contained both natural history objects and a massive library) studying the texts of the classical political economists. The result was a set of notebooks, called the *Grundrisse* (literally, outlines or plans), which are often considered to be the first draft of *Capital*.[13] While the topics Marx covered are wide-ranging, from value and labor to precapitalist forms of economic and social organization and the preconditions for communism, what is of interest here is his announcement of where he thinks the critique of political economy should start: with "socially determined individual production" (ME, 222).

Why is this important? Because it represents Marx's break from the notion of *natural* production, and therefore from the mainstream economics of his day (as of our own). In classical political economy (as in contemporary mainstream economics), capitalism and other economies are considered to be natural, because they are finally reduced to and can be explained by certain given or exogenous factors, such as population, technology, and resources (to which neoclassical economists added given preferences). Also, they take individuals as their point of departure (the most famous example being Robinson Crusoe, a story that is repeated even today in mainstream economics textbooks). Marx's alternative view is that economics should start with social individuals, "individuals producing in society," not given individuals outside of particular historical and social contexts. Moreover, the focus should be on "social production" – different, socially determined ways of producing goods and services – not on any kind of production in general (which students in mainstream economics courses today will recognize in the technical apparatus of isocost and isoquant curves).

Marx also demonstrates his debt to Hegel, in discussing the relationship among production, distribution, exchange, and consumption. Where the classical political economists posit that the goal of production is consumption, and many of the other critics of classical political economy worry about distribution, Marx sees them in terms of a "dialectical unity." In its most general form,

[13] The seven notebooks (ME, 221–93) were written during the winter of 1857–8 but were only published in 1939. The first English-language translation (by Martin Nicolaus) appeared in 1973. The publication of the *Grundrisse* was important not only for readers of *Capital* (and much discussion has ensued about the overlaps and differences between the two), but also for other fields, especially for the new field of cultural studies (in the work of, among others, Stuart Hall and the famous Center for Contemporary Cultural Studies at the University of Birmingham).

> A definite production thus determines a definite consumption, distribution and exchange as well as *definite relations between these different moments*. Admittedly, however, *in its one-sided form*, production is itself determined by the other moments. (ME, 236)

This is a distinction that shows up today in the debate about distribution (through free markets) versus redistribution (through taxes and government programs). What the participants in that debate often forget is the initial distribution of resources and wealth, related to the way capitalist production is organized, which then affects (and, in turn, is affected by) the patterns of consumption, the distribution of income, and the forms of exchange. That initial, profoundly unequal distribution is taken as given by mainstream economists and policymakers.

Marx also announces his break from existing ways of carrying out economic analysis, whether starting from abstract first principles (and deducing the rules that govern reality) or from empirical reality (whereby certain "laws" are extracted). Instead, he argues, the method he proposes is a movement from the abstract to the concrete. In other words, economic analysis is itself a process of production – one that starts from relatively abstract notions and, adding more and more determinations or circumstances, arrives at relatively concrete conclusions ("the way in which thought appropriates the concrete, [which] reproduces it as the concrete in the mind" [ME, 237]). It is not a question of bridging the gap between thought and reality (in terms of some kind of correspondence and validity criterion), but of producing within thought a particular conception of economic and social reality. The implication, of course, is that different economic theories will lead to different, incommensurable conceptions of capitalism and other economic systems.

Finally, in 1859, Marx published *A Contribution to the Critique of Political Economy*. There, he designates his break from the philosophies of both Hegel and Feuerbach with what has become one of his most famous expressions: "It is not the consciousness of men that determines their existence, but their social existence that determines their consciousness" (ME, 4). This is Marx's critique of both Hegel's Absolute Spirit and Feuerbach's alienated consciousness.

A contemporary analogy stems from critical race theory, according to which racism is not the product of individual bias or prejudice, but something deeply embedded in legal systems and policies, which are what need to be changed.[14] It is the same idea that has motivated many working-class movements, from the nineteenth century onwards, which have sought an end to poverty and inequality, improved access to decent

[14] See, for example, Kimberle Crenshaw, Neil Gotanda, Gary Peller, and Kendall Thomas, eds., *Critical Race Theory: The Key Writings That Formed the Movement* (New York: Free Press, 1996).

housing and healthcare, and a substantial role in economic decision-making not by hoping their employers would change their minds and treat them more generously, but by ruthlessly criticizing and seeking to transform the existing economic and social systems.

Looking Ahead

At the end of the Preface to *A Contribution to the Critique of Political Economy*, Marx appends a quotation from Dante Alighieri's *Divine Comedy*, which can also serve as a warning to readers of this book as we embark, starting in the next chapter, on a detailed study of the basic concepts and method of Marx's critique of political economy:

> "Here one must leave behind all hesitation;
> Here every cowardice must meet its death."[15]

Suggested Readings

Joyce Appleby, *The Relentless Revolution: A History of Capitalism* (New York: W.W. Norton, 2010).

Jonathan Beecher, *Charles Fourier: The Visionary and His World* (Berkeley: University of California Press, 1990).

Friedrich Engels, *The Condition of the Working Class in England*, ed. Victor Kiernan (New York, Penguin, 2009 [1845]).

Eric Hobsbawm, *The Age of Capital: 1848–1875* (New York: Vintage Books, 1975).

Stephen Hymer, "*Robinson Crusoe* and the Secret of Primitive Accumulation," *Monthly Review* 23 (1971): 11–36.

Chris Jennings, *Paradise Now: The Story of American Utopianism* (New York: Random House, 2016).

Fred Moseley and Tony Smith, eds., *Marx's* Capital *and Hegel's* Logic: *A Reexamination* (Boston: Brill, 2014).

Robert Owen, *A New View of Society and Other Writings*, ed. and intro. Gregory Claeys (New York: Penguin, 1991).

David F. Ruccio, "Capitalism," in *Keywords for American Cultural Studies*, ed. Bruce Burgett and Glenn Hendler, 3rd ed., pp. 40–3 (New York: New York University Press, 2020).

David F. Ruccio and Jack Amariglio, *Postmodern Moments in Modern Economics* (Princeton, NJ: Princeton University Press, 2003).

Henri Saint-Simon, *Henri Saint-Simon (1760–1825): Selected Writings on Science, Industry, and Social Organization*, trans. and ed. Keith Taylor (New York: Routledge, 2016).

Sean Sayers, "Alienation," in *Routledge Handbook of Marxian Economics*, ed. David M. Brennan, David Kristjanson-Gural, Catherine P. Mulder, and Erik M. Olson, pp. 135–43 (New York: Routledge, 2017).

[15] The lines are from Canto III of "Inferno" (as Virgil's reply to Dante, who has just read the inscription over the Gates of Hell). The original is: "*Qui si convien lasciare ogni sospetto/ Ogni viltà convien che qui sia morta*" (ME, 6).

PART II
CONCEPTS AND METHOD

Chapter 4

COMMODITIES AND MONEY

We now know a great deal about the influences on Marx's writings, including British political economy, German philosophy, and French socialism, as well as the larger economic and social milieu of the development of capitalism during the first half of the nineteenth century. We also have a good sense of the path Marx took prior to formulating his critique of political economy. We were able to trace the trajectory of his criticisms of existing ideas in the following manner: starting with social criticism (in the letter to Ruge), Marx proceeded to focus on social labor (in the Paris manuscripts), social practice (in the theses on Feuerbach), and social production (in the *German Ideology*). Then, as we will see in *Capital*, Marx shifts his attention to social class.

In the next three chapters, in working our way through Marx's critique of political economy, we will follow (more or less) the plan of *Capital*. Much of our attention will be directed to the steps taken in the first volume, but we will also cover a variety of topics from volumes 2 and 3. Then, in the third and final part of this book, we will be prepared to look at some of the significant applications, debates, and consequences of Marx's critique of both mainstream economic theory and capitalism.

Before proceeding, we need to remember the warning included in the first chapter of this book: that the same words often have different meanings in different theories. Just as the idea of capitalism varies from one theory to another, so do the other concepts economists use. This is particularly true in the debate between Marx and classical political economy, since Marx borrowed many of the words he uses directly from the mainstream economists he was criticizing – value, price, labor, capital, and so on. But those words acquire new meanings within Marx's critique. So, we will have to be particularly attuned to those theoretical shifts, as well as to how those exact same words have acquired different meanings in today's world (in the basic theory and textbooks of contemporary mainstream economics as well as in the speeches of politicians, investigative reports and commentary in print and broadcast media, and social media feeds).

In terms of his own approach, Marx starts with the language of mainstream economics – but then ends up in a very different place. For example, as we will see in this part, Marx utilizes the labor theory of value first deployed by the classical economists and then shows how, even under their own strong assumptions, capitalism is characterized by class exploitation.

The Wealth of Nations

Readers of *Capital* are often surprised by where Marx starts his critique of political economy. He doesn't begin where one might expect – with class, history, or communism. Instead, it is a bit of a shock to read the opening sentences of the first chapter of volume 1:

> The wealth of those societies in which the capitalist mode of production prevails appears as "an immense collection of commodities"; the individual commodity appears as its elementary form. Our investigation therefore begins with the analysis of a commodity. (KI, 126)

The question is, why? Why start with the commodity? As we learned in an earlier chapter, wealth is the central concept of classical political economy. It is both the premise and promise of that theory: economic development is defined in terms of the amount of wealth created, and capitalism is celebrated precisely because it is capable of producing more wealth than any other economic system.[1] In other words, Marx starts where the classicals leave off. Their *conclusion* is that capitalism leads to more "wealth of nations," which is equivalent to "an immense collection of commodities." Marx then proceeds to question the conditions and consequences of that wealth.

From the very start, Marx uses the language of mainstream economics and then explores both what it says and what it does not or cannot say. One aspect of that language is that wealth takes a particular form under capitalism: the products of human labor become commodities, that is, goods and services that are bought and sold in markets. That's where Marx begins his investigation. But we learn something radically different is going on in his approach – compared to mainstream economics, then as now – because Marx's analysis in chapter 1 begins with the commodity and ends with commodity fetishism.[2] To put it differently, Marx starts with

[1] To avoid confusion, please keep in mind that the notion of wealth used in classical political economy is a flow of commodities produced over a period of time (say, a year). It is not the contemporary notion of wealth, which is a stock of assets (such as corporate equities, bonds, and real estate) at a particular point in time that yields a financial return to the owner.

[2] Classical political economists began with the division of labor and ended with

the commodity, a common sense within both mainstream economics and capitalism, and then suggests we see it as something quite strange, subject to further questioning.

Before we proceed, here is another important (and often overlooked) caution: nothing in the treatment of commodities and commodity exchange in this chapter presumes the existence of capitalism. It is just about objects that are bought and sold in markets, no matter how they are produced. Yes, they might be capitalist commodities but, at this point in the analysis, they might also be slave commodities, feudal commodities, or for that matter communist commodities. To be sure, the point of Marx's analysis is to eventually get to capitalism (because he's referring to the wealth of societies in which "the capitalist mode of production prevails") but that's a task that is only accomplished through the steps covered in the next chapter. Here, the focus is only on the movement, step by step, from the commodity to the role of money in generalized commodity exchange.

The Commodity

To start with, Marx follows the classical economists in positing the two-fold nature of commodities: they have use-values and exchange-values (KI, 125–8). Their use-values are intrinsic to the commodities as external objects; they have some kind of usefulness to those who purchase them. The commodities' exchange-values, on the other hand, are distinct from the use-values and the nature of the commodities themselves; they refer to the terms by which different commodities can be exchanged with one another in markets.

Thus, Marx identifies an initial tension in the commodity (*C*): it has a use-value (*UV*), which is realized qualitatively in the private act of consumption, and an exchange-value (*EV*), which is realized quantitatively in the social act of exchange (see figure 4.1). And, here's the key: use-value and exchange-value are distinct from and incommensurable with one another.[3]

Use-value thus depends on a particular transformation of nature, which determines the social usefulness of an object. For example, wood can be used to make a table or a door, which are qualitatively different use-values.

---

commodities. The only difference today is that mainstream economists begin with scarcity (defined in terms of limited means and unlimited desires) and finish, just as the classicals did, with "an immense collection of commodities."

[3] This was also the case in classical political economy. However, today, mainstream economists are determined to show that use-value and exchange-value are equal. This takes place during the course of individuals' choices in maximizing utility subject to a budget constraint; in equilibrium, price is equal to utility (technically, as we saw in chapter 2, the ratio of prices, p_1/p_2 is equal to the ratio of marginal utilities, MU_1/MU_2).

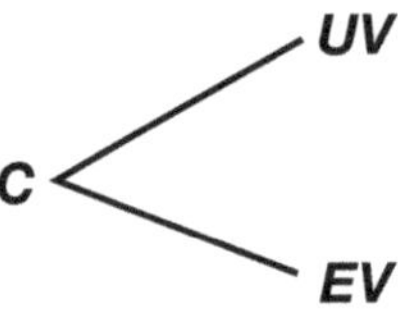

Figure 4.1 Two-fold nature of the commodity

By the same token, use-value denotes a relationship between a commodity and the individual consuming it, what I referred to above as the private act of consumption. Once the commodity is purchased, the individual realizes its use-value while consuming it (in other words, they eat at the table or use the door to enter or exit a room).

But, to be clear, there is nothing given or universal about use-value. It can and often does change depending on the historical and social circumstances. Thus, for example, smoking cigarettes went from being an elite custom to a widespread social practice and, today, it has become a largely circumscribed or prohibited activity. Bananas, too, have had different social lives: more than a thousand different varieties have long served as staples of people's diets around the world; later, one variety (first the Gros Michel, then the Cavendish) was transformed into a favorite snack for US consumers. In general, a historical change in social practices can be expected to lead to changes in use-values.[4]

The key for Marx is that use-values are the "material bearers" of exchange-values (KI, 126). In other words, the existence of different use-values makes exchange possible. It is one of the conditions of existence of the non-accidental exchange of commodities that characterizes capitalism.[5] But commodities cannot exchange as different use-values, since they are qualitatively different and have nothing in common.

That creates a contradiction, based on the following propositions concerning, for example, the exchange of shirts and oranges:

1. Use-values must be different for exchange to take place (nobody exchanges one shirt for one shirt).
2. But use-values must be abstracted from in order for the exchange of equivalents to take place (there's no sense in which one shirt can be

[4] While Marx's notion of use-value bears a passing resemblance to contemporary mainstream economists' concept of utility, the two could not be more different: whereas use-value is historically and socially determined, utility is taken to be exogenous, determined outside markets and taken as given.

[5] To be clear, objects can have use-values without having exchange-values (KI, 131). Self-sufficient farmers or children doing chores in their households create use-values but, since they are not traded in markets, what they produce (food or doing the dishes) does not have an exchange-value.

equal to three oranges because they are different use-values and used for different purposes).

3. Thus, all commodities exchange as equals only in terms of something they have in common, a third element, which is neither one nor the other.

In terms of this third element, one shirt IS worth three oranges! But not as use-values, only as exchange-values. It is a contradiction worthy of Hegel (and probably an exchange that might take place in Siberia), which can only be resolved by identifying what that third element is.

For the classical political economists, that common element is labor (hence, their use of a labor theory of value). Commodities can be exchanged as equivalents because they embody equal amounts of society's labor. One shirt is worth three oranges because it took equal amounts of human labor to produce them (KI, 127–31).

Exchange-Value and Value

It is important before going any further to clear up a common misunderstanding (especially for those who read *Capital* itself along with this book). Marx refers to both exchange-value and value, and uses them more or less interchangeably at this stage of the analysis. So, we need some clear definitions: exchange-value refers to the form of value in exchange, and thus an amount of labor for which a commodity is exchanged. Value, on the other hand, refers to production, and thus the amount of labor embodied in a commodity while it is being produced.

Each commodity therefore has two numbers attached to it: exchange-value (or value in exchange) and value (or value in production).[6] They are clearly not the same (because it is quite possible and, as Marx will show, quite common for the amount of labor embodied in production to be different from the amount of labor for which the commodity exchanges once it is traded in a market). And that difference can matter a great deal – say, if a producer expends 100 hours of labor to produce a commodity and only gets the equivalent of 20 hours in selling it.

However, to avoid unnecessary complications at this early point in the analysis, Marx *assumes* that, quantitatively, the two can be treated as equal. The amount of value in production (*W*) is equal to the amount of value for

[6] The classicals also attached two numbers to commodities: labor embodied (in production) and labor commanded (in exchange). But they ran into theoretical difficulties trying to reconcile the two notions of labor value. That's one of the tasks Marx sets out to accomplish – to investigate the conditions and consequences of different values and exchange-values. In contemporary mainstream economics, however, commodities only have one number: the value or market price determined by supply and demand.

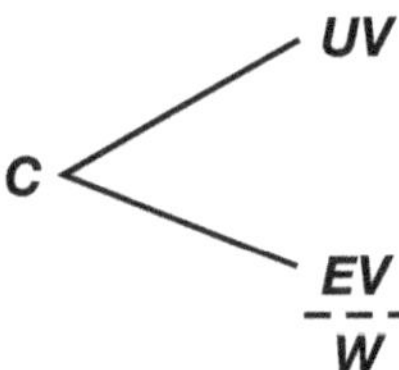

Figure 4.2 Exchange-value and value

which the commodity exchanges (*EV*) – with a dashed line between them in figure 4.2 indicating the assumption, at this stage, of their quantitative equality. Later in the analysis, Marx deliberately relaxes this assumption and analyzes both the reasons for and the implications of those two numbers being different.[7]

So, what is this human labor that Marx argues serves as the basis, the accounting scheme, for a commodity's value (KI, 129)? It is an amount of "socially necessary abstract labor time." Thus, (a) it is measured in hours; (b) it is a portion of society's total labor, reduced to the same standard; and (c) it is an amount that is deemed to be "socially necessary," depending on a wide variety of factors (including the average degree of skill and intensity of labor, productivity, technology, and so on). Thus, exchange-value is measured in terms of the number of hours of socially necessary abstract labor-time for which a commodity is exchanged, while value is an amount of socially necessary abstract labor-time embodied in the commodity during the course of production.

Neither value nor exchange-value is therefore considered to be given, as a technical datum. Rather, each is socially determined, affected by all the other economic and noneconomic processes in society: value, of course, by the average conditions of production at any point in time; and

[7] This is particularly important in thinking about the relationship among the three volumes of *Capital*. Mainstream economists have often criticized Marx's treatment because the assumption of the first volume (that exchange-values equal values) doesn't hold in the third volume (where, in general, exchange-values do not and cannot equal values). What those critics overlook is the fact that Marx wrote the manuscript for volume 3 before volume 1 was ever published. So, what is that variation based on? It rests on a change in the assumptions concerning the way exchange and production interact. Marx assumes exchange-value and value are equal in volume 1 to get the analysis started; then, in volume 3 (after having discussed circulation or exchange in volume 2), he gives up that assumption. We can see this theoretical development by examining the subtitles of the three volumes: "The Process of Production of Capital" (volume 1, assuming certain characteristics of exchange), "The Process of Circulation of Capital" (volume 2, assuming the characteristics of production from the previous volume), and then "The Process of Capitalist Production as a Whole" (volume 3, in which each – production and exchange – affects the other). This is a good example of Marx's approach of moving from the relatively abstract (in volumes 1 and 2) to the relatively concrete (in volume 3).

exchange-value, by another set of factors, from the market structure to advertising.

What about an inefficient producer, someone who spends more time in producing an object than other producers (KI, 129)? Does their commodity have more value and exchange-value? Well, no. A commodity-producing society has a kind of disciplinary mechanism, in that each producer's commodity is exchanged in the same market as those of other producers. Therefore, they exchange at the average of their individual expenditures of labor – and the inefficient producer turns out to have spent part of their time in socially *un*necessary labor.

Concrete and Abstract Labor

If labor is going to be used as the measuring rod for commodity values, it needs to analyzed in the same terms as the two-fold nature of the commodity (KI, 131–9). Therefore, it is important to distinguish abstract labor (*AL*), which is the basis of exchange-value and value, from concrete labor (*CL*), which serves to create use-values (see figure 4.3).

When labor is examined in this dual sense, concrete labor (say, the labor of a shirt-maker or orange grower) creates different use-values, while abstract labor (society's homogeneous mass of labor) is the basis of exchange-value and value. The argument is the same as with the two-fold nature of the commodity: different concrete labors are necessary for commodity exchange to take place but it is necessary to abstract from the qualitative differences among specific skills to analyze the labor that is made equivalent through commodity exchange.

The process of commodity exchange is what reduces complex labor to simple, abstract labor. Thus, for example, healthcare produced by doctors and nurses is exchanged on markets with childcare and landscaping produced by undocumented immigrants. This all occurs, Marx argues, "behind the backs of the producers" (KI, 135).

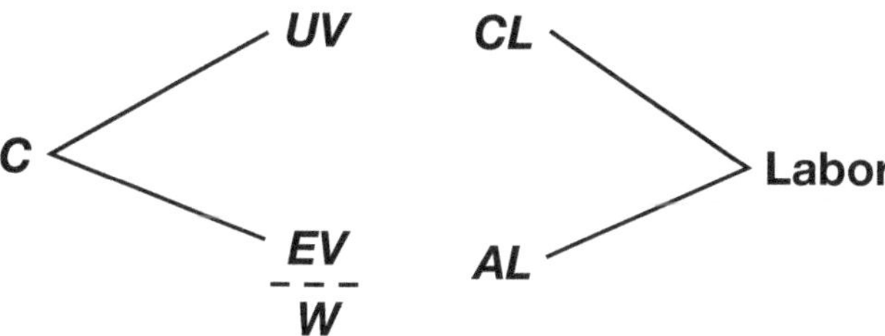

Figure 4.3 Two-fold nature of the commodity and labor

Assumptions

The dual character of labor is not enough for commodity exchange to take place. The classical political economists assumed a specific set of other conditions, including: (a) a social division of labor, such that separate producers trade different commodities in markets; (b) private property, which means that commodity owners have the right to buy and sell their commodities; and (c) equal exchange, in other words, commodity exchangers trade equal amounts of value, and thus get what they pay for.

Marx carries over these same assumptions into his critique. Basically, what he's saying is, "I'll give the classical political economists their strongest possible case and then I'll show that, even under such idealistic assumptions, things can go wrong." In particular, he shows that commodity exchange (even before he arrives at capitalist commodity exchange) is inherently unstable, and that capitalist commodity exchange (once he gets there) is based on social theft.

All three assumptions are crucial. There's no commodity exchange unless different producers take to market their different commodities. And commodity exchange cannot take place unless those different producers actually own their commodities – both before the exchange, such that they have the right to sell them, and after the exchange, such that they can realize the commodities' use-values.[8]

The third assumption is the decisive one. Marx is not arguing that, in the real world, market exchanges always result in equal exchanges. That would be ludicrous.[9] All he is saying is that the classical political economists presume equality in market exchanges (as do contemporary mainstream economists) and therefore his critique will be most robust if he allows them their quixotic view of capitalist markets. Later, after arriving at his preliminary conclusions, Marx will relax the assumption of

[8] In the real world, of course, neither condition is absolute. For example, a social division of labor may exist but one entity may produce and exchange many different commodities. That's the case when large corporations (say, in the food industry) create or acquire many different production lines, often under different brand names. Similarly, private property rights are often circumscribed by rules and regulations (such as when, for example, products need to be tested and certified by government agencies). In both cases – the social division of labor and private property – the assumption is historically and socially determined and contested.

[9] There are many different forms of imperfect competition in real-world capitalism, in Marx's time as in our own. Oligopolies and monopolies (markets with a few large sellers and one seller, respectively) abound, which means that market prices are above the prices that would obtain under perfect competition, thus preventing equal exchanges. In a later section of volume 1 of *Capital* (and as we will see below, in chapter 6), Marx demonstrates that capitalism has an inherent tendency to create various forms of imperfect competition.

equal exchange and examine the conditions and consequences of unequal exchanges.[10]

Use-Value and Exchange-Value

Having established the contradictory, two-fold nature of the commodity, the next step is to work through the effects of that tension – to pull them apart. For example, it is quite possible for the use-value of a commodity to rise while its exchange-value and value fall. This is certainly the case in recent decades with computers: their social usefulness has risen (as many of us are required, at work as well as in our leisure time, to use various computerized electronic devices), while their per unit value and exchange-value (and thus market price) have decreased substantially over time.

In general, Marx's approach calls for him to identify tensions and contradictions, and then investigate their consequences, with the aim of focusing on sources of further change and development. This stands in sharp contrast to the work of mainstream economists, who concentrate on equilibrium situations and merely assume that some kind of movement takes place in order to arrive at a new equilibrium.[11]

While a commodity cannot have an exchange-value if it has no use-value (it can't be sold unless someone is willing to buy it, for its social usefulness), an object can have a use-value without being a commodity (because, while it may be useful, it changes hands through an activity other than a market, such as sharing, gifting, and other non-market practices). Moreover, Marx argues, labor is the source of exchange-value (and value) but it is *not* the only source of use-values; nature provides the raw materials for human labor to transform raw materials into commodities and therefore contributes to the creation of use-values (KI, 133–4).

Language of Commodities

It is the complex, contradictory combination of use-value and exchange-value/value that serves as the basis of the "language of commodities."

[10] This is another example of Marx's method, of moving from the (relatively) abstract to the (relatively) concrete. In other words, his analysis of capitalism changes as he alters the assumptions and introduces new determinations.

[11] While classical political economists tended to focus on long-run equilibrium, what is of most interest for contemporary mainstream economists is short-run equilibrium. What the two traditions share, however, is the idea of equilibrium – not only of individual markets, but of the economy as a whole. In contemporary mainstream economics, this is known as a Walrasian general equilibrium (after one of the first neoclassical economists, Léon Walras); in classical political economy, as we will see below, this is Say's Law.

In its simplest form, one commodity (C_1) is directly exchanged for another (C_2):

4.1 $$C_1 - C_2$$

More technically, a certain amount of one commodity (xC_1, where x is the amount of commodity 1) is worth or exchanges for an amount of another commodity (yC_2, where y is the amount of the second commodity): $xC_1 - yC_2$ or $xC_1 = yC_2$. Marx refers to the first as the relative value, and the second the equivalent value: commodity 1 therefore finds its equivalent in a certain amount of commodity 2, while the amount of commodity 2 is relative to the value of commodity 1.

Under the assumption of equal exchange, the exchange-value of the first commodity (one shirt, from the previous example) is equivalent to or expressed in terms of the second commodity (three oranges). What this means is a change in the social productivity of labor will change the relative form of value. So, xC_1 might become equal to, for example, $2yC_2$ or $0.5xC_1 = yC_2$ depending on a change in the value of C_1 or C_2 or both.

Figure 4.4 illustrates three possibilities (where the Greek letter delta, Δ, denotes a change). A change in the value of either or both commodities will change the exchange relationship between them (KI, 140–54). This captures and reinforces the idea that there is a social connection between the owners of different commodities: the relative value depends on the equivalent value, and vice-versa. For example, if the value of commodity one changes (ΔW_1), while the amount of value embodied in the second does not (W_2), then the ratio at which the two commodities exchange also changes. The same is true if the value of the second commodity or of both commodities changes. For example, if labor productivity in the making of shirts doubles (such that each shirt embodies half the amount of labor as before), then each shirt will be worth, and thus exchange for, half the number of oranges as before. Or, by the same token, it takes twice as many shirts to exchange for the same number of oranges. Thus, the

Relative Value (C_1)	Equivalent Value (C_2)
ΔW_1	W_2
W_1	ΔW_2
ΔW_1	ΔW_2

Figure 4.4 Relative and equivalent value

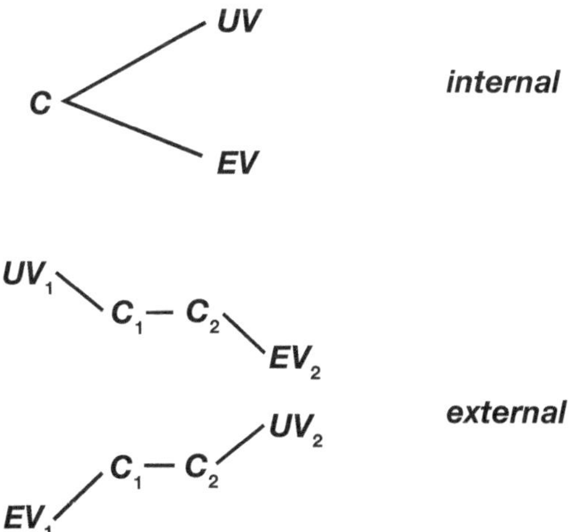

Figure 4.5 Internal and external opposition

exchange relationship goes from $1C_1 = 3C_2$ to $1C_1 = 1.5C_2$ or, what is the same, $2C_2 = 3C_2$.

Moreover, the existence of even such a simple or barter exchange of two commodities transforms the *internal* opposition of use-value and exchange-value/value into an *external* opposition (see figure 4.5).

The idea is that each commodity enters into the exchange in a one-sided fashion. Thus, for example, from the perspective of the owner of commodity 2 (C_2 or, e.g., oranges), what they care about is the use-value of the first commodity (the usefulness of C_1 or the shirt, which is why they want to purchase it) and the exchange-value of their commodity (EV_2, which needs to be realized in order to purchase the first commodity). Exactly the opposite occurs in the case of commodity-owner 1.[12]

To put it differently, in order for such a simple exchange to take place, the owners of the two commodities need to find someone who wants what they have and has what they want. If by chance or time and effort they manage to do that, then an exchange can take place.

But, of course, in a society in which "wealth ... presents itself as 'an immense collection of commodities'," each commodity (C_1) can be exchanged for many other commodities (C_2 through C_n). Marx refers to this as the total or expanded form of value (KI, 154–7), in which case the "accidental relation between two individual commodity-owners disappears" (KI, 156).

If one of those commodities is – by "social custom" (KI, 162) – accepted in exchange for all the others, then we have what can be called a "universal equivalent" (see figure 4.6).

---

[12] I have eliminated from figure 4.5 the expression for value (*W*), which is assumed to be quantitatively equal to exchange-value (*EV*), in order to make things easier to see.

$$yC_2 — xC_1$$

$$zC_3 —$$

•

•

•

Figure 4.6 Universal equivalent

A particular amount of one commodity (xC_1) can be exchanged for any and all other commodities (yC_2, zC_3, and so forth). In such a case, the first commodity (perhaps gold, silver, or some other commodity) is the equivalent form of value for the other commodities. In short, the first commodity now serves as money (M).

What this means is that the simple commodity form ($C_1 - C_2$ or barter) is actually the source of the money form (whereby C_1 or M can be used to purchase C_2, C_3, and all other commodities). It is the use of money that makes such a generalized exchange of commodities possible.[13]

Commodity Fetishism

There's a great deal more to explore in the case of generalized commodity exchange, with the introduction of money. But, for the time being we must pause, leave that analysis for the next section, and consider the issue of commodity fetishism.

It is perhaps the most read (certainly by scholars and students outside of economics, in cultural studies, literary criticism, and so on) and, at the same time, most misunderstood part of the first chapter of *Capital*. The section itself is certainly odd, at least when compared to the texts of mainstream economics. But that is actually the point. Marx takes a common sense – a generally unexamined assumption of mainstream economic theory, in his time and in our own, as well as in daily life under capitalism – and then makes it seem strange. The idea that it is natural to obtain objects via commodity exchange is simply taken for granted in

[13] This, it should be noted, is a logical explanation or derivation of money in terms of commodity exchange. It is not a historical account such as one finds in David Graeber's book, *Debt: The First 5,000 Years*, in which money arises not in terms of exchange (as a solution to the problems associated with mainstream economists' "fantasy world of barter"), but as a way of quantifying and reinforcing debt obligations.

classical political economy and in contemporary mainstream economics; it is also accepted without major questions or objections by most people, who rely on going to market (in person or, increasingly, online) to obtain a large portion of the goods they need or want to consume. In both cases, in economic theory and in quotidian existence, people see themselves as commodity exchangers.

That's what Marx calls commodity fetishism – the agency or subjectivity associated with commodity exchange. And it is more than a bit strange, especially since in most societies throughout human history objects changed hands outside of markets. They shared them or gifted them or appropriated them (or had them taken from them) without any kind of market; they engaged in non-market exchanges (or, in the case of self-sufficient individuals, households, or communities, with no exchange at all). Or objects changed hands through individual markets, especially in long-distance trading, but not in and through a full-blown market system (in which land, labor, and money are converted into and traded as commodities). The emergence of a market system, what Marx refers to as the generalized exchange of commodities across society, is a relatively recent phenomenon (and, of course, is still not the case for many people, at least in certain spheres of their lives).[14] What that means is that, for commodity exchange to take place, people need to have a certain set of skills or characteristics – specific ways of behaving and seeing themselves and others. Without those qualities, commodity exchange is literally impossible.

In the part on commodity fetishism, Marx refers to it as a "definite social relation between men themselves which assumes here, for them, the fantastic form of a relation between things" (KI, 165), which is "inseparable from the production of commodities" (KI, 165). The social relations between human beings takes the form of the exchange between the objects they own, $C_1 - C_2$. So, with commodity exchange, we end up with material relations between persons and social relations between things. We confront one another as commodity-owners, and commodity fetishism is the set of attributes of the subjects who are engaged in commodity exchange.

"So what?" is one possible response. "That's just the way people are." Well, Marx responds, yes and no. Yes, commodity fetishism is necessary for people to exchange goods and services in markets. But, no, commodity fetishism just can't be assumed, as some kind of universal – transcultural or transhistorical – human nature. That's why it needs to be understood as a

[14] Public goods are an example of non-commodities, which have use-values but are not traded in markets. Many are provided as government services (from flood control to street lighting); others are non-governmental collective goods (such as knowledges and languages).

fetish, which according to dictionary definitions involves the worshipping of an inanimate object for its supposed magical powers. It is, in other words, the attribution of inherent value or spirit to an external object.

Commodity fetishism is therefore a polemic against the classical political economists (which is obvious from the footnotes in that part of *Capital*). It is a critique of the idea of *homo economicus*, the idea that people have (as Adam Smith wrote) a "natural propensity to truck, barter, and exchange."[15] By extension, it is also a critique of the self-interested rational actor, which is simply presumed by neoclassical economists today.[16] In both cases, human beings are assumed to be characterized by a fetish of the commodity, an ability and willingness to buy and sell goods and services in markets.

But there is another target of Marx's critique, which is often overlooked: Feuerbach. Marx is not arguing that commodity fetishism is a false consciousness or a distorted view of the world (as Feuerbach argued in terms of a belief in God, which people only needed to become aware of in order to overcome their alienation). Commodity fetishism is not a mistaken notion. That is how a commodity-exchanging world really is. It is a particular way of looking at and behaving in the world without which commodity exchange simply could not exist.

There are two consequences of this view: First, commodity fetishism must come into existence historically for commodity exchange to take hold. Second, commodity fetishism needs to be reproduced socially in order for commodity exchange to continue to exist. So, commodity fetishism is one possible outcome of historical and social processes. And there is no necessity for it to either emerge historically or to persist socially. But, if they do not occur, then commodity exchange isn't possible.

So, what does commodity fetishism consist of? Later in volume 1, Marx summarizes the fetishism of commodities in terms of four elements: "Freedom, Equality, Property, and Bentham" (KI, 280).

- Freedom: commodity exchange requires a particular set of freedoms – to sell and buy goods and services, to realize their exchange-values and use-values, as free individuals.
- Equality: participants in commodity exchange see each other as equals; they also believe the commodities they exchange are worth equal amounts of value.

[15] In the opening paragraph of chapter 2 of Book I of *The Wealth of Nations* (p. 117), Smith describes how the division of labor is not the result of some far-seeing wisdom but the outcome of a natural "propensity to truck, barter, and exchange one thing for another."

[16] Behavioral economics was created as a compendium of all the ways people do *not* make rational decisions when it comes to consuming commodities. However, behavioral economists have not sought to eliminate the assumption of rational actors, but instead to "nudge" people to make rational decisions.

- Property: the institution of private property (and, along with it, a set of laws and a system of law enforcement) means not only that commodity-exchangers have the right to sell their commodities, but that consumers have the right to realize the use-value of the commodities they purchase.
- Bentham: associated with the utilitarian Jeremy Bentham (and brought into classical political economy by John Stuart Mill), the idea is both that external objects are capable of satisfying human needs and that each individual need only pay attention to their own interests and not those of anyone else in order to maximize society's welfare.

Individuals literally see the equality established between the objects they exchange as essential aspects of the objects themselves.[17] On top of that, in an economic and social system based on commodity exchange, the tendency is to believe that everything needs to be governed by the rules of commodity exchange. So, for example, instead of the commons or public ownership, private property. In the place of Social Security, private retirement accounts. The climate crisis can be solved through "cap-and-trade" programs. The value of social programs should be evaluated through cost–benefit analysis (according to which both costs and benefits can be calculated and compared through real or imputed market values). Each is an example of what Marx refers to as the fetishism of commodities – or what we might today call "market fetishism."

But commodity fetishism is not in any sense guaranteed by the existence of commodity exchange. It is behavior that is certainly learned through economic activities, by participating on a regular basis in market exchanges, but it is not a simple reflection of the economy. Historically, commodity fetishism was the outcome of a wide variety of economic, political, and cultural changes: the birth of the individual, the creation of certain freedoms, the imagining and celebration of equality among human beings, the separation of people from nature and thus the objects they could consume, and so on.

Today, socially, commodity fetishism is reproduced in the economy (via consumerism and the idea that you get what you pay for), in culture (in terms of consumer sovereignty, rationality, and programs of financial literacy), and in politics (such as the freedoms, notions of equality, and individual interests represented and embedded in democratic institutions). The result is that everything – from food, clothing, and shelter through healthcare, childcare, and hospitality services – can and should be obtained

[17] However, as Arjun Appadurai has argued, there is nothing simple or straightforward about external objects becoming commodities. In his view, all things have a "social life," and can make the journey from commodity to non-commodity and back again. Moreover, some kinds of goods and services (e.g., art, politics, and nature) are destroyed when turning them into market transactions.

through private markets.[18] And, if not through commodities, then through public programs that mimic the results of the market. That, readers will recognize, is the basis for neoliberalism (which of course is not a recent invention, starting in the 1970s, or even the 1940s, as many presume). It has been a project for remaking the world (in terms of expanding the role of property rights, individual decisions in private markets, and decreasing social regulations) since the advent of generalized commodity exchange.[19]

Why, else, does commodity fetishism matter? Beyond serving as a condition of existence of commodity exchange (and therefore, as we will see, of capitalism), it offers some pretty big promises – especially, of freedom and equality for all human beings. Commodity fetishism has therefore served as the spark for a wide variety of economic and social struggles. The movement for Indian independence is a good example: both salt (which was a staple of Indians' diets and which Britain's Salt Act of 1882 prohibited them from collecting or selling) and textiles (the production of which within India was proscribed by the British, so that the cotton would be exported to British textile mills) served as the basis of significant moments of anticolonial rebellion (leading to the great Salt March of 1930 and the call for the production of homespun or khadi cloth). The US Civil Rights movement is another example: during the famous lunch-counter and bus demonstrations of the 1950s and 1960s, one of the demands was to eliminate Jim Crow laws and to expand the right, the freedom, and equality of African-Americans to purchase commodities. Both of those movements, and many others like them, were enabled by and justified in terms of commodity fetishism. However, we also have to recognize that important parts of those same movements chafed at the restrictions imposed by commodity fetishism and sought to move beyond them, to demand forms of economic and social justice that a market economy simply could not deliver. Thus, under Nehru, the Indian National Congress, India's largest political party, adopted socialism as a framework for economic and social policies in 1936; while in the United States, leading Civil Rights figures such as Martin Luther King Jr. and Malcolm X later in

[18] Readers might try the following thought experiment: where would you draw the line between commodities and non-commodities? Consider these goods and services: a loaf of bread, a jacket, a house or apartment, sex, and body parts. Which, if any, should be on the non-commodity side – and, if any of them is, why not the others?

[19] Neoliberalism is one side of what Karl Polanyi, the Hungarian economic historian and anthropologist, referred to as the double movement of capitalist markets: during some periods, the advocates of laissez-faire (or what we now call neoliberalism) attempt to "disembed" the economy from society, often with strong state intervention, in order to establish a self-regulating market system; during other periods, liberal reformers push back and attempt to "re-embed" the economy through the creation of social regulations and protections (such as labor laws and trade tariffs). In both cases, however, the goal is to subordinate society to the dictates of a market economy.

their lives linked poverty and Black oppression directly to the injustices of capitalism.

Moreover, commodity fetishism, however prevalent in Marx's time and in our own, is neither absolute nor guaranteed. The same society that presumes and produces the elements of commodity fetishism also creates other ways of reading the "social hieroglyphic" (KI, 167) of the commodity (just as the same society that brought into being classical political economy also engendered the Marxian critique of political economy). Thus, for example, in Marx's time as in our own, movements have formed to abolish sweatshops, to reorganize production into cooperatives and worker-owned enterprises, to protect the natural environment from being treated as a commodity (or from being despoiled by efforts to produce more commodities), and so much more.[20] The demands of each of those movements have represented ways of imagining and enacting alternative arrangements for producing and exchanging goods and services, alongside and beyond the limits of commodity fetishism.

Say's Law

Commodity fetishism is one of the conditions of existence of commodity exchange, in addition to private property and a social division of labor. One commodity is traded for an equivalent exchange-value (and value). So, according to the assumptions of the classical political economists, there's no cheating and you can't get a commodity with a smile (i.e., without offering an equal exchange-value). Moreover, as we saw, the commodity is a contradictory unity of use-value and exchange-value. That means commodity exchange is a combination of a private act (of realizing a commodity's use-value, of consuming the product of a concrete labor) and a social act (of realizing a commodity's exchange-value, in terms of a portion of society's abstract labor).

In a world of simple commodity exchange – of exchanging one commodity for another, each considered in a one-sided fashion – there is a remarkable result: "every consumption is a production." Or, what is the same, "every purchase is a sale." This is what has become known as Say's Law. According to the classical economist Jean-Baptiste Say (and neoclassical economists today), as we saw in chapter 2, an economy based on commodity exchange

[20] One of the obstacles such movements face is the fact that commodities do not come stamped with their origins. We may know from labels on commodities or their packaging what countries they were produced in, what materials were used to make them, even what percentage of daily caloric requirements are satisfied by a typical serving (in the case of commercially produced food products). But we do not generally know *how* the commodities were produced – whether they were created and distributed on the basis of child labor, slavery, capitalist exploitation, or democratic communities of workers.

is characterized by a general balance such that all the commodities that are produced are in turn purchased. In other words, supply is presumed to create its own demand. The argument is that during the course of producing commodities incomes are generated, which are then used – via workers' consumption, business investment, and landlords' purchases of luxury items – to demand all the commodities on the market. The result is that no commodities are left over. Therefore, there will be no unused resources and no unemployment.

Of course, there's no guarantee that commodities actually are exchanged (because of the need for a double coincidence of wants, which limits at any particular point in time and place the use-values that are desired and possessed). But if a commodity exchange does take place – if $C_1 - C_2$ does, in fact, happen – then the commodities that are produced do change hands and all of their values are realized and Say's Law holds.

However, as we saw just before we embarked on the discussion of commodity fetishism, it is quite possible that a certain commodity is socially designated as the universal equivalent. That is what we call money, the universal equivalent of value. It is the commodity that can be exchanged for the socially necessary abstract labor embodied in any and all other commodities. If money mediates exchange, if one commodity serves as a means of payment, then the form of the exchange process is fundamentally altered. We go from (simple) barter to (generalized) commodity exchange – from $C_1 - C_2$ to

4.2 $$C_1 - M - C_2$$

The first commodity (C_1) is exchanged for money (M), which can then be used to purchase another commodity (C_2).

What happens when money is introduced? On one hand, money facilitates exchange. It overcomes the limitations of barter exchange (by avoiding the need for that double coincidence of wants). Therefore, it serves to broaden commodity exchange in both time and place. Exchanges can take place whenever and wherever money is present, instead of requiring that the two commodity-owners meet at a particular place and at a specific time in order to directly exchange their commodities. That's how commodities from around the world can appear on markets a long time after and in a place distant from where they were produced. It is also how markets can be created for everything from shirts and oranges to healthcare and carbon credits. The use of money makes that possible. On the other hand, money is a destabilizing factor. As we will see below, the use of money in exchange widens the contradiction between use-value and exchange-value. It therefore has the effect of undermining or exceeding Say's Law. One commodity can be exchanged for money but the money need not be used to purchase another commodity. So, it is quite possible, in monetary exchange, for commodities to be produced but not sold (or, in anticipation of not being sold, of not being produced in the first place).

Here, at this point in the analysis, what we are referring to is commodity money (such as gold, silver, and so on). This is not fiat money, that is, money (such as currency, checking accounts, and so on) that is created by government decree and used to pay taxes. Step by step. We will deal with the additional concrete effects of fiat money after discussing the implications of commodity money.

At this stage, money is treated like all other commodities. It has a use-value, an exchange-value, and a value. But there is one key difference: the use-value of money *is* its exchange-value. The social usefulness of money is the fact that it represents a command over any portion of society's abstract labor. Money is therefore the only commodity whose use-value is equal to its exchange-value. All the previous assumptions about commodities are carried through, such that a certain amount of commodity one is sold (at its exchange-value, equal to its value) for a specific sum of money (zM), which is then used to purchase a second commodity (also at its exchange-value, equal to its value): $xC_1 = zM = yC_2$.

From here, now that we have the use of money as the means of payment, we can derive for the first time the price of commodities. The "normal price" of commodities, the monetary equivalent of exchange-value, is the amount of money (e.g., gold) per unit use-value of a commodity, calculated by multiplying the exchange-value per unit use-value of a commodity by the amount of money divided by its exchange-value:

4.3 $$\text{normal price} = \frac{EV}{UV} \times \frac{M_{gold}}{EV} = \frac{M_{gold}}{UV}$$

The amount of money per unit use-value (M_{gold}/UV), the normal price of commodities, therefore represents the role of money as a measure of value or unit of account in generalized commodity exchange.

And "market price"? Due to a whole variety of circumstances, affecting either the demand side and/or the supply side of the market, the market price may be different from the normal price. Whatever deviations between the two prices that might occur in a market are, according to Marx, "inherent in the price form itself" (KI, 196).[21]

With the appearance of money, the concept of a commodity price now exists. We can therefore see that some things can have prices but no values or exchange-values. This might occur if no labor is embodied in the object,

[21] Moreover, as in classical political economy, commerce is such that market prices oscillate around normal prices. But the adjustment processes (of market prices from above or below the normal price) do not necessarily lead to an equilibrium. The constant interaction between production and exchange produces both departures from and tendencies toward the equality of market price and normal price.

such as virgin land, or because no amount of society's abstract labor can produce another one, such as in a rare piece of art like the *Mona Lisa* – or, for that matter, "things such as conscience, honour, etc." (KI, 197). Such items "can be offered for sale by their holders" (KI 197), with a price attached. But they are not considered to be commodities, with a value and exchange-value, like a truck or healthcare services.

Sale and Purchase

The existence of money also means that we can break up the circuit of monetary exchange ($C_1 - M - C_2$) into two separate moments. There's the sale of the first commodity for money ($C_1 - M$), and then the use of money to purchase the second commodity ($M - C_2$).

4.4 $$C_1 - M \,//\, M - C_2$$

During the course of the first moment, the sale ($C_1 - M$), the commodity-owner trades their commodity for money. What that means is the social nature of the commodity is realized by the transformation of a quantity of abstract labor into money. In other words, the private performance of labor is validated as social labor in and through the exchange of the commodity for money. During the second moment, the purchase ($M - C_2$), money is used to purchase a use-value, for the private act of consumption. The original owner of the first commodity uses the alienated form of the commodity, now money, to obtain some kind of useful good or service.

In other words, the opposition between the moments of sale and purchase – between $C_1 - M$ and $M - C_2$ – is resolved by selling the first commodity for its exchange-value and using the money they receive to purchase another commodity for its use-value. This is selling ($C_1 - M$) in order to buy ($M - C_2$). If sales and purchases of this sort continue, then we have a repeated series of commodity exchanges throughout society. The producer of the shirt sells their commodity for money, and then uses the money to purchase oranges – or, for that matter, any other commodity. Then, the seller of that commodity (be it oranges or anything else) can turn around with the money they now have and purchase another commodity. And so on and so forth. This is generalized (monetary) commodity exchange.

Mainstream economists generally presume that this sequence of the sale and purchase of commodities continues without interruption. That's the assumption of Say's Law, which serves as the basis of both classical political economy and contemporary neoclassical microeconomics (but, as we have seen, not the other side of mainstream economics, Keynesian macroeconomics). "Consumptions are productions" and "purchases are sales," *ad infinitum*. Their policy advice is thus straightforward: give free reign to markets. If markets for commodities exist, they should function without regulation or intervention; and, if they don't exist, they should be created. The mainstream view is that, if markets are allowed to operate freely, there will be no interruptions, no unemployment, and no economic downturns (except, perhaps, for some exogenous event). The presumption of Say's Law is therefore one of the reasons for the celebration of free-market capitalism.

Marx's view is, not surprisingly, quite different. Yes, the circuit of monetary exchange ($C_1 - M - C_2$) does, in fact, make general commerce possible, precisely because of the temporal sequence of sale and purchase. It enhances production, extends the social division of labor, and widens and deepens commodity markets. It overcomes the limitations of barter exchange and thus leads to the formation of all kinds of new markets for new commodities in new places. What's not to celebrate?

But the existence of money, and the separation of sale and purchase, also creates the possibility of crises. Whether on Black Friday of 1929, the 1973 oil crisis, the stock market crash of October 20, 1987, the Enron collapse, the failure of Lehman Brothers in 2008, or the travel industry in the midst of the Pandemic Depression, markets opened with many sellers but no buyers. In all those cases, the sequence of commodity exchanges simply could not continue. The sellers of commodities were not able to realize in the form of money the value of the commodities they put up for sale, and therefore could not turn around and engage in purchases of other commodities.

As Marx argues,

> Nothing could be more childish than the dogma that because every sale is a purchase, and every purchase a sale, the circulation of commodities necessarily implies an equilibrium between sales and purchases. (KI, 208)

Within a system of generalized commodity exchange, there is no rule or mechanism that ensures that the sequence of commodity exchanges will in fact take place or continue. For example, commodities may be offered on the market but potential buyers either don't have the money (e.g., if they are poor and are forced to choose between, say, paying the rent or purchasing food) or they choose not to use their money to make a commodity purchase (because, if they are rich, they don't have to). Since money is a store of value, it is also possible for the owner of a commodity to sell their commodity and then to stop, to decide not to make an additional purchase, and to hold their money for a longer or shorter period of time, awaiting other opportunities. Finally, those who have gained money from commodity sales can decide to hoard their money, to amass a monetary fortune as a stock of wealth – a drive to accumulate that has no limit.[22] In

[22] The small group at the top who amass such wealth are able to engage in commodity purchases, if and when they want, without any commodity sales – either because of earnings on their holdings or because they are able to borrow against their wealth.

all three cases, the existence of money has the effect of interrupting the sequence of commodity exchanges.

Money serves both to facilitate and to undermine commodity exchange – thus demonstrating that, in a society based on generalized commodity exchange, private decisions have social ramifications. Perfectly rational private choices (like slowing production and laying off workers) may create social disasters (as we routinely see in economic recessions and depressions). Decisions that lead to private benefits for some often have tremendous social costs for everyone else. And then something has to be done, whether poor relief (such as in the Speenhamland system at the end of the eighteenth century and during the early-nineteenth century) or public works (as with the Works Progress Administration in the 1930s) or a giant financial bailout (which, in the United States, took the form of the Troubled Asset Relief Program during the Second Great Depression).

This is what Marxian economists mean by the "anarchy of production." In a system based on private, individual commodity production and exchange, there is no necessary coordination of sales and purchases. The existence of money makes the instability of such a system possible. That's particularly the case with, looking ahead, capitalism.

This leads to one of the key debates between mainstream and Marxian economists. For mainstream economists (from Adam Smith and David Ricardo to Milton Friedman and Paul Krugman), crises are exogenous; they emanate from somewhere outside of capitalism – from some kind of "mistake" or unexpected occurrence (often attributed to a natural disaster or government intervention). In fact, the possibility of an internally generated crisis doesn't even exist in their theories and models. That's because, in their view, money is merely a veil. It is not present in mainstream economists' most basic conception of markets. There (e.g., in the usual supply and demand graphs and sets of equations), the prices that exist are only relative prices, the ratios by which commodities exchange for one another; they are not monetary prices.[23] It should come as no surprise, then, that mainstream macroeconomists did not include a separate (and possibly unstable) financial sector in their models in the run-up to the crash of 2007–8.

In Marxian approaches, money is there from the start, at the beginning of generalized commodity exchange. So, the possibility of economic crises is inherent in the commodity form. Such crises are therefore, from a Marxian perspective, endogenous to capitalism – perhaps not as a necessity but always there as a real, persistent possibility.

[23] Readers might want to perform this experiment the next time they attend a lecture about markets: ask the speaker, "where's the money?"

Contradictions in Monetary Exchange

Let us continue to explore the distinctions between simple commodity exchange ($C_1 - C_2$) and monetary exchange ($C_1 - M - C_2$).

In simple commodity exchange or barter, supply creates its own demand; while in generalized commodity exchange, with the use of money, it is possible to sell without purchasing. What this does is point to the existence of different incentives in buying and selling, and thus the distinction between general commodity-owners and the owner of money. Once production takes place, the goal is to sell the commodity, to realize the commodity's value through exchange. In other words, commodity-producers don't want to hold inventories. To do so is to fail to convert their individual, private labor into social labor – to not have the labor they perform validated by the rest of society. But the introduction of money also means that it is possible to make a sale without purchasing, to sell one commodity for money without turning around to purchase another commodity. That decision, to sell without purchasing, is up to the private producers of the commodities.

For example, consider a commodity purchase ($M - C_2$) as an investment decision. The choice not to purchase inputs, raw materials, and so on, which may be perfectly rational in many situations (when, e.g., consumer or producer confidence is shaky), may result in layoffs in the industries that provide those inputs, raw materials, and so on. The result is an interruption in the flow of commodities. Some producers are left holding money, others are left with their commodities. That's when the illusion of the independence of commodity producers is shattered. The situation of each and every commodity-owner turns out to be a function of, to depend crucially on, the decisions of all other commodity-owners.

What if the commodity-seller hoards the money they receive? That is possible when money serves not just as a unit of account and means of exchange, but as a store of value. If the money-commodity-owners take a portion of their money out of exchange (because its value as the universal equivalent persists, even when no commodity exchange is taking place), the contradictions of monetary exchange are brought to the fore – the contradiction between use-value and exchange-value, between the private act of consumption and the social act of exchange.

That possibility stands in sharp contrast to simple commodity exchange, when the decision to sell is also simultaneously the choice to purchase. Now, with money, it is possible to satisfy one's needs by using money to purchase commodities from others. However, to be able to buy without selling, the one who has money must have sold previously without buying. And if they hoard that money, then the amount of money necessary for the circulation of commodities is diminished.

The question then is: how much money is required, as a means of payment, for all commodity sales and purchase to actually take place? That depends on both the value of the commodities and the value of money (KI, 212–20).

Consider the following hypothetical example of two commodities and gold:

4.5
$$\frac{EV_1}{EV_{gold}} = \frac{8}{2} = 4_{gold} = P_1$$

$$\frac{EV_2}{EV_{gold}} = \frac{4}{2} = 2_{gold} = P_2$$

Assume the value of commodity one is 8 hours, that of commodity two 4 hours, and the value of a unit of commodity money (e.g., an ounce of gold) is 2 hours. Then the total value exchanged is 12 hours, and 6 units of money are needed to complete the exchange of the two commodities. In other words, the amount of money is the sum of the two prices (assuming, that is, the velocity of money, the rate at which money is exchanged, is one). If some of that money is hoarded, then the circuit of commodity exchange is curtailed. Not all of the commodities can be traded, because there is not enough money to realize their values – unless we see an increase in the velocity of money or the monetary authority puts more money into circulation.[24]

So, according to Marx, the so-called quantity theory of money is a truism. It is true by definition that, to use the symbols of mainstream economics, the amount of money (*M*) is equal to the price of commodities (*P*) times the number of commodities (*Y*) divided by the velocity of money (*v*):

4.6
$$M = \frac{(P \times Y)}{v}$$

But we can't stop there. We still need a theory of *M*, *P*, *Y*, and *v* in order to determine the dynamics of a system of generalized commodity exchange. Marx is, in effect, building that theory from the simplest category, the commodity.

Contemporary mainstream economists turn that definition into a causal theory of inflation, based on a notion of exogenous money. They assume the total amount of commodities (*Y*) corresponds to full employment; the velocity of circulation of money (*v*) is fixed; and the causality runs from left to right, from a change in the supply of money (ΔM) to a change in prices (ΔP). That's how they derive their quantity theory of inflation:

[24] The monetary authority's insertion of more money into commodity circulation is the basis of "quantitative-easing." That's when a central bank purchases government bonds or other financial assets in order to inject money into the economy to attempt to create the conditions for commodity exchange to continue without interruption.

$$4.7 \qquad \Delta M \rightarrow \Delta P$$

In their view, an increase in the amount of money necessarily causes an overall rise in the prices of commodities. This is the theory of inflation that is then used to attack monetary and fiscal authorities (when, e.g., they lower interest rates, engage in quantitative-easing, or run budget deficits) for creating the inevitability of runaway price increases.

Nonmainstream economists (such as Modern Monetary Theorists, whose work we return to in more detail in chapter 8) contest this notion of exogenous money, arguing instead that money is created – and is therefore endogenous – through the activities of the banking system. Bank lending creates deposits, and therefore increases the supply of money. And, because the supply of loans is driven by demand, the only threat of inflation is when an increase in the amount of money in circulation runs up against the constraint of real resources (such as the full employment of the labor force). Marx held much the same view: the direction of causality runs not from money to prices, but the reverse, from the price level (and the level of economic activity more generally) to money.

Marx also rejected cost-push theories of inflation, because in his view an increase in wages is not the cause of a surge in prices. In his debate with the English socialist John Weston, who had earlier argued in favor of the idea that "a general rise in the rate of wages would be of no use to the workers," Marx responded:

> a struggle for a rise of wages follows only in the track of previous changes, and is the necessary offspring of previous changes in the amount of production, the productive powers of labour, the value of labour, the value of money, the extent or the intensity of labour extracted, the fluctuations of market prices, dependent upon the fluctuations of demand and supply, and consistent with the different phases of the industrial cycle; in one word, as reactions of labour against the previous action of capital. By treating the struggle for a rise of wages independently of all these circumstances, by looking only upon the change of wages, and overlooking all other changes from which they emanate, you proceed from a false premise in order to arrive at false conclusions.[25]

In other words, workers' demands for higher wages do not cause an increase in the price level, but are instead a response to the previous actions of capitalists (which are themselves responsible for changes in M, v, Y, and P). Moreover, even if a pay raise for workers does increase the demand for wage-goods, and thus leads to an increase in their prices for a while, low-cost producers will expand production while others find new, cheaper ways of producing those commodities, at which point prices will

[25] *Value, Price and Profit*, p. 56. This is the transcript of a two-part lecture Marx delivered to the First International Workingmen's Association, which took place in June 1865, one year before the first volume of *Capital* appeared. It was eventually published as a book after Marx's death, in 1898, by his daughter Eleanor Marx Aveling.

actually fall. The only ones who might suffer are the producers of luxury commodities, if the profits of capitalists are dented by the increase in workers' wages and the recipients of surplus-value end up demanding fewer luxury goods and services.

Problems in Commodity Exchange

To summarize, even at this early stage in the analysis, there are three potential problems in the circuit of monetary exchange:

First, the commodity-owner may not be able to complete the sequence because they can't sell their commodity for money. This is what is called a realization problem – a conflict between use-value and exchange-value – which arises when potential buyers don't have the money to purchase commodities or when others choose not to engage in commodity purchases.

Second, money introduces the problem of time. As we saw above, the act of sale can be separated from the act of purchase. So, it is quite possible for commodity-producers to successfully sell their commodities and then to wait, for a shorter or longer period of time, before purchasing other commodities.

Finally, the hoarding of money creates another crisis potential. If the producers who sell their commodities store that realized value in the form of money, then the required amount of money falls short of the sum of values that is available on the market. This is when the accumulation of money, not the exchange of commodities, becomes the goal. Those who have been successful in selling their commodities come to obey the admonitions to abstain, to save instead of consume – and the circuit of commodity exchange is interrupted.[26]

All three of these moments create the possibility, but again not the necessity, for economic crises. That ever-persistent fragility is inherent in monetary exchange, even before we get to capitalism.

Looking Ahead

There is, of course, one more possibility associated with the use of money in commodity exchange: credit. A loan creates a debt that needs to be repaid, which only makes sense for those engaged in commodity exchange if an additional sum of money – a surplus-value – can be found within the system. For Marx, credit-money serves as a bridge from generalized

[26] Then, those who are appointed (or who appoint themselves) to protect commodity exchanges step in to call for exactly the opposite – for individuals and companies to abandon their hoards and to spend their money in the purchase of more commodities.

commodity exchange to specifically capitalist commodity exchange. But we have to leave the discussion of how that works for the next chapter.

Suggested Readings

Jack Amariglio and Antonio Callari, "Marxian Value Theory and the Problem of the Subject: The Role of Commodity Fetishism," in *Fetishism as Cultural Discourse*, ed. Emily Aptera and William Pietz, pp. 186–216 (Ithaca, NY: Cornell University Press, 1993).

Arjun Appadurai, "Introduction: Commodities and the Politics of Value," in *The Social Life of Things: Commodities in Cultural Perspective*, ed. Arjun Appadurai, pp. 3–63 (Cambridge: Cambridge University Press, 1986).

David Graeber, *Debt: The First 5,000 Years* (Brooklyn, NY: Melville House, 2012).

Costas Lapavitsas, "Money," in *Routledge Handbook of Marxian Economics*, ed. David M. Brennan, David Kristjanson-Gural, Catherine P. Mulder, and Erik M. Olson, pp. 69–79 (New York: Routledge, 2017).

Karl Marx, *Value, Price and Profit*, ed. Eleanor Marx Aveling (New York: International Publishers, 1935).

Karl Polanyi, *The Great Transformation: The Political and Economic Origins of Our Time*, intro. Fred Block, Foreword by Joseph E. Stiglitz (Boston: Beacon Press, 2001 [1944]).

Bruce Roberts, "Abstract Labor," in *Routledge Handbook of Marxian Economics*, ed. David M. Brennan, David Kristjanson-Gural, Catherine P. Mulder, and Erik M. Olson, pp. 59–68 (New York: Routledge, 2017).

Bruce Roberts, "Value and Price," in *Routledge Handbook of Marxian Economics*, ed. David M. Brennan, David Kristjanson-Gural, Catherine P. Mulder, and Erik M. Olson, pp. 80–9 (New York: Routledge, 2017).

Chapter 5

SURPLUS-VALUE AND EXPLOITATION

In the previous chapter, we saw how Marx started his critique of political economy, with the commodity – an apparently simple category that, upon further inspection, reveals how historically and socially contingent and potentially unstable commodity exchange actually is.

In particular, Marx shows how the commodity is characterized by an inner tension between use-value and exchange-value (and value), an opposition that is externalized and made sharper by the exchange of one commodity for another. Moreover, commodity exchange is characterized by commodity fetishism, a particular way in which mainstream economists assume that economic agents naturally think and act in order for the exchange of commodities to take place. Marx's critique is that, instead of being a feature of some kind of universal human nature, commodity fetishism emerges only under specific historical conditions and may (but need not) be reproduced within a society based on commodity exchange.

Then, once money is introduced as the universal equivalent, it becomes clear that Say's Law, which is simply presumed within mainstream economics, can only hold under nonmonetary or barter exchange. Once money is introduced, all bets are off and commodity exchange becomes fragile and carries within itself the potential for crisis.

All of that pertains to commodity exchange, even before we get to capitalism. There is nothing particularly capitalist about any of that discussion of the commodity, commodity exchange, commodity fetishism, and monetary exchange (although Marx clearly had his eye on the role commodity exchange plays within capitalism). That changes in this chapter, when for the first time we see how Marx produces the concept of *capitalist* commodity exchange.

To be clear, the analysis in chapter 4 is a logical but not historical analysis. In other words, it is not that Marx is focusing on precapitalist forms of commodity exchange, as they existed historically (say, in Ancient Greece or Rome) or today (in large parts of the world, where commodity exchange among noncapitalist producers is still quite prevalent). Instead, the point is that Marx is building toward a *concept* of capitalism, which includes (but is not limited to) generalized or monetary exchange. Therefore, all of the issues concerning commodity exchange covered in the previous chapter carry over into this chapter. Here, we will see how Marx develops additional concepts in order, for the first time, to be able to talk about a specifically capitalist mode of production.

Readers will get a sense of how different Marx's notion of capitalism is compared to the ideas about capitalism that are prevalent within mainstream economic theory, in his time as in our own. This is not only a key theoretical difference – what Marx means by capitalism compared to how the classical political economists and contemporary mainstream economists use that term (or, in many cases, avoid the use of that name, preferring instead to analyze what they call "markets" or "free enterprise" or some such notion). The different meanings of the word capitalism are also based on and reveal contrasting ethical theories. Thus, for example, whereas mainstream economists argue that everyone gets what they deserve within capitalism, Marx's view is quite different: capitalism is based on the exploitation of workers, and therefore on a basic economic and social injustice. Much of that theoretical and ethical debate hinges on the notion of surplus-value, as well as how "wages" (workers) and "profits" (capitalists) are differently understood within Marxian and mainstream economics.

The major analytical steps covered in this chapter include: (a) credit, debt, and capital, (b) the difference between labor and labor power, (c) the extraction of labor from labor power leading to surplus-value, (d) the value of a capitalist commodity, (e) the idea of class exploitation, (f) the different forms and conditions of surplus-value, and (g) the relationship between workers' wages and exploitation.

Credit and Debt

At the end of the previous chapter, we discussed three potential problems that are inherent in monetary exchange. Now, let's consider a fourth potential source of crisis: the creditor-debtor relationship.

Suppose a commodity is sold before money is actually received by the seller. This introduces credit and debt into monetary exchange. Money is owed to the original commodity-owner but they end up having to extend credit to the person they sold it to. The new commodity-owner, the one who purchased the commodity, is therefore in debt.

This new relationship is the source of the kinds of debt problems that regularly plague capitalism. We see them all the time: bankruptcies of family farms, government deficits, home mortgages, buying stocks on margin, student loans, and so on. Without analyzing the new fragilities introduced by credit and debt, it would be impossible to understand the causes of capitalist instability, such as the first Great Depression or the crash of 2007–8.

According to Marx, credit-money springs directly out of the function of money as a means of payment. It involves a promise to pay, and therefore only a "nominal means of purchase" (KI, 234). The seller must wait for the material transfer of the money commodity to serve in its role as the actual means of payment. The original producer has given up their commodity but they aren't able to realize the value embodied in that commodity – and they can't until money actually changes hands.

On one hand, debt (like money) serves to expand commodity exchange. Households and firms that don't have the financial means can borrow money and then make commodity purchases. Debt thus allows otherwise-ineligible buyers to enter the market or to expand their time there. That's why such financial innovations as letters of credit, installment credit, credit cards, home mortgages, car loans, and student loans are so important. They allow commodity exchanges to take place even when individuals and corporations don't have the requisite money on hand.

Many students, for example, are able to purchase a university education based on loans (and their universities are only too happy to facilitate such loans, which allow students to pay the often-elevated fees for tuition, room, and board). Afterwards, of course, the graduates are required to look for jobs (instead of, for example, taking time off to travel, volunteer on a project to help the needy, or do nothing at all), in order to earn a wage or salary to repay their loans. That indebtedness can cause other problems in commodity exchange, as when graduates are so burdened with repaying their student loans they can't pay their rent or purchase a home.

On the other hand, the circuit of commodity exchange ($C_1 - M - C_2$) will be interrupted if the debtor will not or cannot pay. In that case, the original commodity-owner has given up their commodity, without managing to receive an equivalent amount of value in return. If payment isn't received, they can't turn around and purchase another commodity. That's a problem that needs to be solved – say, by an individual bankruptcy proceeding or a more general bailout of lenders and debtors. It is also why a commodity-purchaser who promises to pay needs to be examined carefully. The buyer must be worthy of credit, which is why there are credit ratings and consumer credit checks, government supervision of banks and other financial institutions, and much more – all in an attempt to make sure debtors fulfill their obligations and creditors are repaid. Even then, conditions might change, and those who were able to repay their debt at one point in time simply cannot at another point in time. And what happens when debtors can't repay their loans, and don't have access to a bankruptcy proceeding or government bailout? In India, for example, tens of thousands of farmers have committed suicide in the past 30 years, the prime reason being their inability to repay their debts.

Logically, once debt exists, there are two alternative scenarios. One possibility is for the owner of the original commodity, who has sold their commodity (C_1) without realizing its exchange-value, to pass on the debt to the owner of another commodity (C_2). Both commodities thus change hands. But it's neither barter nor the bodily form of money. The "ideal form of money" or, what is the same, the nominal means of payment is holding up the system of commodity exchange. Still, even though both commodities have been sold, no exchange-values have been realized. If this pattern is repeated many times, and debtors aren't able to pay, then the circuit is interrupted. Another crisis of commodity exchange ensues.

The only way to realize the value of a commodity is in the bodily or material form of money. If a commodity is *not* sold for money, the commodity has a use-value but no exchange-value. And if this occurs on a widespread basis in a commodity-producing society, that society may succumb to a generalized crisis. As Marx put it, the contradiction between use-value and exchange-value is raised to the "level of an absolute contradiction" (KI, 236).

There is, of course, a second alternative. Assume the first commodity is bought on credit. Then the buyer (who is also now a debtor) must acquire the money commodity to repay the debt by selling the commodity they just bought. If they manage to do so, they get their money back and retire the debt. So, we have:

5.1 $$\boxed{M} - C - M$$

where $\boxed{M}$ signifies money in the form of credit.

The problem is, once the debtor repays the money they borrowed by selling the commodity they purchased, they haven't managed to acquire anything. They are left with no use-value and no exchange-value. Nothing has happened. The circuit turns out to have been a waste of time.[1]

Unless ...

As readers will have guessed, the only way such a situation makes sense is if the indebted commodity-purchaser is able to sell the commodity for *more* money than they borrowed. Then we have something different:

5.2 $$\boxed{M} - C - M'$$

where M' signifies an amount of money greater than the original amount borrowed, $\boxed{M}$.

---

[1] It does make sense, of course, for those who lend the money, and receive interest payments from the debtors. Later, in volume 3 of *Capital*, Marx introduces finance capital and, with it, a new class position of recipient of a portion of the surplus for lending money. We explore this feature of capitalism below, in chapter 6.

The debt can be repaid and the money commodity-owner ends up with an additional amount of money (ΔM equal to the difference between M' and $\boxed{M}$), which they can then use to purchase another commodity. (Technically, the indebted commodity-exchanger needs to end up with a sum of money that is greater than the amount they borrowed plus any interest on the loan.)

We now have a different kind of commodity exchange: buying in order to sell, as against selling in order to buy. The commodity-exchanger buys the initial commodity for its exchange-value, not its use-value. That is, they purchase it for its social use, not its private use. This is the case when, for example, someone borrows money to purchase a house not to live in it, but to "flip" it. They obtain it for its exchange-value not its use-value.[2] They hope to sell it for more than they paid for it (and, of course, for more than they borrowed).

Money as Capital

So, buying in order to sell ($M - C - M$) emerges directly from selling in order to buy ($C - M - C$). But the former doesn't make the same sense as the latter. If the participant in commodity exchange sells in order to receive money to purchase another commodity, they end up with a use-value they can consume. However, buying in order to sell only makes sense if they end up with more money, and thus more exchange-value (i.e., $M - C - M'$).

$M - C - M'$ turns out to be the general formula for capital, where M' is greater than M.[3] Money, in this case, begets more money, an extra amount of value, a "surplus-value" (KI, 251). That's why Marx refers to this as a process of "self-valorization" (KI, 255). It is when exchange-value becomes the "driving force and motivating force," the "determining purpose" of its own expansion (KI, 250).[4] Readers will recognize this as the prime directive of capitalism – to make a profit.

What, then, is the relationship between commodity exchange ($C - M - C$) and the circuit of capital ($M - C - M'$)? It's a contradiction. (Again!)

As we saw in the previous chapter, Marx's analysis of commodity exchange presumes (at least at this stage in the analysis) equal exchange. That's what the classicals assumed (as do mainstream economists today).

[2] A similar argument is often used to justify student loans and paying for a university education: graduates' earnings will, over a lifetime, be higher than what workers with only a secondary school education are paid. The result: a university education is, like the flipped house, reduced to its exchange-value.

[3] Mathematically, $M' = M + \Delta M$, where ΔM is the increase in the amount of money.

[4] How can we measure the process of self-valorization? Using the notation from before, the index of success is $\rho = \Delta M/M$ (where ρ, the Greek letter rho, is the rate of self-valorization, ΔM the increase in the amount of money, and M the original amount of money).

So, $C - M - C$ is actually $C = M = C$ (where, as before, the equals signs designate equal amounts of value). Thus, for example, a commodity that took 10 hours to produce is exchanged for an amount of money that embodies 10 hours, which in turn is used to purchase another commodity that also took 10 hours to produce.[5] The problem is, money as capital appears to violate the assumption of the exchange of equivalents. It simply can't be the case that $M = C = M'$, if the amount of money at the end (M') is greater than the amount of money at the beginning (M). Mathematically, it just doesn't work.

Moreover, if we maintain the heroic assumption of equal exchange, then the additional amount of money, the extra or surplus-value, cannot be explained by any kind of swindle in the realm of circulation. It is not created by merchants buying cheap and selling dear, or by bankers lending money and charging interest, or for that matter by producers overcharging their customers. All those ways of acquiring or capturing extra amounts of value do of course exist in real-world capitalism. But they are ruled out at this point in the analysis by the assumption of equal exchange. All that happens when merchants, bankers, and powerful producers get something extra is they shift the amount of value each participant gets (more for the merchants, bankers, and overcharging producers and less for their customers) but the total amount of value remains the same.

As Marx explained,

> However much we twist and turn, the final conclusion remains the same. If equivalents are exchanged, no surplus-value results, and if non-equivalents are exchanged, we still have no surplus-value. Circulation, or the exchange of commodities, creates no value. (KI, 266)

Marx's argument (KI, 266–7) is that, while historically merchant capital (buying cheap and selling dear) and interest-bearing capital (lending money to make more money) appear *before* capitalism, theoretically they come *after* the explanation of surplus-value (because, under capitalism, they involve distributions of surplus-value).

Production

Surplus-value therefore *appears* in the market, in the realm of circulation, but it is *not explained* by what happens in the exchange of values.

---

[5] To be clear, the equal exchange of values does not mean that the number of use-values remains constant. For readers familiar with the mainstream theory of international trade, the theory of comparative advantage, the number of use-values produced will increase if producers specialize and trade according to their relative advantages. But trade according to comparative or relative advantage does not increase the amount of value produced and exchanged.

Surplus-value must originate elsewhere, outside markets, in the realm of production.

We start (as before) by dividing the general formula for capital into two moments, purchase and sale:

$$M - C_1 // C_2 - M' \quad (5.3)$$

Between the two is production. Value continues to be defined in terms of labor (as embodied socially necessary abstract labor-time). Therefore, the only way to go from the first commodity (C_1) to the second (C_2), where the second commodity contains more value than the first, is to perform labor and increase the amount of value embodied in the commodity. And this can only occur during the course of production. So, we end up with

$$M - C \ldots P \ldots C' - M' \quad (5.4)$$

where P represents the process of production.

If that increase in value does take place, then both exchanges can satisfy the assumption of equal exchange (such that $M = C$ and $C' = M'$). The source of the additional amount of money is thus the extra value that is embodied in the second commodity during the course of production. Surplus-value, Marx concludes, therefore appears in exchange but actually originates in production.

Marx's conclusion about capitalist production being the source of surplus-value is, of course, dependent on all the prior assumptions. He follows the classical political economists in assuming that commodity exchanges are equal exchanges, that labor is the source of value, and so forth. But he arrives at a very different place: the source of capitalist profits or surplus-value can only be the extra amount of labor performed (and thus value created) during the course of capitalist production.

Labor and Labor Power

The next key question is: is there a commodity that can be bought at its value (since we are still assuming equal exchange) and then consumed such that, in the act of consumption, it creates even more value? Let's remember that to consume is to realize a commodity's use-value. So, in this case, the act of consuming the use-value must create more value and exchange-value for the purchaser of the commodity. The answer, for Marx, is clear: labor power. If labor power is purchased at its value, it can be put to work to create more value. That ability to create more value is its use-value.

Marx in fact only takes credit for introducing a small modification into classical political economy: the difference between labor and labor power.

Labor power is defined as laboring capacity, a set of mental and physical abilities that allows someone to work and perform labor. *Labor*, on the other hand, is the actual work performed, the time spent laboring and creating value. The idea is that capitalists purchase labor power – and, after the commodity exchange is completed, they get labor in production. So, labor power, but not labor, has to exist as a commodity. The owners of labor power (in short, workers) must be able to alienate their ability to perform labor.

Logically, workers must be:

1. free to sell their labor power (i.e., labor power is a commodity); and
2. forced to sell their labor power (i.e., it has no use-value to them).

Only if workers are forced to have the freedom to sell their labor power can there be a surplus-value. And only if there's surplus-value can there by capitalism.[6]

Therefore, the emergence of capitalism requires the birth of the freedom to buy and sell labor power. It is another condition, in addition to and an extension of all the social attributes defined by commodity fetishism. Indeed, it is one of the freedoms that separates capitalism from other modes of production, such as feudalism (where workers are tied to the land and are forced to pay rent – in kind, money, or labor – to landlords) and slavery (where workers themselves are bought and sold as human chattel). Once labor power exists as a commodity, workers aren't forced to pay rent and aren't traded on slave markets; it is their ability to labor that is bought and sold for a specific period of time (say, an 8-hour workday). After that, labor power needs to be replenished so that it can be sold the next day, and the day after that, and so on. And, for that, workers are paid a wage or salary to purchase what they need to maintain their social existence as workers.

The idea that workers are *forced* to have the freedom to sell their ability to labor is an admittedly provocative phrase – one that stands in stark contrast to the notion, enshrined within mainstream economics, that capitalism is only about freedom and choice. The usual presumption is that workers are free to get a job or not (and, by the same token, employers are free to hire them or not). If they decide not to work, that's their own free choice. However, from Marx's perspective, workers are actually coerced into exercising that freedom because, if they don't own an office or factory, if they don't have access to the means of production, their ability to perform labor is of no use to them. They *must* sell their labor power to

[6] Here, Marx is making a logical argument, based on the distinction between labor and labor power. Only later, as we will see in chapter 9, in the discussion of the so-called primary accumulation of capital, will Marx offer a historical analysis of the economic and social conditions whereby labor power becomes a commodity.

someone else – in order to receive a wage or salary to purchase commodities to support themselves and their families.[7]

If labor power is available as a commodity and capitalists have the wherewithal to purchase it, how much do they have to pay for it? On the assumption of equal exchange, capitalists have to pay wages equal to the value of labor power. As with all other commodity exchanges at this stage of the analysis, the exchange-value of labor power (in short, a worker's wage or salary) is assumed to be quantitatively equal to its value.

So, what is the value of labor power? It is the quantity of socially necessary abstract labor-time necessary to sustain the workers, the owners of labor power. Labor power is therefore the same as all other commodities, with one key exception: labor power itself is not produced. Instead, the value of labor power is determined by the value of the commodities that make up the workers' wage bundle.[8]

Thus, the value of labor power has a "historical and moral element" (KI, 275). It's the amount of value that is *socially* necessary to reproduce the sellers of labor power. The value of labor power is therefore a historical and social convention, an average for workers in a particular place and at a specific point in time. For example, the value of labor power in the United Kingdom in 2020 is different from what it was in 1950 or what it is today in Brazil.

Importantly, the value of labor power is not a minimum amount, in the way that the classical political economists thought about it (as a subsistence wage) or some international agencies currently do (often measuring it as a caloric minimum). Nor is it, as contemporary mainstream economists maintain, an amount of money that is equal to workers' (marginal) productivity. The value of labor power is, instead, a historical and social convention – a product of all the changes within capitalism that have taken place that go into determining what the standard of living of workers can and should be. It is therefore affected by everything, from how the commodities in the wage bundle are produced and the degree of unionization of the labor force to minimum-wage laws and the changing structure of workers' families (see figure 5.1).

The analysis of the commodity labor power proceeds along the same lines as that of the other commodities: it has a use-value and an exchange-value (equal, at this stage of analysis, to its value) (see figure 5.2).

---

[7] By the same token, one can also argue that capitalists are forced to have the freedom to purchase labor power – because, as we will see below, they can only appropriate surplus-value by extracting labor from labor power.

[8] Mathematically, the value of labor power (V) is equal to the dot product of two vectors, one for the exchange-value per unit use-value of the commodities that make up the customary standard of living of workers ($\mathbf{e}$) and another for the number of use-values in the wage bundle ($\mathbf{q}$): $V = \mathbf{e} \bullet \mathbf{q}$.

Here's a useful thought experiment: what is the value of labor power in your country at the time you are reading this book? To calculate this, you need to add up the value of the commodities – food, clothing, shelter, and so on – that make up the typical worker's wage bundle.

Here's a hypothetical example (where US dollar values are calculated for one year):

Housing	$14,000
Transportation	6,680
Food	5,120
Insurance/pensions	3,720
Healthcare	3,200
Clothing	1,200
Other*	5,680
Total	$40,000

*Including education, entertainment, childcare, and other expenses.

Workers in this example would have to receive US$40,000 a year (or US$19.23 an hour) in the form of wages or a salary to purchase the commodities necessary to maintain their customary standard of living.

Figure 5.1 Value of labor power

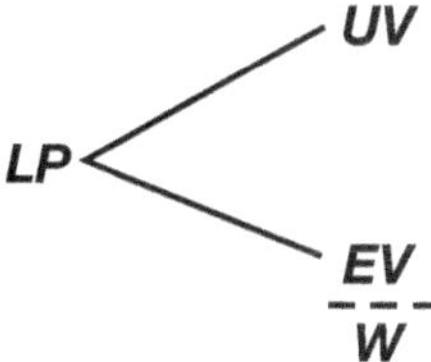

Figure 5.2 Labor power as a commodity

The exchange-value (and value) of labor power is realized in the market, as workers sell their ability to work to capitalists. However, the use-value of labor power, the performance of labor, is realized outside of exchange, in the realm of production. We can thus define the productive consumption of labor power as the extraction of labor from labor power by those who have purchased the workers' ability to perform labor.

What does the workers' circuit of commodity exchange look like? If they sell their labor power (*LP*), they turn around and use the money they receive (*M*, equal to the value of labor power) to purchase the commodities necessary to reproduce their social existence (*C*). Workers therefore sell their labor power and purchase wage goods following the familiar sequence of generalized monetary exchanges: $C - M - C$.

Exploitation

And capitalists? In order for them to sell commodities, they have to purchase commodities. In other words, they have to use their money to invest, which leads to higher employment, more commodities produced and exchanged, more factories and offices, and so on – all the things usually associated with capitalist growth. And, of course, more profits for capitalists. It's another way to talk about capital as the self-expansion of value.

What this means is that capital is a social relation, not a thing or piece of equipment. The idea that money or the equipment purchased with that money is productive of surplus-value or capitalist profits is "capital fetishism." According to Marx's critique of political economy, capital is instead defined as the productive consumption of labor power, the realization of the use-value of workers' ability to labor. That's all capitalists have to do, to consume labor power productively, by uniting labor power with the instruments or means of production and raw materials in order to engage in capitalist commodity production.

Capitalists, as they are defined here, perform no labor. Instead, after purchasing the commodity labor power, they extract the workers' labor from labor power. A portion of that labor is paid to workers, equal to their value of labor power. That's referred to as necessary labor. The rest, the extra or surplus labor, goes not to the workers, but to the capitalists.

In fact, that's Marx's definition of exploitation: capitalists appropriate the extra labor of workers for doing *nothing*. And that exploitation occurs even under the radical assumption of equal exchange, that all commodities – before and after production takes place – exchange at their values. So, capitalism, even under the best-case scenario, where everyone gets what they deserve in exchange, is based on the exploitation of workers.

The idea that capitalism involves exploitation is a direct rebuke to mainstream economics – both classical political economy and contemporary mainstream economic theory. In both traditions, capitalist profits represent the return to capital, and therefore the just reward to capitalists. For Smith, Ricardo, and the other classical political economists, the "normal return" to capital (including interest on the plant, tools, and machinery owned by the capitalists and the wages of superintendence) is simply added to workers' wages and landlords' rents to make up the value of commodities. Contemporary mainstream economics is a bit different: profits are seen as the reward for not-consuming (i.e., interest on savings or abstinence), which in turn is equal to the marginal (physical) productivity of capital. The idea is that households that engage in not-consuming (or, as we say in everyday language, of not being "piggy") sell their savings to firms and receive interest payments equal to the return on capital.[9] Therefore, in both traditions of mainstream economics, profits are what capitalists get when they do something – when they abstain from consumption and, instead, invest in capital equipment and supervise the production process. That is the fetishism of capital.

Marx's view is quite different: capitalists obtain their profits for literally doing nothing, because they are involved in a social relationship that gives them the right to appropriate the surplus labor of their workers. Therefore, as we discuss in some detail below, from a Marxian perspective, capitalist profits or surplus-value violate one of the key ethical principles of capitalism, the presumption that everyone gets what they deserve. In order for capitalism to exist, that principle must be violated on a regular basis.

Exploitation is, of course, a loaded expression. Within the terms of capitalism, as reflected in mainstream economic theory, everyone receives a flow of value or income that corresponds to a "doing," which is therefore equal to something they contribute. Workers do work, and receive wages; capitalists do savings and investment, and receive profits; and landlords do make their land available, and receive rents. Utilizing those same terms, Marx argues that capitalists appropriate value – a surplus-value – for merely occupying the position of capitalist – that is, for no kind of doing at all. They therefore engage in a relationship of exploitation.

Surplus-Value

Let's see how this works.

Money operates as capital if and when the value of labor is greater than the value of labor power. That self-expansion of value is created in production, and then realized (if and when the resulting commodities are sold) in markets.

Perhaps the best way to illustrate this is in terms of a timeline (see figure 5.3). Once the labor power exchange is completed (workers sell their ability to work for a wage or salary for a specific period of time), the process of production is started and work is done. Labor is performed and value is created during the entire day, *x* to *z* (say, 10 hours). During the first portion of the day, *x* to *y* (e.g., 6 hours), the workers create value equal to the value of labor power, the value they were paid to work that day. But they don't

[9] Notice, then, in contemporary mainstream economics, there is no separate class of capitalists (as is the case in classical political economy). Instead, households sell their savings to firms, who in turn pay those households a market-determined rate of interest on the funds they choose not to use for present consumption – one part of the lower loop of circular flow that we saw above in the markets of factors of production of figure 2.2.

NL
SL
x
y
z

Figure 5.3 Necessary and surplus labor

put down their tools and stop working then. They continue to work and to create value for the rest of the contracted workday, from *y* to *z* (e.g., 4 hours). During that second period, they are working not for themselves but for their employers.

So, the workday as a whole is not necessary labor-time. Rather, during the first part of the day, the workers perform necessary labor (*NL*), equal to their wages or the value of their labor power; during the second part, they perform even more labor, a surplus labor (*SL*). Together, the two parts equal the total amount of living labor (*LL*): $LL = NL + SL$. Therefore, the amount of surplus labor is the living labor minus the necessary labor: $LL - NL = SL$. If the value workers created during the workday were equal to necessary labor (such that $LL = NL$), there wouldn't be a surplus-value – and thus no profits.

Another way to put it is, the first part of the workers' day represents paid labor (*PL*) and the second part is unpaid labor (*UL*). So, in slightly different form, $LL = PL + UL$. A third way is to look at the commodities produced during the course of the workday. Some of them are necessary product (*NP*), while the others are surplus product (*SP*). Together, they make up the total product (*TP*): $TP = NP + SP$.

However we look at it, surplus labor or unpaid labor or surplus product is therefore the source of surplus-value, the extra amount of value that is the basis of capitalist profits.

Whence we can define the rate of surplus-value (s') as the ratio of surplus labor and necessary labor or, what is the same, unpaid labor and paid labor or necessary product and surplus product:

5.6 $$s' = \frac{SL}{NL} = \frac{UL}{PL} = \frac{SP}{NP}$$

All three ratios are therefore equivalent ways of representing the rate of exploitation (KI, 320–39).

Those ratios also represent the condition for class struggles – struggles over the process of appropriating (and, as we will see in the next chapter, distributing) surplus labor. Once exploitation exists, workers and capitalists can be expected to struggle over the degree or rate of that exploitation, thus leading to changes in those ratios. They may also struggle over whether or not exploitation should exist in the first place.

Capitalist Production

The process of capitalist production involves, of course, more than the extraction of labor from labor power. Workers need to be brought together with the means of production and raw materials so that new commodities can be produced. Those commodities can then be sold so that capitalists can realize, in the form of money, the commodities' value and exchange-value.

What Marx calls "industrial capital" (as against merchant capital, finance capital, and other forms of capital) expands upon the original definition of capitalist production (*M* – *C* ... *P* ... *C'* – *M'*) to include the value of all the necessary commodity purchases and sales, as illustrated in figure 5.4.

The idea is the following: capitalists use money to buy, at their exchange-value equal to their value, three groups of commodities (*C*): means of production (*MoP*), raw materials (*RM*), and labor power (*LP*). Then, labor is performed and new commodities are produced (*P*); the value (and exchange-value) of the resulting commodities capitalists expect to sell (*C'*) includes the value of the means of production (*MoP*), raw materials (*RM*), and labor (*L*). Those commodities can then be exchanged for more money (*M'*) than what the capitalists started with (*M*).

Readers will immediately notice that the only difference between the value of the commodities the capitalists purchase (*C*) and those they sell (*C'*) is the difference between the value of labor power (*LP*) and the value of labor (*L*). In other words, if the value of labor is greater than the value of labor power, the capitalists have managed to capture an extra value, a surplus-value. The possessor of money thus "functions as a capitalist" (KI, 254).

Here's the way this works (KI, 307–19): the means of production (*MoP*) depreciate in value as they are utilized in production, and their value is transferred to the finished commodities. So, while the building, tools, and machinery need to continue to exist as use-values, their value is embodied in the commodities that are produced and then sold on the market. Raw materials (*RM*) are a bit different, since they change form as use-values but, like the means of production, they transfer their value to the output. That's why Marx refers to the money spent on both the means of production and the raw materials as *constant capital* (*c*). The value of the means of production and raw materials is transferred to, and thus remains constant in being embodied in, the newly produced commodities.

$$M - C \begin{Bmatrix} MoP \\ RM \\ LP \end{Bmatrix} \ldots P \ldots \begin{Bmatrix} MoP \\ RM \\ L \end{Bmatrix} C' - M'$$

Figure 5.4 Capitalist production

The money spent on workers' wages and salaries is different: it gives capitalists access to the commodity labor power but the productive consumption of labor power is what gives rise to labor; thus, it is the value of labor, not the value of labor power, that is embodied in the produced commodities. The money that is used to purchase labor power is referred to as *variable capital* (v). The money capitalists advance in the form of wages, to purchase labor power, leads to a variable amount of value – even more value – embodied in the commodities that are produced.

And Marx's conclusion? It is the difference between the value of labor and the value of labor power that accounts for capitalists' profits in the form of surplus-value (s).

Value of Capitalist Commodities

Until this point, the value and exchange-value of commodities (however they are produced) were defined as quantities of socially necessary abstract labor-time. Now, for capitalist commodities, we can make that more concrete. The value of commodities produced under capitalist conditions is a combination of dead labor (DL) and living labor (LL) – labor embodied in the means of production and raw materials and labor that is performed during the course of production. Thus, we have labor that is transferred to the new commodities plus new value that is created while capitalist production is taking place.

So, the value, W (assumed still to be equal at this stage to its exchange-value, EV) of capitalist commodities can be represented in the following manner:

5.7 $$EV = W = DL + LL$$

or, what is the same,

5.8 $$EV = W = c + v + s$$

where c is dead labor, the value of constant capital, and $v + s$ is living labor, variable capital plus surplus-value.

To be clear, the entire sum of the value of variable capital and surplus-value ($v + s$) is created during the course of the workday, as labor is extracted from labor power. One portion (v) is paid to the workers, while the other portion (s) is appropriated by the capitalists.

What, then, is the appropriate measure of capitalist success? What index can be used to represent the ability of capitalists to fulfill their role as capitalists? The usual way (within both mainstream economic theory and capitalism) is the rate of profit. We can use that same index but interpret it now in specifically Marxian terms. We end up with the following expression:

5.9 $$\rho = \frac{s}{K} = \frac{s}{c + v}$$

where ρ, the Greek letter rho, is the rate of profit.[10] The rate of profit, in Marxian terms, is the ratio of surplus-value (s) to the total capital advanced by capitalists (K, which is equal to $c + v$). The more surplus-value, the higher the rate of profit; the more capital they need to spend, the lower the rate of profit. This index is exactly equal to the self-valorization of capital ($\Delta M/M$), the rate at which money begets more money, as before.

To put it differently, capitalists start with an initial sum of money or capital, which they use to purchase the elements of constant capital and variable capital. What they end up with are commodities whose value comprises those elements of capital plus an additional value. Their success at deploying their capital to appropriate surplus-value is thus measured in terms of the rate of profit.

Now, for the first time in this presentation of Marx's critique of political economy, we have specifically capitalist production!

Capitalism

It has been a long but careful, step-by-step analytical process. We should therefore stop for a moment and consider what makes this a concept of capitalism. According to Marx's method, this is an initial, relatively abstract concept that will be further explored and made more concrete in the pages and chapters ahead.

At this point, what we have is a notion of capitalism that is defined by two different circuits of commodity exchange – representing the different positions, actions, and interests of workers and capitalists. Workers sell their labor power in order to receive money to purchase a bundle of commodities that will sustain their social existence. Therefore, they are engaged in what is now the familiar sequence of monetary commodity exchanges:

5.10 $$LP - M - C$$

Workers sell their labor power for its exchange-value (equal to its value) and end up with a bundle of use-values they can consume.[11]

---

[10] With a bit of algebraic manipulation, we can also show that $\rho = s'(1 - k)$, where $s' = s/v$ and $k = c/(c + v)$. We will see the importance of this expression in chapter 6, when we discuss the tendencies of movement in the rate of profit. For now, interested readers can see that the rate of profit will increase as the rate of exploitation (s') increases and decrease as the ratio of constant capital to total capital (k) increases.

[11] Note that workers here occupy a position in a society in which, by assumption, all the products of labor take the form of commodities. That's why the value of labor power is the sum of the values of all the commodities in the customary wage bundle. What is

Capitalists, for their part, use their money capital to purchase commodity inputs (including means of production, raw materials, and labor power) in order to produce the commodity outputs they can sell at their value and realize a profit:

5.11 $$M - C - M'$$

Workers have to sell in order to buy. Their success is defined by their ability to sell their labor power, so that they can purchase commodities to sustain themselves as owners and sellers of labor power. Capitalists, in contrast, buy in order to sell – and to sell the commodities they produce at a profit. They can accomplish this only if they are successful in extracting more labor value than they used to purchase labor power, so that they end up with a surplus-value.

What this means is that, on top of all the conditions of monetary or generalized commodity exchange discussed above, we now have two new characteristics or conditions of specifically capitalist production:

1. The buying and selling of labor power as a commodity imply the buying and selling of wage goods.
2. By the same token, capitalist production means that the means of production and raw materials are available as commodities.

Together, these conditions underline the importance of the circulation of commodities for "those societies in which the capitalist mode of production prevails." Both wage goods and producer goods have to be available as commodities, so that they can be purchased by workers and capitalists, respectively.[12] Moreover, the surplus-value embodied in capitalist commodities is only socially recognized when those commodities are sold, and their value and surplus-value realized in the form of money. Only then, when they sell the output, can capitalists receive their monetary profits.

Parallel to the discussion of the two-fold nature of the commodity, and in contrast to the way production is analyzed within mainstream economics, the production of capitalist commodities represents the unity of two distinct processes, labor and valorization. Labor is performed and, at the same time, value is created. Even more important, more value is created than capitalists advance in purchasing the initial set of commodity inputs. So, capitalist production involves the production of both value and surplus-value.

---

missing here, of course, is the production that does not take the form of commodities – household production (a topic we return to in chapter 7) but also government-provided goods and services.

[12] To be clear, these commodities need not be capitalist commodities. The only conditions are that wage goods and producer goods be available as commodities – but they may be produced under noncapitalist conditions. Historically, for example, cotton produced by slaves in the US South was sold for use in capitalist textile mills in Manchester and other English cities.

It is the drive to extract surplus-value that, according to Marx, serves to define the capitalist (KI, 990):

> The self-valorization of capital – the creation of surplus-value – is therefore the determining, dominating, and overriding purpose of the capitalist; it is the absolute motive and content of his activity.[13]

Which leads us to the next question: is it possible for capitalists to raise the rate of surplus-value?

Absolute Surplus-Value

As we have seen, during the course of the workday, the capitalist extracts labor from labor power. Or, as Marx puts it, in words reminiscent of John William Polidori, capital "only lives by sucking living labour, and lives the more, the more labour it sucks. The time during which the labourer works is the time during which the capitalist consumes the labour-power he has bought from him" (KI, 342).[14]

Therefore, one way for capitalists to raise the rate of exploitation is by "sucking" more living labor, which they can accomplish by extending the length of the workday. That's what Marx refers to as *absolute surplus-value* (KI, 283–426). It's a change in the absolute amount of time during which living labor is performed. So, if the amount of necessary labor remains constant, an extension of the workday (say, from 10 to 12 hours) will result in more surplus labor.

We can see this by using a timeline (figure 5.5) similar to the one we introduced above, modified only by using the symbols for variable capital (v) and surplus-value (s) in place of necessary and surplus labor.

It is clear, then, that if the workday is increased (from $x-z$ to $x-z'$), and workers are paid the same as before (so v remains constant), the number of hours during which workers labor not for themselves but for their

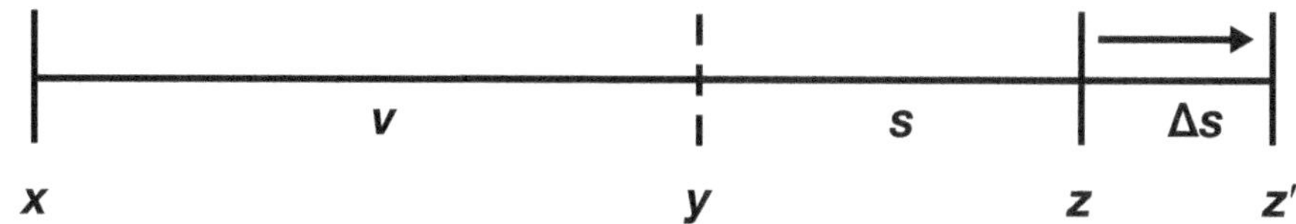

Figure 5.5 Absolute surplus-value

[13] The following point is often overlooked in Marx's discussion of capitalists. On the very same page of *Capital* on which Marx characterizes that capitalist imperative, he also writes: "the capitalist is just as enslaved by the relationships of capitalism as is his opposite pole, the worker, albeit in a quite different manner" (KI, 990).

[14] Polidori was the English author of "The Vampyre," the first published modern vampire story (in 1819).

employers also increases (it goes from s to $s + \Delta s$).[15] Therefore, since the denominator remains constant and the numerator increases, the rate of surplus-value (s/v) itself increases.[16]

Absolute surplus-value will also rise with an increase in the number of workers employed by capitalists. Even if the rate of exploitation remains constant, more workers performing surplus labor for capitalists will increase the mass of surplus-value capitalists are able to capture. Once again, what is considered an indicator of progress within mainstream economic theory – in this case, an increase in employment – is an economic and social problem – that is, it leads to more exploitation – within Marxian economic theory.

If the existence of exploitation represents the theoretical possibility of class struggle within capitalism, then absolute surplus-value is a particular form of that struggle. It shows how the interests of workers and capitalists diverge – or, to put it differently, how the two classes struggle over conflicting rights. Whereas workers are in favor of limits on the length of the workday, capitalists would like to see it expand as long as possible.

That, as it turns out, is the source of the series of struggles that first broke out during the nineteenth century, when workers made known their grievances against working from "sunrise to sunset." Those struggles culminated in early May 1886 near Haymarket Square in the midwestern US city of Chicago, Illinois, when workers went on strike demanding an eight-hour workday. The movement was then taken up by other workers both inside and outside the United States. While no law has ever been passed in the United States limiting the length of the workday, the Haymarket protest became the origin of International Workers' Day held on May 1 around the world – everywhere but in the United States.[17]

Relative Surplus-Value

What happens if it becomes difficult for capitalists to extract absolute surplus-value by extending the length of the workday – if, for example,

[15] Even if workers' pay increases (so that v rises) – for example, if they are paid a higher rate for overtime – the rate of surplus-value will rise if the increase in pay is less than the increase in the time spent performing surplus labor. And even if the rate of exploitation does not rise, it will still be the case that, as the workday expands, the mass of surplus-value appropriated by capitalists will increase.

[16] Readers can consult Appendix 1 at the end of this chapter to see how absolute surplus-value works using a numerical example.

[17] In the United States, Labor Day is a federal holiday celebrated on the first Monday in September. It was formally adopted in a law signed by conservative Democratic president Grover Cleveland in 1894 in order to distance it from the radical (socialist, anarchist, and communist) associations with International Workers' Day.

customs and traditions or legislation or collective-bargaining agreements prevent it – or because they decide not to hire more workers or, for that matter, if a growing portion of the working-class is simply not available because of poor health and even death due to being overworked? Are there any alternatives for capitalists to appropriate more surplus-value?

One possibility open to capitalists is to extract *relative surplus-value* (KI, 429–639). This occurs when the relative portions of the workday are changed, thereby decreasing the time workers labor for themselves and increasing the time spent creating surplus-value.

As we can see in this new timeline (figure 5.6), the portion of the day spent creating value equal to variable capital decreases (changing from $x-y$ to $x-y'$) and the portion of the day devoted to surplus-value increases (going from $y-z$ to $y'-z$). As a result, even though the workday and the total amount of value created remain constant, paid labor or the amount of variable capital (v) falls and unpaid labor or surplus-value (s) rises. Therefore, since the denominator decreases and the numerator increases, the rate of surplus-value (s/v) itself grows.

The problem is, within mainstream economics, employers can't just lower workers' wages or take items out of the wage bundle. Mainstream economists presume that wages are set not by individual capitalists, but by supply and demand in the market for labor power. So, under what conditions might the value of labor power fall?

Let us remember that the value of labor power (v) is a bundle of commodities (wage or consumer goods), each with a particular exchange-value. If we hold the number of use-values in the wage bundle constant (workers purchase and consume the same number of items), then a decrease in the exchange-value of one or more of those commodities will lower the value of labor power. And, as the value of labor power falls, capitalists have to put up less money (and therefore less variable capital) to purchase the commodity labor power.[18]

So, the question about relative surplus-value is actually a question about the dynamics of capitalism: what might cause the elements of the wage bundle to decrease in value? As it turns out, there *is* such a mechanism:

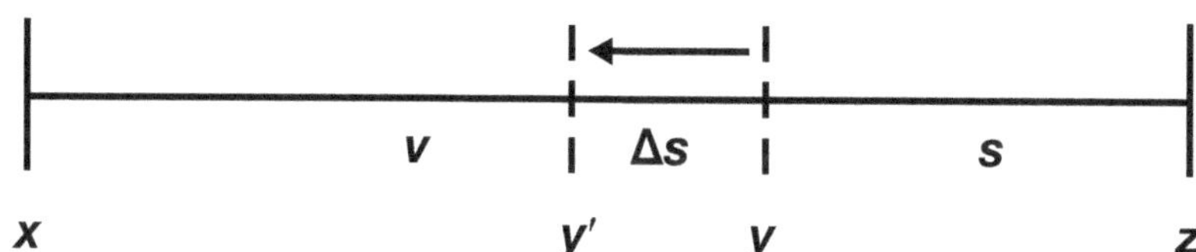

Figure 5.6 Relative surplus-value

[18] Readers can refer to footnote 8 above for the mathematical expression of the value of labor power.

increased productivity in the wage-goods industry. An increase in the amount produced per worker in the sector that produces the commodities workers purchase as part of their consumption bundle (so, food, clothing, and shelter but not yachts, private jets, and mansions) will lower the amount of value embodied in each commodity in the wage bundle. And, as the value of labor power falls, employers need to come up with less money to gain access to labor power. Thus, the relative portions of the day spent creating value equal to variable capital and surplus-value will change. The result will be an increase in the rate of surplus-value.[19]

Here, again, we have an aspect of capitalism that is celebrated by mainstream economists (and regularly reported in the media as a good thing) – an increase in productivity – which is, from a Marxian perspective, something that represents a social theft from a majority of the population – as the value of labor power falls and workers are subject to an increase in capitalist exploitation.

Capitalist Competition

Not only do mainstream economists applaud increases in productivity (because, they argue, it leads to more use-values and thus higher national output); they also extol the virtues of competition.

Both liberal and conservative mainstream economists, in Marx's time and in our own, see competition as one of the positive features of capitalism, a key source of both its fairness and its dynamism. If competition exists between firms in an industry, it is credited with creating and maintaining equality among market participants (since none of them is able to exercise market power over others); it is also an incentive for firms to innovate – to develop cheaper ways of producing goods and services, to come up with new products, and so on. And if perfect competition doesn't exist (if, for example, there are oligopolies and monopolies), it should be created or restored (e.g., through antitrust laws) and then left alone. Competition is either the condition of capitalist markets (for conservative mainstream economists) or the goal of such markets (for liberal mainstream economists).

However, according to Marx's critique of political economy, that same competition turns out to be a mechanism for creating relative surplus-value.

Let's see how that works. Competition is defined as a particular social interaction among capitalist enterprises based on their ability to realize additional surplus-value in the form of super-profits. Until now, the assumption was that a capitalist's profits represented the surplus-value

[19] Readers can consult Appendix 1 at the end of this chapter to see how relative surplus-value can be extracted using a numerical example.

they extracted from their own workers. However, in an industry made up of various competing enterprises (as assumed within mainstream economic theory), it is likely that profits will be distributed between enterprises. Firms or enterprises that manage to outcompete others within that industry will not only get the surplus-value from their own workers; they'll also be able to capture some of the surplus-value created within other firms. In other words, they will be able to obtain more surplus-value – their "normal" profits plus above-normal or super-profits.

That's one of the reasons the two numbers attached to commodities – value and exchange-value – are so important. It is quite possible (and, under the conditions of capitalist competition, generally expected) that one firm will be able to lower the value of the commodities it produces, and yet sell that commodity like all the other firms at the average exchange-value for that industry. With competition, then, the value of an individual firm's commodities is not necessarily equal to its exchange-value, which also means that the amount of surplus-value it realizes when selling its commodities need not be equal to the amount of surplus-value it appropriates from its workers. Some firms will be unable to realize all the surplus-value they extract from their workers, and that surplus-value will be captured by one or more other firms that have secured a competitive advantage.[20]

So, competition is an incentive for capitalist enterprises to innovate, just as in mainstream economic theory. But both the goal and the effects of competition within Marxian economic theory are quite different. First, firms face both a carrot and a stick to undercut their competitors – to capture some of the surplus-value produced within other enterprises and to avoid such a distribution of "their" surplus-value to other capitalists. The discourses of capitalism and mainstream economics thus function to make a virtue out of the social necessity to innovate. Second, if one firm outcompetes others within an industry, and obtains additional surplus-value, they are able to use those additional profits to drive the other, less successful firms out of the industry. The effect is to destroy the very competition they started with. We will see how this works below, in chapter 6.

Subsumption of Labor

Now that we know it is possible for capitalists to extract more surplus-value – via absolute and relative surplus-value – the question is: what are the conditions within a capitalist society that make these forms of exploitation possible?

[20] Readers can consult Appendix 1 at the end of this chapter to see how, using a numerical example, surplus-value is distributed among firms.

Marx, in a section on the "Results of the Immediate Process of Production," explains that the formal subsumption of labor and the real subsumption of labor are the preconditions for absolute and relative surplus-value.[21] At the simplest level, the formal subsumption of labor refers to the expropriation of the direct producers *outside* production, while the real subsumption of labor involves the expropriation of the direct producers *inside* production.

The process whereby labor becomes subsumed to capital, in both senses, is a story about labor relations and technological change that are endogenous to capitalism, parts of its economic and social history. In this, Marx's approach differs from that of mainstream economists, who presume the existence of wage-labor and focus on choices profit-maximizing capitalists make from an exogenous set of available technologies (determined, for example, by engineers).

For Marx, the formal subsumption of labor involves laborers, the sellers of labor power, going to work for capitalists and not for themselves or someone else (such as feudal landlords or slaveowners). It is the beginning of capitalism, in the absence of any changes in the existing state of production and technology, in which workers are separated from the means of production. They no longer own or have access to the means of production. Therefore, since their labor power has no use-value for them, the direct producers are forced *en masse* to have the freedom to sell their ability to work to capitalist employers. That's what makes the extraction of absolute surplus-value possible.

But the significance of the formal subsumption of labor goes beyond that. It means that the Industrial Revolution – the set of profound changes in how workplaces were organized and in the makeup of the technologies that were utilized in production, extravagantly represented in London's Crystal Palace during the Great Exhibition of 1851 – is a product of capitalism, not its origin or cause. It comes *after* capitalism, the formal subsumption of labor, and the extraction of surplus-value already exist.

A good example of the formal subsumption of labor is the so-called putting-out system. This is when, starting in the seventeenth and eighteenth centuries, employers "put out" materials to rural producers who usually worked in their homes (but sometimes labored in workshops or in turn put out work to others). Finished products were returned to the employers for payment on a piecework or wage basis. The putting-out system differed from the handicraft system of home production in that the workers neither bought materials nor sold products. Thus, the direct producers only received the equivalent of their necessary labor, the rest

[21] Sometimes known as the "lost chapter" of *Capital*, it was written between June 1863 and December 1866 and was first published in 1933, in German and Russian. An English translation appears as an Appendix to the Ben Fowkes translation of volume 1 of *Capital* (pp. 948–1084).

– the surplus-value – being appropriated by the capitalists. It served to undermine the restrictive regulations of the urban artisanal guilds and led to the first widespread industrial employment of women and children.

Once the formal subsumption of labor has occurred – once the workday is divided into two parts, necessary and surplus labor, within capitalism – it becomes possible to change how capitalist production itself is organized, and to create the real subsumption of labor. Then, relative surplus-value can be extracted.

The first step is cooperation, the creation of the collective laborer. Masses of labor power are collected under one roof, in the same workplace, which makes it possible to incorporate a sequence of work shifts, to save on fixed costs, to reduce waste in the use of raw materials, and so on. Now, production depends less on the endeavors of individual workers and more on the assemblage of many direct producers.

The next step is the technical division of labor, a reorganization of the labor process with an eye toward greater efficiency. This is the creation of the detail laborer, the worker who is employed in one part of a much larger production process – of the sort that is celebrated in Adam Smith's famous example of the pin factory and indicted in Charlie Chaplin's film *Modern Times*. The range of skills of craftworkers is made irrelevant, and the emphasis instead is on the flow of production through subdivided tasks and more detailed skills.

This technical division of labor is distinguished from the social division of labor, which as we saw above is a condition of commodity exchange. The social division of labor presupposes the dispersion of the means of production among many capitalists, who produce and exchange different commodities. The technical division of labor, on the other hand, is based on the concentration of means of production in the hands of capitalists (and not of others, especially the direct producers). Thus, in Marx's view, capitalism represents a contradictory combination of anarchy and despotism (KI, 450) – the absence of coordination outside of production and the absence of democracy inside production.

Finally, according to Marx, is the step defined by machinery or modern industry. This is the Industrial Revolution per se, which presupposes the formal subsumption of labor, the creation of the collective laborer, and the technical division of labor. Now, capitalists can substitute constant capital for variable capital, new machines for human laborers, in search of super-profits. This is when, in the search for higher levels of productivity, workers become appendages of the machines they work with. The result is that the machines set the pace of work, call for certain specialized tasks, and create a continuous flow of production. It also leads to new forms of surveillance (either by supervisors, who monitor the pace of work, or by the machines themselves, which include ways of measuring the output).

The advent of modern industry also ushers in a reorganization of the economy as a whole into separate sectors or departments – one producing consumer goods (whose values determine the value of labor power), the other producer goods (and therefore the elements of constant capital). Only then can we say that capitalism – generalized commodity exchange based on absolute and relative surplus-value – is fully constituted.

But the process doesn't stop there. It continues with the advent of machinofacture, the "production of machines by machines" (KI 506). Just as manufacturing industry is distinguished from handicraft production by the deskilling of the labor process involved in manufacturing, machinofacture is distinguished from earlier stages of manufacturing by the fact that in machinofacture machinery replaces not just a less sophisticated tool of production, but the human hand itself.

Again, we should note, modern industry can be employed in the production of services as well as goods. Gigantic iron mills and automobile factories may be the quintessential examples in period photographs and the textbooks of mainstream economics. But the technologies and forms of workplace organization of manufacture are also deployed in many other areas – from healthcare and education to sports and fast food. In each case, the craftspeople (such as doctors and nurses, teachers, athletes, and chefs), who utilize a range of skills and have some autonomy in controlling the pace of their work, are expropriated within production and, as a result, become appendages to the machines and software utilized in producing a wide variety of goods and services.

A similar process continues today, with the introduction of new forms of automation and digital technologies. Just as in the first Industrial Revolution, new production methods and new ways of organizing workplaces are redefining the process of work and the possibilities of exploiting workers during the immediate process of production. For example, with the further development of machinofacture, the conditions are eventually created for the introduction of artificial intelligence, when not only the human hand, but the human brain, is replaced in the production of machines by machines.[22]

That's why contemporary capitalism is both radically different from and, in other ways, exactly the same as it was in the nineteenth century when Marx first formulated his critique of political economy.

[22] The most recent stages of machinofacture, which has less and less need for workers' hands and brains, pose a dilemma for contemporary societies: what role is left for all those workers? As it turns out, capitalists have come up with an answer – to increase the volume of data (which some capitalists can collect, process, and sell as commodities to other capitalists). But, with that, another problem arises: how will the population earn enough income to participate in the bandwidth?

Exploitation and Real Wages

One of the major claims of mainstream economists, then as now, is that capitalism "delivers the goods." In particular, the argument goes, increases in productivity lead to higher real wages for workers over time.

As we have seen in recent decades, in the United States and in many other countries, workers' real wages have failed to keep pace with the growth in productivity. That's one of the main reasons why inequality has been growing to such obscene levels, with a growing gap between the top 1 percent and everyone else. Therefore, it's hard to take seriously mainstream economists' presumption and repeated assertions of a correlation between productivity and real wages. Recent history, as we saw in chapter 1, calls that relationship into question.

However, even if real wages were rising, does that mean workers would be better off? The answer is, from a Marxian perspective, yes and no. Yes, in the sense that there will be more use-values, more goods and services, in workers' wage bundles. But the answer is also no, because it is quite possible for growing real wages to be accompanied by more exploitation of workers.

Such a two-fold answer stems from the idea that the value of labor power includes two components: the number of commodities seen as use-values and the exchange-value per unit use-value of each of those commodities. The set of use-values (food, clothing, shelter, etc.) represents the real wage; the sum of those use-values multiplied by their exchange-values is the value capitalists have to pay to purchase labor power and that workers receive in the form of wages and salaries. What that means is, if the exchange-values per unit use-value of the commodities that make up the value of labor power fall more quickly than the real wage is growing, then the value of labor power as a whole will fall – and the rate of exploitation will rise.[23]

Such a combination of rising real wages and a falling value of labor power is actually quite crucial to various forms and periods of capitalism. An increase in real wages means workers can purchase the growing number of commodities that are being produced by capitalist growth. That can occur either when domestic productivity is increasing or when firms in advanced countries are able to offshore the production of consumer goods to other countries where production is cheaper. In both cases, a rising real wage is a condition of existence of mass production wherever it occurs within global capitalism. At the same time, one of the results of a decrease in the value of labor power is that capitalists are able to extract more relative surplus-value and capture more profits, even as the real wages of their workers are rising.

[23] Readers can consult Appendix 2 at the end of this chapter to see the mathematical derivation of this conclusion.

But what if, under other circumstances, workers' real wages are stagnant or even decreasing? Then, in addition to selling their labor power to attempt to maintain a certain standard of living, workers will likely go into debt (on their credit cards, home mortgages, car loans, etc.). To take but one example, by 2007 in the United States, consumer debt had risen to more than 100 percent of income as workers struggled to secure the standard of living they had come to expect by selling their labor power. Of course, workers still need to repay their debts (plus the interest on those debts), which forces them to continue to sell their labor power to their employers. Plus, they have to avoid other forms of debt (e.g., to pay for the escalating cost of healthcare and additional education). So, in many countries, workers have an additional reason to sell their labor power, in order to secure employer-provided healthcare and educational benefits.

Thus, from a Marxian perspective, as long as workers live in societies in which the capitalist mode of production prevails, they are forced to have the freedom to sell their labor power and to be subject to class exploitation.

Looking Ahead

Marx's theory of surplus-value represents both a direct challenge and a radical alternative to the way profits are generally understood within mainstream economic theory and capitalism. It therefore forms an important part of his class critique of political economy.

Although we have covered a great deal of ground in this chapter, it is only the first step. In the next chapter, we will look at how surplus-value, once appropriated by capitalists, is distributed – and what that means for analyzing profits and wages, the ethical implications of different economic theories, and the dynamic movements of capitalism over time.

Suggested Readings

Harry Braverman, *Labor and Monopoly Capital: The Degradation of Work in the Twentieth Century* (New York: Monthly Review Press, 1974).

Michael Burawoy, *Manufacturing Consent: Changes in the Labor Process under Monopoly Capitalism* (Chicago: University of Chicago Press, 1979).

Gugliemo Carchedi, "Exploitation," in *Routledge Handbook of Marxian Economics*, ed. David M. Brennan, David Kristjanson-Gural, Catherine P. Mulder, and Erik M. Olson, pp. 45–8 (New York: Routledge, 2017).

Erik K. Olsen, "Labor and Labor Power," in *Routledge Handbook of Marxian Economics*, ed. David M. Brennan, David Kristjanson-Gural, Catherine P. Mulder, and Erik M. Olson, pp. 49–58 (New York: Routledge, 2017).

John R. Weeks, *Capital and Exploitation* (Princeton, NJ: Princeton University Press, 2014).

Appendix 1: Notes on Absolute and Relative Surplus-Value

These notes use numerical examples to show how, within Marx's critique of political economy, absolute and relative surplus-value work under capitalism. They also include an example of the competition over super-profits that is part of the explanation of relative surplus-value.

We start with the initial situation of a hypothetical capitalist enterprise, along with the underlying assumptions (where all values are converted into US dollars):

$\$80c + \$20v + \$20s = \$120w$

Assume:

number of laborers (l) = 20
length of workday (h) = 10
total person-hours worked ($h \bullet l$) = abstract labor (AL) = 200
number of use-values produced (uv) = 1200

The rest of the terms are defined as in the main text: c is constant capital, v is variable capital, s is surplus-value, w is value, and ev is exchange-value.

Here are the results in this initial situation:

(a) rate of exploitation (s/v) = \$20/\$20 = 100%
(b) value rate of productivity or intensity of labor ($[v + s]/[h \bullet l]$) = (\$20 + \$20)/(10 • 20) = \$.20 per person hour
(c) technical productivity of labor ($uv/[h \bullet l]$) = 1200/(10 • 20) = 6 per person hour
(d) exchange-value per unit use-value or "normal price" (ev/uv) = \$120/1200 = \$.10 per unit
(e) rate of profit ($\rho = s/[c + v]$) = \$20/(\$80 + \$20) = 20%

Absolute Surplus-Value

Here are two examples of absolute surplus-value – one based on a lengthening of the workday, the other based on an increase in the number of laborers.

A. Lengthening of the workday

Assume the workday is increased by 2 hours. Then:

$h \bullet l = 240$
value created = \$48 = $\$20v + \$28s$
c embodied = \$96 (because more constant capital is used up during the extra hours)

Therefore, the new value is \$96*c* + \$20*v* + \$28*s* = \$144*w*. And the results are:

(a) rate of exploitation (s/v) = \$28/\$20 = 140%
(b) value rate of productivity or intensity of labor ($[v + s]/[h \bullet l]$) = (\$20 + \$28)/(12 • 20) = \$.20
(c) technical productivity of labor ($uv/[h \bullet l]$) = 1440/(12 • 20) = 6
(d) exchange-value per unit use-value or "normal price" (ev/uv) = \$144/1440 = \$.10
(e) rate of profit ($\rho = s/[c + v]$) = \$28/(\$96 + \$20) = 24%

Compared to the initial situation, the rate of exploitation has increased (from 100% to 140%) as has the rate of profit (from 20% to 24%).

B. Increased proletarianization

Assume the number of laborers increases by 50 percent. That means:

$h \bullet l = 300$
value created = \$60
c embodied = \$120 (because more laborers have to work with more constant capital)

Therefore, \$120*c* + \$30*v* + \$30*s* = \$180*w*

(a) rate of exploitation (s/v) = \$30/\$30 = 100%
(b) value rate of productivity or intensity of labor ($[v + s]/[h \bullet l]$) = (\$30 + \$30)/(10 • 30) = \$.20
(c) technical productivity of labor ($uv/[h \bullet l]$) = 1800/(10 • 30) = 6
(d) exchange-value per unit use-value or "normal price" (ev/uv) = \$180/1800 = 180/1800 = \$.10
(e) rate of profit ($\rho = s/[c + v]$) = \$30/(\$120 + \$30) = 20%

Compared to the initial situation, both the rate of exploitation and the rate of profit remain the same but the mass of surplus-value has increased (from \$20*s* to \$30*s*).

Relative Surplus-Value

This is an example of relative surplus-value, based on an increase in the technical productivity of labor in the wage-goods industry, i.e., the sector that produces commodities that are included in the value of labor power. The first part illustrates relative surplus-value per *se*, that is, the results of the change in productivity for a firm whose workers purchase the wage goods. The second part represents the competition over super-profits.

Assume the technical productivity of labor has doubled in the wage-goods industry.

A. Firm whose workers purchase wage goods

Assume the technical innovation has spread throughout the wage-goods industry.

Then, the *ev/uv* in that industry will fall by 20 percent, to \$12.

(a) Therefore, \$80*c* + \$16*v* + \$24*s* = \$120*w*
(b) rate of exploitation (*s/v*) = \$24/\$16 = 150%
(c) value rate of productivity or intensity of labor ([*v* + *s*]/[*h* • *l*]) = (\$16 + \$24)/200 = \$0.20
(d) technical productivity of labor (*uv*/[*h* • *l*]) = 1200/(10 • 20) = 6
(e) exchange-value per unit use-value or "normal price" (*ev/uv*) = \$120/1200 = \$0.10
(f) rate of profit (ρ = *s*/[*c* + *v*]) = \$24/(\$80 + \$16) = 25%

Compared to the initial situation, the rate of exploitation has increased (from 100% to 150%) as has the rate of profit (from 20% to 25%).

B. Firm with increase in labor productivity, i.e., super-profits

We begin by assuming the initial situation of a wage-goods industry (say, shirts) with three identical capitalists, each of whom produces one use-value based on the following value equation: \$11*c* + \$2*v* + \$2*s* = \$15*w*.

This is what the industry looks like:

K	Value	UV
K1	$c_1 + v_1 + s_1 = w_1$	1
K2	$c_2 + v_2 + s_2 = w_2$	1
K3	$c_3 + v_3 + s_3 = w_3$	1
	\$33*c* + \$6*v* + \$6*s* = \$45*w*	3

The total value and exchange-value is \$45, the exchange-value per unit use-value (*ev/uv*) is \$15/shirt, which is equal to the "normal price" of wage goods.

Suppose the second capitalist becomes more productive (e.g., with the introduction of new machinery):

K2 \$20*c* + \$2*v* + \$2*s* = \$24*w* 2*UV*

The total exchange-value produced by the industry rises by \$9 to \$54, while the number of use-values produced increases by 1 to 4.

The new industry average exchange-value per unit use-value (*ev/uv*) = \$54/4 = \$13.50 (which is less than \$15, the original "price" of shirts).

K	*UV*	*EV*	*EV/UV*	avg	revenue	$c + v$	$S_{realized}$
K1	1	$15	$15	$13.5	$13.5	$13	$0.5
K2	2	$24	$12	$13.5	$27	$22	$5
K3	1	$15	$15	$13.5	$13.5	$13	$0.5
4		$54		$13.5	$54	$48	$6

The total industry *s* = 6, which is the same as before. But it is now distributed differently among the three capitalists.

K2 gains because K1 and K2 lose. It's a zero-sum game.

	Before Change		After Change	
	s	*s/v*	*s*	*s/v*
K1	$2	1	$0.5	.25
K2	$2	1	$5	2.5
K3	$2	1	$0.5	.25

K2 has gone on the offensive against K1 and K3. They must respond, for example, by copying the innovation.

If they do, the total *EV* = $72, the number of *UV* = 6, and the *EV/UV* = $12 (as in the first part above).

Here, then, are the results of an industry-wide increase in productivity within that industry:

(a) the exchange-value per unit use-value (*ev/uv*) falls from $15 to $12
(b) the rate of exploitation (*s/v*) stays the same
(c) the composition of capital ($k = c/[c+v]$) increases from .85 to .91
(d) the rate of profit ($\rho = s/[c+v]$) decreases from 15.38% to 9.09%

The profit rate falls because more capital is involved in production to get the same surplus-value. Each of the three capitalists must advance $20 + $2 = $22K to get $2*s* instead of $11 + $2 = $13K as before. But dead labor (*c*) does not create value.

Appendix 2: Real Wages and Exploitation

The mathematical proof of the result in the text – that rising real wages are compatible with increased exploitation – is straightforward.

We start with the definition of the value of labor power, $V = \mathbf{e} \bullet \mathbf{q}$ (where $\mathbf{e} = ev/uv$, the exchange-value per unit use-value of wage goods, and $\mathbf{q}$ is the vector of use-values in the wage bundle).

Totally differentiating the expression gives us $dV/V = d\mathbf{e}/\mathbf{e} + d\mathbf{q}/\mathbf{q}$.

Thus, the value of labor will fall if the per-unit exchange-value in the wage bundle falls, even if the real wage rises, as long as the absolute value of the change in the exchange-value per unit use-value is greater than the change in the real wage. Mathematically, $dV/V < 0$ if $de/e < 0$, even if $dq/q > 0$, as long as $|de/e| > |dq/q|$.

Here is the total differentiation of the value of labor power (where ∂ is a partial derivative):

$$V = e \bullet q$$

$$\begin{aligned} dV &= (\partial V/\partial e)de + (\partial V/\partial q)dq \\ &= (q \bullet de) + (e \bullet dq) \end{aligned}$$

Dividing through by V, gives us:

$$\begin{aligned} dV/V &= (q \bullet de)/(e \bullet q) + (e \bullet dq)/(e \bullet q) \\ &= de/e + dq/q \end{aligned}$$

which is the result above.

Chapter 6

PROFITS, WAGES, AND DISTRIBUTION OF THE SURPLUS

In the previous two chapters, we addressed many of the issues that form the core of Marx's critique of political economy.

In chapter 4, readers were introduced to and encouraged to explore in some detail (OK, I will admit, *considerable* detail) Marx's treatment of the commodity, commodity exchange, and the various uses of money, which distinguishes his approach – especially in the discussion of commodity fetishism and the possibility of crises in a market-based economic system – from that of mainstream economists, both in his time and in our own. Then, in chapter 5, I presented Marx's theory of exploitation, examining the key difference between labor and labor power, what this means for analyzing the value of capitalist commodities, and the various ways capitalists are able to extract more surplus-value from their workers.

But those chapters no doubt left readers with many other questions, which I endeavor to answer in this chapter. For example, how does Marx define wages and profits (and, in addition, rent)? How are they different from the way they are understood within mainstream economics? What are the different ethical implications of Marx's theory of value and surplus-value compared to the mainstream theories that are so often taught and utilized within the discipline of economics?

Moreover, while it is clear Marx's critique of mainstream economics is closely related to his class critique of capitalism, we also need to ask how Marx's theory of profits and wages offers a mapping of the class positions that define the economic and social landscape of capitalism. Are there only two classes, workers and capitalists, as is often presumed, or does Marx's analysis produce a class structure of capitalism that is more complex and variegated than that?

In order to get there, we have to ask, what happens to the surplus once it's extracted? How are portions of the surplus-value distributed by capitalists to others who provide some of the conditions of existence of capitalism? The analysis of such distributions connects the approach in volume 1 of *Capital* with that of the other two volumes, especially volume 3. This is important because the analyses in the first and third volumes are often criticized, especially by mainstream economists, for being inconsistent with each other. It also implies additional class positions and serves as a key to understanding the class conditions and effects of the unequal distribution of income and wealth within capitalism.

The distributions of surplus-value, along with the initial appropriation of the surplus, are also crucial in analyzing movements in and changes of capitalism over time. What happens, for example, when a portion of surplus-value is directed toward the accumulation of capital? What are the other possible uses of the surplus within capitalism? Tracing the patterns of appropriations and distributions of the surplus can tell us a great deal about the tendencies of capitalism, especially the particular ways a capitalist economy can and often does enter into crisis.

The analysis of profits, wages, and distributions of surplus-value therefore demonstrates additional differences, in addition to and alongside the ones we have already seen in previous chapters, between Marx's critique of political economy and mainstream economic theory.

Distribution of Income

Marx's critique of mainstream economics is based on a fundamentally different approach to the distribution of income under capitalism. In *Capital*, he presents it as a break from classical political economy. Later, in part II of Engels's *Anti-Dühring*, he shows how it is different from what other radical thinkers were arguing at the time.[1] By extension, we will also discover how it challenges the way contemporary mainstream economists analyze the distribution of income.

To be clear, the distribution of income here refers to the "functional," not the "size" distribution of income. Today, we commonly discuss the distribution of income (to the extent that we do, since income inequality is still mostly overlooked in the research, textbooks, and public pronouncements of mainstream economists) in terms of how much income individuals, grouped into percentiles of the population, receive. So, for example, we occasionally see references to the share of income that goes to the top 1 percent or top 10 percent versus the share earned by the bottom 50

[1] The full title is *Herr Eugen Dühring's Revolution in Science*, which was written as a series of articles and then published as a book in 1878. Eugen Karl Dühring was a German economist and socialist, who was also a critic of Marx's critique of political economy. In the mid-1870s, Dühring's work had become influential among German Social-Democrats, which provoked the critical response by Engels and Marx. In 1880, Engels took three chapters of *Anti-Dühring* and created what would become one of the most popular (and, for many Marxists, controversial) socialist pamphlets in the world: *Socialism: Utopian and Scientific* (ME, 683–717). We return to this pamphlet in chapter 9.

percent or the middle 40 percent of individuals or households. The degree of inequality is thus measured by ratios between those groups (e.g., an "interdecile ratio" such as the 90:10 ratio, which shows the income level of individuals in the top 10 percent of the income distribution relative to the income of those in the bottom 10 percent of the distribution) or by a single summary number (such as the Gini coefficient, which measures the inequality among values of a frequency distribution of levels of income – ranging from zero, where everyone has the same income, to one, where only 1 person has all the income).

In recent years, the discussion of the size distribution of income has certainly expanded, for two reasons: because inequality has reached such obscene levels, with the share of income going to the small group at the top of the economic pyramid growing larger and larger, and because of the pioneering work of Thomas Piketty and the growing set of countries represented in the World Inequality Database, which is regularly updated and made available online.[2]

Figure 6.1 illustrates the changing distribution of income in the United States, from 1913 to 2019. As readers can see, in recent decades, just as during the 1920s, the share of income captured by the top 1 percent (the dotted line in the chart) has been rising, while the share of income going to all of the bottom 90 percent of Americans (the dashed line) has been falling. Between them, there is a short period (25 years or so following World War II), when this tendency was reversed and the difference in the shares of the two groups was becoming smaller.

This is the so-called Golden Age of US capitalism, when the policies of the Depression-era New Deals, as well as the growing strength of labor unions and the unique position of the United States within global capitalism, created a less unequal distribution of income. In retrospect, the period of declining inequality that was long considered the norm, for both US capitalism and mainstream economic theory, turns out to have been the exception between two, much-longer periods of growing inequality.

The functional distribution of income, in contrast, refers to the shares of income captured by different groups, such as factors of production (as they are referred to in mainstream economics) or classes (in Marxian economics). Thus, instead of individuals and percentiles, the focus is on the profit share, the wage share, and the rental share – and thus the distribution of income to labor, capital, and land.

The size distribution of income thus measures how much income individuals are able to capture, while the functional distribution of income reveals the sources of that income, in terms of the class structure of capitalism.

[2] Piketty's pioneering book is *Capital in the Twenty-First Century.* The URL for the World Inequality Database is https://wid.world/.

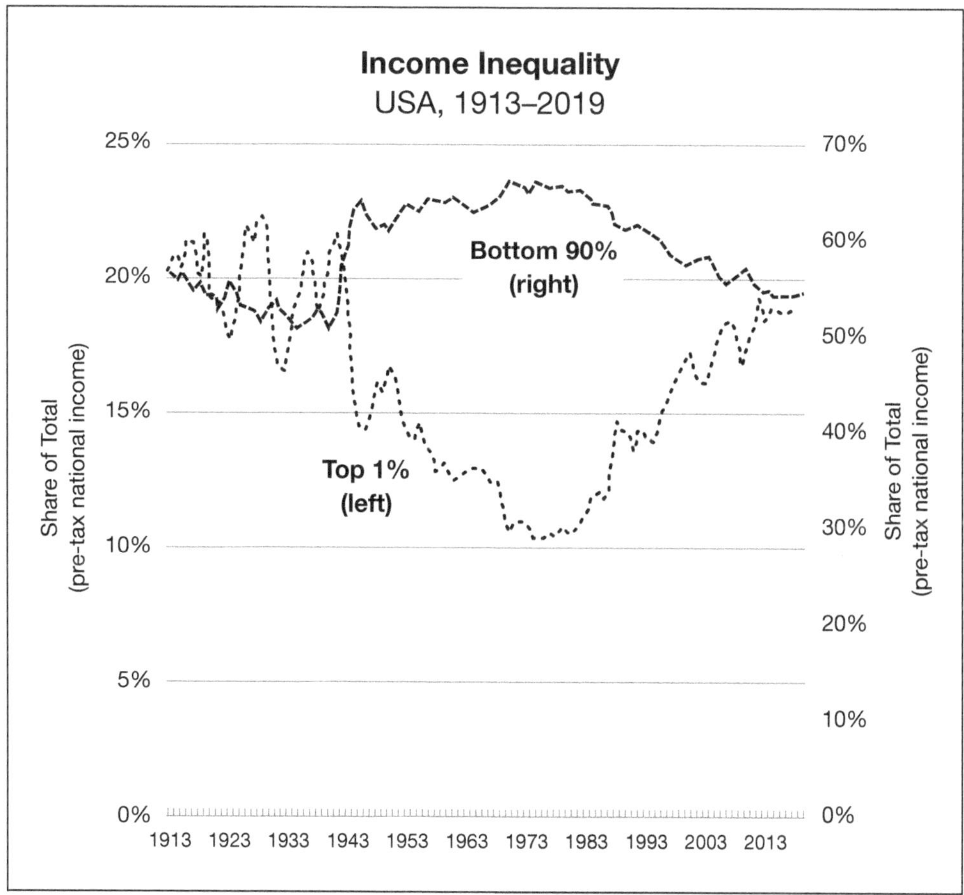

Figure 6.1 Income inequality in the United States
Source: World Inequality Database

The focus in classical political economy, and hence in Marx's critique, is on the functional distribution of income. Below, we will also see how changes in this class distribution of income affect the size or individual distribution of income.

Trinity Formula

The classical theory of the distribution of income, as developed by Adam Smith, was that each factor or class – labor, capital, and land – would receive a share of national income – wages, profits, and rent, respectively – corresponding to the "ordinary" or "average" rates prevailing in the general circumstances of society. Thus, a commodity's "natural price" would be the sum of the natural rates of wages, profits, and rent. In economics, this is generally referred to as an "adding-up" theory of value.[3] What David Ricardo added to Smith's theory was the idea that there might be tradeoffs or conflicts between the different components of income. As we saw in chapter 2, Ricardo was concerned that either wages or rents might cut into profits, and thus slow the growth of capitalism.[4]

While contemporary mainstream economists reject the labor theory of value, their conception of the distribution of income is actually quite similar to that of the classicals. According to the neoclassical marginal productivity theory of distribution, labor, capital, and land are combined (in production functions, given technology) to produce output. Each factor then obtains, within markets, its share of the output corresponding to its marginal contributions to production. Under specific conditions, mainstream economists can then prove that all of the output is exhausted – that is, nothing is left over and therefore no surplus exists – if each factor is paid an amount equal to its marginal product. Finally, each individual obtains a share of income according to the amount of labor, capital, and land they choose to contribute to production.[5]

In their different ways, then, both classical political economy and contemporary mainstream economics are based on what Marx refers to as a Trinity Formula (KIII, 953–70). Each of the three factors receives a share of the total output, which is separately determined (either by "natural" prices or market equilibrium) according to its productivity as a thing – whether labor, capital, or land – that is involved in and contributes its share to production. Moreover, their theory serves to reinforce the

[3] However, at any moment in time, the market price might be different from – above or below – the so-called natural price. This is the reason competition was so important to the classical political economists: it served to bring the market price closer to the natural price, and thus factor payments closer to their natural rates.

[4] Theoretically, Ricardo was troubled by the idea that the size of the national product appears to change when the division of the product into different income shares changed. Thus, he searched for some kind of "invariant standard of value," a project that was later taken up by Piero Sraffa, in his attempt to define a "standard commodity."

[5] Mathematically, marginal productivity theory proceeds in the following fashion: First, factors of production combine to produce outputs, given technology: $Q = Q(hL, K, T)$, where Q is output, $Q()$ the given technology, hL is the amount of labor (where h is the number of hours worked and L the number of laborers), K is capital, and T is land. Second, these factors obtain shares of income equal to their marginal contributions to output: $w = Q_{hL}$, $i = r = Q_K$, and $R = Q_T$, where w is the wage rate, Q_{hL} the marginal product of labor, i the interest rate, r the rate of return on capital, Q_K the marginal product of capital, R the rental rate on land, and Q_T the marginal product of land. According to Euler's Theorem (for a linear homogeneous production function), the total output is exhausted by the summation of the three factors multiplied by their marginal products: $Q = K \bullet Q_K + hL \bullet Q_{hL} + T \bullet Q_T$. Finally, individuals receive incomes according to their given endowments of factors and their choices to sell them to firms in factor markets: $Y_i = K^i \bullet Q_K + hL^i \bullet Q_{hL} + T^i \bullet Q_T$, where Y is income and the subscript and superscript i's the ith individual. Again, there is no remainder, that is, the summation over all individuals exactly exhausts the total output.

historical permanence and universality of the distribution of income to workers, capitalists, and landlords. For both the classicals and contemporary neoclassical economists, the fundamental determinants of the distribution of income remain the same throughout history and across different forms of economic organization.

The alternative is to focus on conflicts and struggles over the distribution of income, to attribute income shares to the social relations that characterize the way production is organized, and to pay attention to the specific historical and social conditions under which production and distribution take place. That's what Marx sets out to do in his critique of the so-called Trinity Formula. His view is that, within capitalism, it is productive labor, not independent factors of production, that creates the income that flows into the hands of capitalists and landlords.[6]

Starting with the same concepts as the classicals, Marx defines profits (π) as consisting of "profits of enterprise" ($\hat{\pi}$) plus "interest" (i), which go to capital, and the rental share or "ground rent" (GR), which goes to land (or, in general, property). Both profits and rents represent distributions of surplus-value produced and appropriated in capitalist production. In addition, workers receive wages equal to the value of their labor power (v).

Together, wages, profits, and rents comprise the net value of output (Y), that is, the value of total output (W) minus the value of intermediate goods or constant capital (c).

Mathematically, using the symbols as defined above:

6.1

$$W = c + v + s$$
$$s = \pi + GR$$
$$\pi = \hat{\pi} + i$$
$$W - c = Y = v + \hat{\pi} + i + GR$$

Thus, the new value added (or, as Marx puts it, the "the value of the annual product") created by productive labor must be equal to the total of the value of labor power and surplus-value or, alternatively, the value of labor power and the sum of the distributions of surplus-value.

Within capitalism, in Marx's alternative to the Trinity Formula, both capitalists and landlords "share in the booty" created by the exploitation of wage-laborers.

Implications

Marx's critique of the Trinity Formula has far-reaching implications, both ethical and analytical.

[6] Productive labor is here defined as labor that is productive of surplus-value. We return to the distinction between productive and unproductive labor below.

The ethical implication is that capitalists and landlords are no more deserving of their profits and rents than the objects they own are responsible for creating new value. *All* of the value that is received by workers, capitalists, and landlords is created during the course of production, by extracting labor from labor power. Some of that value is paid to workers, corresponding not to their labor but to the value of their labor power. In fact, Marx chides mainstream economists, any reference to the "'price of labor' is just as irrational as a yellow logarithm" (KIII, 957). The rest, the surplus-value – the difference between the value of labor and the value of labor power – is appropriated by capitalists and shared by them and landlords (and, as we will see below, by everyone else who manages to obtain a distribution of the surplus-value). Thus, if the sum total of those distributions of surplus-value is increasing, it must be because more surplus labor is being performed, more surplus-value is being pumped out of the direct producers, and more exploitation is taking place.

Marx's critique therefore challenges the ethical presumptions of economic theories, whether mainstream or heterodox, that deny the existence of surplus-value. That's the case at the microeconomic level, as we saw in the previous chapter, where the reference is to the process of production within individual firms. It is also the case at the macroeconomic level, where, as we can now see, the capital and land shares of income represent distributions of surplus-value. This is particularly true, Marx argues, when "vulgar economists" convert the Trinity Formula into an "apologetics" for the grotesque levels of inequality that capitalism has regularly generated over the course of its history.

The other major implication is analytical, when attention does eventually turn (as it did especially during and after both the first and second Great Depressions as well as the Pandemic Depression) to the problems associated with growing income inequality. We know, for example, in many countries the top 1 percent has been receiving a larger and larger share of national income, even while workers' real wages have stagnated. We might ask, therefore, what is the relationship between the changing distribution of income and the rate of surplus-value?

Figure 6.2 represents a hypothetical example of one aspect of the changing distribution of income (say, in the United States or the United Kingdom or any one of a variety of other countries) between 1977 and 2007. In each column, we can see three groups of incomes: the value of labor power (*V*, in dark grey), the income of chief executive officers (CEOs) (in lighter grey), and corporate profits (in off-white). The total income can be divided between the conventional national income accounting categories: the wage share, which goes to everyone who gets a wage or salary (thus, *V* plus CEOs), and the profit share (Profits). Alternatively, in Marxian terms, we can see the share comprising distributions of surplus-value (Profits plus CEOs) and the value of labor power (*V*).

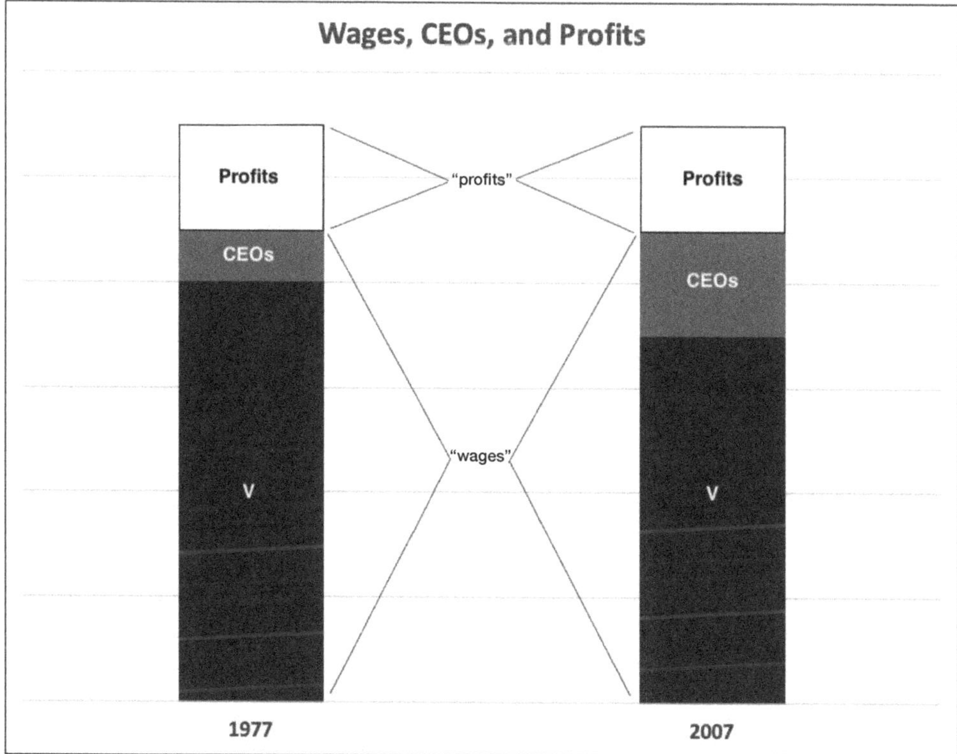

Figure 6.2 Wages, CEO salaries, and profits

It is clear from this example that, even with constant profit and wage shares (which is a standard assumption within mainstream economic theory), there can be an increase in the rate of exploitation. In other words, the combination of the grey wage rectangles remains constant (which is the way wages are normally calculated within national income accounts, where the incomes of CEOs are included in "wages"), as do the off-white rectangles (comprising corporate profits). However, as we can see, between 1977 and 2007, the share accounted for by the value of labor power fell, while the total of surplus-value (CEO salaries plus Profits) rose.

The conclusion? It is quite possible for the wage–profit ratio to remain constant but the rate of surplus-value – and therefore the degree of class exploitation – to rise.

The growing gap between workers and capitalists has become even more dramatic than that in recent decades, since the wage share has actually fallen and the profit share has increased – across the world and in many individual countries. For example, as is clear from figure 6.3, the profit share (the black line, measured on the right side) and the wage share (grey

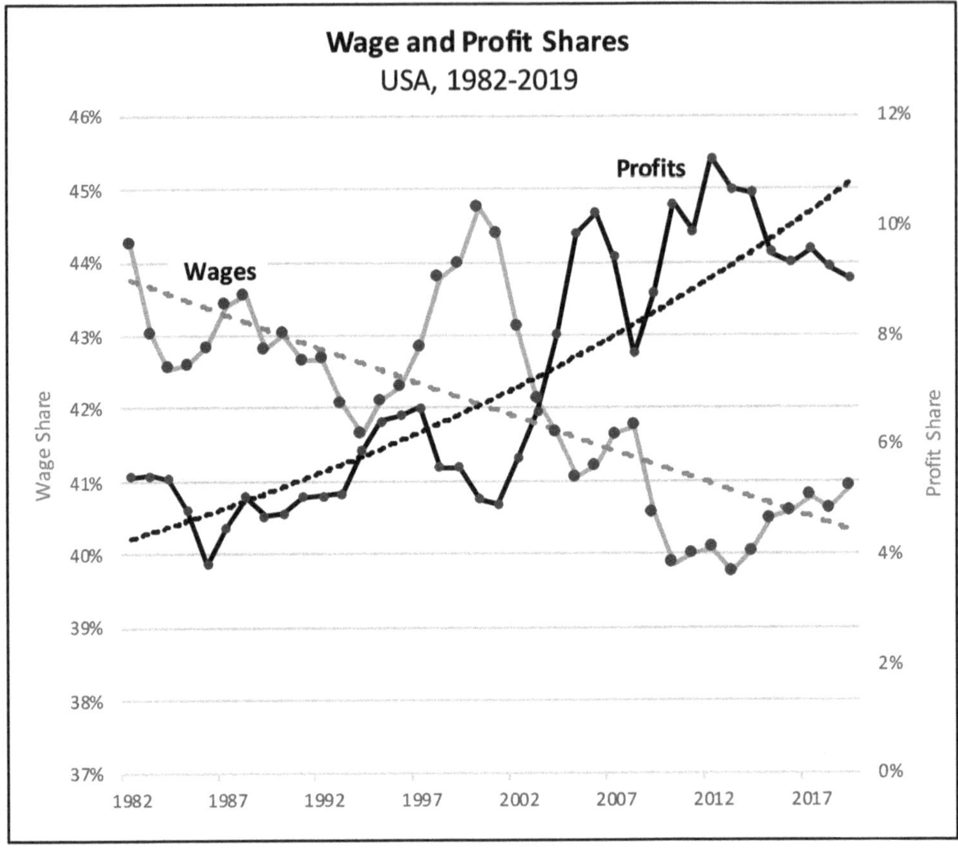

Figure 6.3 Wage and profit shares

Source: Bureau of Economic Analysis

line on the left side) in the United States have been moving in opposite directions since the early 1980s (and probably longer, but the existing data set only begins in 1982). The (exponential, dashed) trendlines for the two series of data illustrate the diverging movements in the wage and profit shares even more dramatically.

If we consider the fact that some distributions of the surplus (such as CEO salaries) are included in the wage share and excluded from the profit share, we can conclude that the rate of exploitation has risen even more than is represented in the changing wage and profit shares. Ignoring the problems inherent in the Trinity Formula therefore hides from view both the ethical and analytical implications of Marx's critique of capitalist exploitation.

Simple Reproduction

From Marx's critique of the Trinity Formula, we learned that the surplus-value appropriated from workers is captured as both a profit share by capital and a rental share by landlords.

The next question is: what is done with that distributed surplus-value? Marx focuses on one of those distributions, the profit share, because the general presumption of the classical economists was that the rental share was used to purchase more property and to engage in conspicuous consumption, thereby contributing nothing to the maintenance or reproduction of capitalism. As for the profit share, it might also be directed to conspicuous consumption, that is, it might be consumed instead of being invested. This is the situation Marx refers to as "simple reproduction" (KI, 711–24) – the reproduction or continued existence of capitalism on the same scale (as against expanded reproduction, as we will see below, which leads to the growth of capitalism).

The point is, even if capitalist profits are "eaten," and not used to purchase additional amounts of capital, capitalism itself can still be maintained or reproduced – thus putting the lie to the idea that capitalists' thrift or investors' acumen is somehow responsible for capitalism's success.

How does that work? Expanding on the role of time that was implicit in the discussion of commodity exchange, we can trace capitalist production through different periods. In the first period, capital is used to purchase and deploy a certain amount of constant and variable capital. Once production takes place, the capitalist has a bundle of commodities whose value is equal to the initial amount of capital plus surplus-value. If that surplus-value is used for consumption or otherwise set aside or hoarded, the capitalist still has an amount of value equal to the initial capital, which can be used to purchase the same amount of constant and variable capital, which when set to use in production leads to more surplus-value. This can go on through successive periods, *ad infinitum*, thus leading to the reproduction of both capital and not-capital, the capitalists as well as the workers.[7]

The key is that the capital ($K = c + v$) remains in the capitalists' hands and not with the laborers. Therefore, the capitalists can continue to engage in productive consumption and to maintain their role in the circuit of capitalist commodity production ($M - C - M'$). As for the laborers, they, too, maintain their position, as not-capital, and continue to engage in

[7] Mathematically, this is what simple reproduction looks like (where, as before, K is total capital, c is constant capital, v is variable capital, W is the commodity's value, and s is surplus-value, and the superscripts refer to time periods, 1 through n): $K^1 = c^1 + v^1 \rightarrow W^1 = c^1 + v^1 + s^1$. All of s^1 is consumed. So, $c^1 + v^1 = K^2 = c^2 + v^2 \rightarrow W^2 = c^2 + v^2 + s^2$. And so on, such that $c^{n-1} + v^{n-1} = K^n = c^n + v^n \rightarrow W^n = c^n + v^n + s^n$.

individual consumption (*LP* – *M* – *C*) in order to reproduce and sell their labor power to the capitalists.

Perhaps even more important, the workers continue to be forced to have the freedom to sell their labor power to their capitalist employers precisely because they don't have capital. Since their labor power has no use-value for them, their only possibility is to exchange their labor power for a wage equal to the value of labor power and to work not for themselves, but for someone else. Even at the level of simple reproduction, then, capitalist production maintains the separation between labor power and the conditions of labor. Capitalists continue to have the means to purchase labor power, while the owners of labor power must sell their ability to work to someone else precisely because of their status as not-capital.

Mainstream economists, both liberal and conservative, celebrate this situation – arguing that workers' having jobs gives structure and dignity to their lives (and, of course, is one of the conditions for the continued growth of capitalism). Marx, however, sees a different result: the reproduction of the division between capital and not-capital maintains not dignity, but a particular form of capitalist dependence, of wage-laborers on their capitalist employers. It's not just that workers are laboring; they are laboring for someone else, who are thus able to appropriate the workers' surplus labor in the form of surplus-value.

That's one of the reasons mainstream economists, pundits, and politicians often criticize so-called entitlement programs, because they believe workers only prove their moral worth in and through the market. To thrive, you must work. (Although, they fail to add, you must work for someone else.) And if you do not work, then you forfeit whatever help your fellow citizens decide to give, whether in the form of child tax credits, anti-poverty transfer payments, or a universal basic income. To take without working, they argue, is to undermine and weaken the very fabric of society. The Marxian critique of political economy challenges that argument and actually reverses it: when it comes to surplus-value, it is the capitalists who are the takers and the not-capitalists, the workers, who are the makers.

The possibility of simple reproduction also leads to a change in the conception of the relationship between property and labor (KI, 730). In one tradition, that of natural law, associated with Thomas Aquinas and John Locke and then carried on in classical political economy, private property is grounded in labor.[8] In Marx's alternative view, property is a historical and social institution, developed and maintained on the basis of unpaid or

[8] According to the natural law tradition, private property (as against the long-standing Christian interpretation of the biblical admonition in favor of stewardship of the common) is justified by (a) the sanctity of human agreement (akin to acting in conformity with natural law) and (b) the idea that individual possession comes about by the exertion of labor upon the earth.

surplus labor. Within capitalism, the owners of capital are able to exercise their property rights utilizing the value and surplus-value created during the course of production. Workers, on the other hand, own only their labor power and the commodities they purchase when they sell their ability to work to capitalists. In other words, workers are limited to the personal property that is associated with their role as performers of unpaid labor for someone else.

Accumulation of Capital

Economic growth is the fundamental premise and promise of both mainstream economic theory and capitalism itself. Those who celebrate the existence of capitalism – whether in the academy, the media, the government, or the business sector – presume that the capitalist way of organizing economic and social life has, more than any other system, an intrinsic dynamism that leads to economic growth. That growth, they promise, gives rise to more production, more jobs, and, in general, a higher standard of living for all who choose to play a productive role within capitalism.

Such arguments also serve to extol the role of capitalists, who, even when they are primarily driven by self-enrichment, and not dedicated to the betterment of those around them, occupy a crucial position in marshalling savings (their own or the savings of others) and investing in new, better means and methods of production. That's what makes capitalists, even when their high incomes and extraordinary wealth place them far above the vast majority of people, "respectable" (KI, 739).

Marx takes on this argument, in one of the most cited (and, at the same, most misinterpreted) passages in volume 1 of *Capital*:

> Accumulate, accumulate! That is Moses and the prophets! "Industry furnishes the material which saving accumulates." Therefore, save, save, *i.e.*, reconvert the greatest possible portion of surplus-value or surplus product into capital! Accumulation for the sake of accumulation, production for the sake of production: this was the formula in which classical economics expressed the historical mission of the bourgeoisie in the period of its domination. Not for one instant did it deceive itself over the nature of wealth's birth-pangs. But what use is it to lament a historical necessity? If, in the eyes of classical economics, the proletarian is merely a machine for the production of surplus-value, the capitalist too merely a machine for the transformation of this surplus-value into surplus capital. Classical economics takes the historical function of the capitalist in grim earnest. (KI, 742)

The usual interpretation of this paragraph is that Marx is asserting that capitalists have an imperative to use their profits, their share of the surplus-value, for investment and thus to accumulate capital. But there's another way of reading that passage: Marx is actually criticizing mainstream economists (the classical political economists then, and by extension mainstream economists today) for imagining that capitalists operate like machines in automatically accumulating capital – and thus spurring capitalist growth.

Mainstream economists are the ones who operate with the presumption – in their theories, models, and public pronouncements – that capitalists will always and everywhere engage in the accumulation of capital. Moreover, they continue, everyone benefits, via "trickledown" economics, from the growth that stems from the accumulation of capital. That becomes the warrant for arguing in favor of policies that help capitalists fulfill their "historical mission" as, in contemporary language, "job creators." Marx, on the other hand, makes no such assumption. It is quite possible, in specific times and places, for capitalists *not* to use the surplus-value appropriated from wage-laborers to accumulate additional capital.

Instead of accumulating additional capital, capitalists may divert portions of the surplus toward other uses. These include financing mergers and acquisitions, repurchasing equity shares, and paying dividends to shareholders. When that happens, some corporations grow much larger (as they merge with and acquire the assets of other corporations), the stock market soars (as corporations intervene to purchase their own shares), and owners of corporate stocks become wealthier (both because stock prices rise and higher dividends are paid to them), while job growth slackens, the workers' share of national income decreases, and the distribution of income and wealth becomes more and more unequal. In such situations, it becomes increasingly difficult for mainstream economists, pundits, and politicians to defend the role of capitalists as innovators and job creators.

Productive and Unproductive Labor

As it turns out, that was one of Smith's worries about the future of capitalism: that capitalists' profits would be used for consumption and not investment.

Smith discussed the issue in terms of the difference between productive and unproductive labor. Unproductive labor, in his view, was labor involved in consumption activities – for example, the labor of servants and other staff involved in maintaining the lavish lifestyles of the wealthy recipients of surplus-value. Productive labor, on the other hand, was involved in production activities – capitalist production, production that led to more goods and services, more markets, and more jobs. In other words, only productive labor would lead to that "immense collection of commodities" that fulfills the premise and promise of capitalist growth.

As in many instances, Marx took over the classicals' terminology and then transformed it, to arrive at radically different conclusions. Marx redefined productive labor as productive of surplus-value; while unproductive labor is all labor within capitalism that is not involved in the production of surplus-value. In other words, the distinction between productive and unproductive labor is not what workers do but, instead, how they do it. If they are engaged in labor that results in surplus-value, their labor is defined as productive; if not, it's unproductive labor.

That's the case in the example above, of corporate CEOs. They labor but they do not produce commodities and thus do not create surplus-value. In other words, the labor of CEOs (and of managers generally) is not embodied in the commodities that are produced by the corporations that hire them. Instead, their salaries represent distributions of surplus-value, because they provide conditions (such as managing the enterprise on a day-to-day basis) that facilitate the continued appropriation of surplus-value. They perform labor that is essential for the operation of capitalist enterprises but it is, in Marx's view, unproductive labor.[9]

Only labor that is directly involved in creating value during the course of producing capitalist commodities, whether goods or services, is considered productive labor. Other labor is not. So, for example, within capitalist enterprises, labor that is involved in managing, accounting, purchasing, selling, advertising, and so on, is *not* productive labor. Marx does, however, make a distinction between two different aspects of management: One concerns labor that is involved in supervision anytime many detail workers cooperate to accomplish a task, "as with the conductor of an orchestra" (KIII, 507). That is classified as productive labor. The other kind of supervision stems from the opposition between the direct producers and the capitalist appropriators of surplus-value, which is unproductive labor. Their salaries represent distributions of the surplus that is created by the workers. Marx's view was that "The greater this opposition, the greater the role the work of supervision plays" (KIII, 507) – as much in capitalism as under slavery. His counterexample is a cooperative factory, in which the workers are able to hire managers to supervise their combined and cooperative labor but have no need either for capitalists or for the supervision of the class divisions inherent in a production process organized along capitalist lines (KIII, 511).

Outside capitalist enterprises, there is also a great deal of unproductive labor – labor that is not productive of surplus-value but, instead, is exchanged for a portion of surplus-value. This is the case, for example, of labor involved in finance (or, more generally, what is referred to as FIRE, that is, finance, insurance, and real estate), merchants, government officials and public-sector workers, and so on. All of them may be involved

[9] In fact, in recent decades, a larger and larger share of the income captured by the top 1 percent represents "earned income," that is, income that stems from a distribution of surplus-value based on work. Whereas at one time (e.g., during the first Gilded Age), the incomes of those at the top mostly came from returns on their accumulated wealth, now (during the second Gilded Age), while they continue to derive income from their wealth holdings, the source of a large percentage is labor involved in managing capitalist enterprises (as chief executive officers, chief financial officers, computer and information systems managers, and so on).

in activities that secure the conditions within which capitalist exploitation can continue to take place but they don't produce surplus-value. That's why the work they do is considered unproductive labor.

Thus, for example, banks supply money to capitalists in order to finance the accumulation of capital or other activities (such as dividends, mergers and acquisitions, management salaries, and so on). For this, they receive a portion of surplus-value in the form of interest payments. Similarly, merchants, who make sure capitalist commodities are sold and their value realized, receive a distribution of surplus-value, amounting to the difference between the commodities' value and the lower price merchants pay for those commodities. Government workers, for their part, provide education to future workers and infrastructure (such as roads, bridges, ports, and airports) to allow for the transportation of capitalist commodities within and between nations – and taxes on the surplus are used to finance those activities.

The list could go on. The point is, a good deal of the labor performed within economies organized along capitalist lines is unproductive labor – labor that is not productive of surplus-value but, rather, is paid for out of distributions of the surplus.

Capitalist Enterprises

Focusing on the appropriation and distribution of surplus-value leads to a radically different conception of capitalist enterprises.

Within mainstream economics, capitalist enterprises have long been invoked as a kind of black box, a site where factors of production are combined (via production functions, given technology) to produce outputs. It was just presumed that perfectly competitive firms would follow a rule of maximizing profits, given prices determined in markets, by choosing a level of output (and therefore amounts of the factors of production and technologies from an exogenously determined "technology shelf").[10] That's it. Inside the firm, nothing much else of interest took place.[11]

[10] Mathematically, the idea is that perfectly competitive firms choose a level of output at a point where p (the output price, determined by supply and demand in markets, which, by virtue of the definition of perfect competition, firms take as given) = MR (marginal revenue, the extra revenue from the last unit of output sold) = MC (marginal cost, the extra cost from producing the last unit of output) = D (the perfectly elastic demand for output each firm faces). In order to produce those levels of output, firms choose a technology and purchase factors of production at the point where each factor payment equals the extra revenue brought in. Thus, they demand labor to the point that w (the wage) = MRP_L (the marginal revenue product of labor), capital such that i (the price of capital) = MRP_K (the marginal revenue product of capital), and land such that R (the rental rate on land) = MRP_T (the marginal revenue product of land).

[11] More recently, mainstream economists decided to take a look inside the black box. But all

Capitalist enterprises figure more prominently in everyday language. Oftentimes, especially in the business press, they are conceived as sites of creativity and entrepreneurship – and therefore where capitalists are justly rewarded for devising new commodities and better ways of producing those commodities. (Some mainstream economists have picked up on this idea and introduced entrepreneurship, either as a special kind of human capital or a separate factor of production, as the source of short-run, above-normal profits.) Capitalist entrepreneurs are thus celebrated as innovators who, under considerable uncertainty and risk, are the source of the new ideas and business procedures that allow their enterprises to prosper (or, if they fail, to lead their enterprises to ruin).

A third view, also present in everyday economic discourses, is that corporations are increasingly powerful entities. As they grow larger, giant corporations are able to muscle aside business rivals (Walmart's role in undermining small retailers is the classic example) and to play a more significant role in determining the fate of local communities and indeed of entire nations. Such a critical view is only reinforced if and when attention is directed at corporate lobbying (the results of which show up in government legislation) and corporations are afforded the rights of persons (especially in financing political and media campaigns).

Marx's critique is aimed at all three sets of discourses – of mainstream economists, the mainstream media, and the proverbial "person in the street" – resulting in a very different, class conception of the firm. Here, we focus on the "industrial capitalist enterprise," where "industrial" refers not to the common usage (of industry or manufacturing), but to a firm in which the production and appropriation of surplus-value take place. Thus, for example, an industrial capitalist enterprise (which can be involved in the production of goods or services) is distinguished from other kinds of capitalist enterprises, such as banks (which are involved in the buying and selling of money), merchants (which buy and sell commodities), and so on.

According to Marx's class critique, industrial capitalist enterprises are sites of both the production/appropriation and distribution/receipt of surplus-value (as well as many other nonclass activities, of course). For example, as illustrated in figure 6.4, they include the extraction of labor from labor power and thus the process of exploitation (s/v). They also comprise various distributions of the surplus-value: some inside the firm (indicated by the dashed arrows, for example, to management, accounting, sales, purchasing, and research and development); others to entities

they found was a "principal-agent problem," where it was possible for the "agents" (e.g., the managers) to act in their own interests and, in doing so, to behave in a manner inconsistent with the interests of the "principal" (the owners of the firm). Thus, for example, corporate managers might approve a massive project that gives them more authority or prestige instead of adopting other measures that would maximize shareholder value.

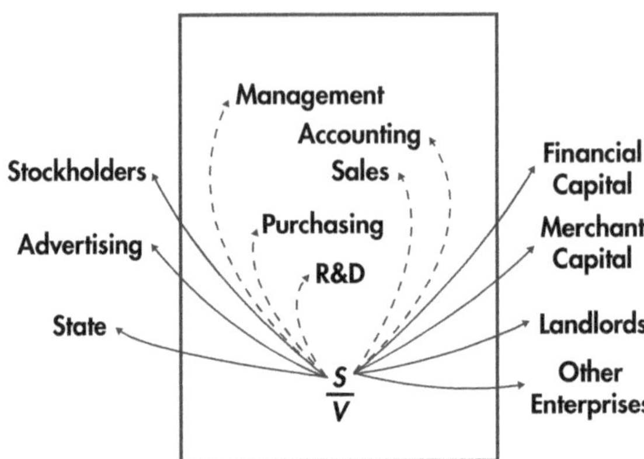

Figure 6.4 Industrial capitalist enterprise

outside the firm (following the solid arrows, for example, to financial capital, merchant capital, landlords, other industrial capitalist enterprises, stockholders, advertising agencies, and the state).

So, as against the view that serves as the basis of mainstream economic theory, the industrial capitalist enterprise is not a black box, but a complex economic and social institution in which many different activities and flows of surplus-value take place. Moreover, in contrast to the single rule presumed by mainstream economists – that corporations are always and everywhere profit-maximizers – Marxian economists argue that corporations follow many different strategies. That's in part because, within mainstream economics, the profits that are supposed to be maximized are ill-defined, especially in terms of the time dimension. Over what period of time are profits supposed to be maximized – a quarter or a fiscal year or a ten-year span? Moreover, corporations in the real world often follow other strategies that don't involve maximizing profits. They may, for example, seek to grow larger than their rivals or to enhance their reputation and prestige or to boost their stock price – or any one of a large number of other possible strategies.

As for the everyday notion that focuses on and celebrates capitalist entrepreneurship, the Marxian argument is that, while innovation may in fact take place within capitalist enterprises (thus allowing some enterprises to flourish and others not), the innovations are not the source of surplus-value. They are, instead, the means whereby capitalists – some of them, and perhaps not others – are able to capture the surplus-value that is created during the course of extracting labor from labor power. Moreover, the capitalists themselves are not necessarily responsible for those innovations. Instead, as we saw above in chapter 5 (and as we will discuss in more detail in chapter 7), the industrial capitalist is defined as the appropriator and distributor of surplus-value – no more, and no less. It may be the case that some capitalists (especially in smaller firms) occupy other positions within an enterprise, such as manager or innovator, and receive a distribution of surplus-value for doing so. But it is also the case that new ideas can and often do come from other areas, both inside and outside enterprises – such as CEOs and managers, research and development departments, academic research units, and government programs.

Much the same is true of the money that is put at "risk" in the creation and operation of capitalist enterprises. There may be cases, perhaps many (again, in smaller capitalist enterprises), in which the individuals who occupy the position of capitalist also put up their own money to finance the commodity purchases of labor power, means of production, and raw materials. Then, of course, their initial capital is at risk: if the enterprise fails, they lose their money; if it succeeds, they are rewarded with a portion of the surplus-value, as a form of interest on the money advanced. But, in the case of larger modern corporations, the capitalists generally do not own the capital or put any of their own savings at risk. In fact, the money to start or expand an enterprise is often raised from initial public offerings of stock, bank loans, venture capital funds, and public subsidies. They, not the capitalists, are the ones whose money is exposed to risk, for which they receive a cut of the surplus-value (or, with subsidies, it is the government that shoulders the costs, in the form of lost tax revenues).

Finally, Marxian economists are certainly sympathetic to the idea that corporations exercise an inordinate amount of power within capitalist societies – in large part, because most of the surplus is generated within their confines, and they have a great deal of control over what is done with the surplus. In fact, as we will see below, Marx analyzed the formation of large, powerful corporations, through the concentration and centralization of capital. But, Marxian economists hasten to add, corporations also exercise considerable power on the inside, over their own employees. Even if labor contracts are free and voluntary (and, as we have seen, Marx casts doubt on that idea, since workers within capitalism are forced to have the freedom to sell their ability to work), once those contracts are signed, workers labor under a system of command and control – doing the tasks that are assigned to them, taking orders from their supervisors, working at a pace dictated by the speed of the machines of which they have become appendages, and so forth – with little or no role in making the decisions that govern their work lives. In other words, coercion doesn't have to originate from the government, as libertarians claim; it occurs within markets and, especially, inside capitalist enterprises.

In all three cases, distributed flows of the surplus-value extracted from workers is what is at stake.

We have already briefly discussed three of those distributions of surplus-value: to other industrial capitalist enterprises, via the process of competition over super-profits within industries, thereby compelling firms to respond to the actions of other firms within an industry; to internal management, such as the salaries of CEOs, who direct the activities of firms, carrying out corporate strategies and exercising control over workers on a daily basis; and landlords, in terms of ground rent, who not only own the land, but also the buildings in which goods and services are produced and many of the transportation systems whereby commodities are moved within and between countries. The other payments illustrated above, both inside and outside the firm, also represent distributions of surplus-value appropriated from productive laborers that takes place inside a typical industrial capitalist enterprise.

Moreover, there is nothing fixed about the activities that are located inside or outside a capitalist enterprise. The boundaries of capitalist enterprises can and do change over time. Thus, for example, some capitalist enterprises may decide to add to their involvement in the process of exploiting their own workers the process of money-lending, thus creating a new source of profits (via a distribution of surplus-value produced elsewhere, just like a free-standing bank).[12] Or they may create their own security force, thus bringing inside an activity that is typically provided by the government or state outside the enterprise. The movement can also occur in the opposite direction, as enterprises "outsource" activities traditionally supported by distributions of surplus-value inside the firm. Thus, an enterprise might contract other firms – for example, in accounting or human resources – to carry out those activities, and make additional distributions of surplus-value to them.

What this means is capitalist enterprises don't have a single, stable identity. Still, to be considered industrial capitalist enterprises within a Marxian approach, they must include among their myriad activities the production and appropriation of surplus-value.

Struggles over Distributions of Surplus-Value

That doesn't mean, of course, that there won't be conflicts over the distribution of surplus-value, either within industrial capitalist enterprises or with recipients of surplus-value outside those enterprises. On the contrary!

[12] A famous example is General Motors, which was the world's largest automaker from 1931 through 2007, having engaged in the exploitation of generations of autoworkers – and, of course, been the site of some of the most famous strikes in the history of the United Automobile Workers union. However, in the 1990s, it expanded the activities of the General Motors Acceptance Corporation beyond lending to car buyers, which became a major source of profits for the parent corporation.

We would generally expect such conflicts to erupt, depending on the specific conditions within those enterprises and in the wider economy and society. Just as wage-laborers and capitalists engage in struggles over exploitation (as we saw in the case of absolute and relative surplus-value in chapter 5), so the various recipients of surplus-value can be expected to struggle over the portions that are distributed to them.

One classic example at the microeconomic level, in terms of individual enterprises, is the struggle between industrial capitalists and merchant capitalists. Merchants often attempt to squeeze the producers of capitalist commodities in order to receive a larger share of surplus-value (which, let us remember, they receive as the difference between the amount they pay for the commodities and the value they realize when the commodities are finally sold). Larger merchants (e.g., Walmart, Amazon, Alibaba, Ikea, and Tesco) can exercise their market power to strengthen their ability to bargain with the producers of commodities – by depriving producers of the possibility of selling their commodities, by threatening to purchase commodities from other producers, and so on. And the larger the share of surplus-value that goes to merchant capitalists, the less there is for other recipients of the surplus-value distributed by industrial capitalists.

Another example, at a macroeconomic level, in terms of a national economy, is the struggle between industrial capitalist enterprises and finance capital over the terms of money-lending. In general, industrial capitalists want "cheap money," at low interest rates, to finance the conditions for exploitation. Financial capitalists, on the other hand, benefit from higher interest rates, which means they obtain a larger share of the surplus-value from industrial capitalists. Such struggles can then flare up, not only between individual banks and industrial capitalist enterprises (which are sometimes resolved, at least for a time, by placing a representative of the bank on the board of directors of the industrial enterprise), but also at the national level, over the course of monetary policy (and therefore over the policies adopted by a country's central bank).

Much the same can occur over tax policies, as industrial capitalist enterprises call for lower rates on corporate income, which means state officials are forced to cut back on government projects and programs – or to engage in deficit-financing in order to carry out those initiatives. But, of course, if capitalist enterprises purchase the resulting government debt, they can have their proverbial cake and eat it, too: they are able to distribute less of their surplus-value (through lower taxes) and, at the same, they create an additional source of profits (via interest payments on the loans they make to the state).

Workers, too, may participate in the struggles over distributions of the surplus-value. They might, for example, call for a decrease in payments to internal management such that more of the surplus-value can be distributed to projects they favor – whether an increase in jobs or the financing of projects that favor workers and their families, such as the creation of child-care centers or more generous healthcare or pension benefits.[13]

And, of course, such struggles over distributions of the surplus-value can rebound back on the rate of exploitation. If banks, merchants, or internal managers succeed in capturing a larger share of the surplus, industrial capitalist enterprises may respond by attempting to extract more surplus-value from their productive laborers. New struggles over the rate of exploitation inside the industrial capitalist enterprises may then break out, affecting both the appropriation and distribution of surplus-value going forward.

Expanded Reproduction

When one of the distributions of surplus-value is directed to the accumulation of capital, then, Marx argues, we need to look at the effects of the reproduction of capitalism on an expanded scale (KI, 725–61).

First, we need to define the accumulation of capital. If the original capital deployed by capitalists or capitalist enterprises is $K = c + v$ (where, as before, K is capital, c is constant capital, and v is variable capital), then the accumulation of capital means more capital, an addition to the existing amount of capital, and therefore $\Delta K = \Delta c + \Delta v$ (where the deltas indicate change, so ΔK is the increase in the total amount of capital, Δc the increase in constant capital, and Δv the increase in the amount of variable capital). We can then calculate the rate of accumulation of capital (a common term in mainstream economics, particularly when it comes to economic growth), in Marxian terms, as $K^* = \Delta K/K = (\Delta c + \Delta v)/(c + v)$.

It is clear, then, that, in contrast to simple reproduction (where the surplus-value is used not for investment, but for consumption), expanded reproduction involves using a portion of the surplus-value to purchase additional amounts of constant and variable capital, thereby leading to the growth of capitalism that is so celebrated within mainstream economics, in Marx's time as in our own. Just like simple reproduction, the accumulation of capital reproduces the separation of the direct producers from the means of production. The only difference is that it does so on a larger and larger scale.

The accumulation of capital actually involves two distinct processes: (1) a distribution of surplus-value, and (2) purchases of additional amounts of

[13] A good example is the historic 1946 Krug-Lewis agreement, according to which the United Mineworkers of America secured a share of surplus-value to provide pensions and medical care for retired miners, widows, and dependants.

constant and variable capital. On one hand, the accumulation of capital is a distribution of part of the surplus-value that is not used for other purposes – whether internally (e.g., to pay the managers) or externally (such as taxes to the state).[14] On the other hand, it involves purchasing additional commodities: additional means of production and raw materials and additional units of labor power (either more hours or the labor power of more laborers or both).

For mainstream economists, the accumulation of capital is the key to capitalist growth – and the accumulators, the capitalists, are celebrated as "job creators." As for Marx: the "accumulation of capital is ... multiplication of the proletariat" (KI, 764). That's because the accumulation of capital increases both the demand for and supply of labor power.[15] It increases the demand for labor power directly: because Δv represents an increase in capitalists' demand for labor power. It also increases it indirectly, because Δc, an increase in the demand for constant capital (means of production and raw materials), also means more demand for labor power (as a "derived demand," given the ratio of constant to variable capital or c/v). That is, given the existing ratio of constant to variable capital, more labor power is needed to work with the larger amounts of means of production and raw materials to produce capitalist commodities.

The accumulation of capital also operates on the other side of the labor power market, in terms of the supply of labor power.[16] As capitalists innovate (e.g., to compete for super-profits) – and, as we saw in chapter 5, use a portion of the surplus-value to purchase new, more productive elements of constant capital – they succeed in undercutting other producers (both capitalist and noncapitalist), who now join the pool of wage-laborers and are forced to have the freedom to sell their labor power to someone else. The accumulation of capital also induces migrations of workers both

[14] Mathematically, if $s = D_I + D_0 + D_M + D_R$, where s is surplus-value, D_I the distribution of surplus-value to internal management, D_0 to the stockholders or owners, D_M to money-lenders, and D_R the distribution of surplus-value to all others (landlords, merchants, government officials, and so on), then $\Delta K = \Delta c + \Delta v = \beta D_I = s - [(1 - \beta)D_I + D_0 + D_M + D_R]$, where β is the share of the surplus-value distributed to internal managers that is used for the accumulation of capital.

[15] Readers will notice that I am using supply and demand to illustrate Marx's treatment of the market for labor power. While some might consider it irregular, I do so for two reasons: First, it's a convention at least some readers will recognize. Second, and perhaps more important, supply and demand do play a role in Marx's discussion of the prices of commodities but not in the same way they are understood and utilized within contemporary mainstream economics. They are not, for example, reduced to given preferences, technology, and resource endowments, but instead are determined by history and society.

[16] This is another point of criticism of the work of mainstream economists, who presume that the supply of and demand for labor are independent of one another. For Marx, they can't be independent, precisely because both are determined, at least in part, by the accumulation of capital.

within countries and across national boundaries, thus increasing the supply of labor power in other areas and sectors. Finally, the accumulation of capital often leads to changes in the labor force participation rate, as people who are not at the moment sellers of labor power (e.g., women involved in domestic labor, students and other young people, and the elderly) leave their previous positions outside the labor-power market and expand the supply of labor power.

In such circumstances, it is quite possible for the accumulation of capital to lead to increases in both the demand for labor power (from *D* to *D′* and then *D″*) and the supply of labor power (from *S* to *S′* and *S″*) in the chart of the market for labor power. The result, illustrated in figure 6.5, is that the wage (or the price of labor power, P_{lp}) remains equal to the customary value of labor power (*v*) but the proletariat has multiplied (growing from *LP* to *LP″*). Thus, the expanded reproduction of capitalism means more laborers are separated from the conditions of their labor – and thus are forced to have the freedom to work not for themselves, but for their capitalist employers.

That is one scenario. But it is also possible, under other circumstances (especially during a phase of the business cycle of more rapid economic growth), for the increase in the demand for labor power to outstrip the supply of labor power. If that occurs, if the accumulation of capital proceeds at a quickened pace (e.g., during a period when more surplus-value is directed away from other distributions to the accumulation of capital), such as the situation illustrated in figure 6.6, then the proletariat will grow and the price of labor power will be bid up above the value of labor power

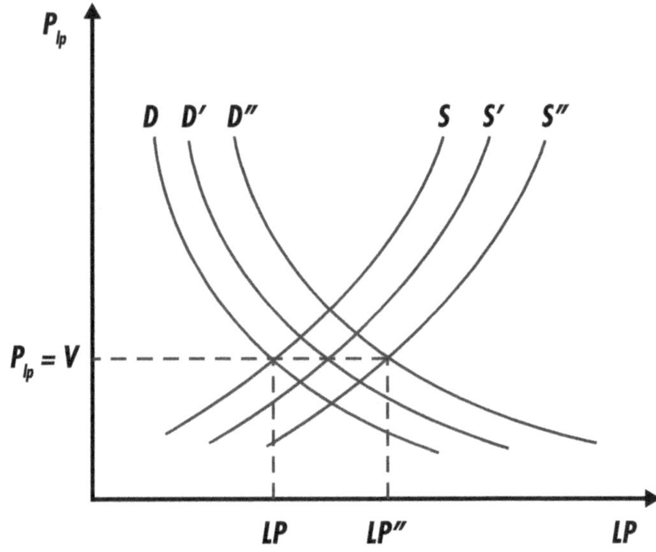

Figure 6.5 Market for labor power: increases in demand and supply

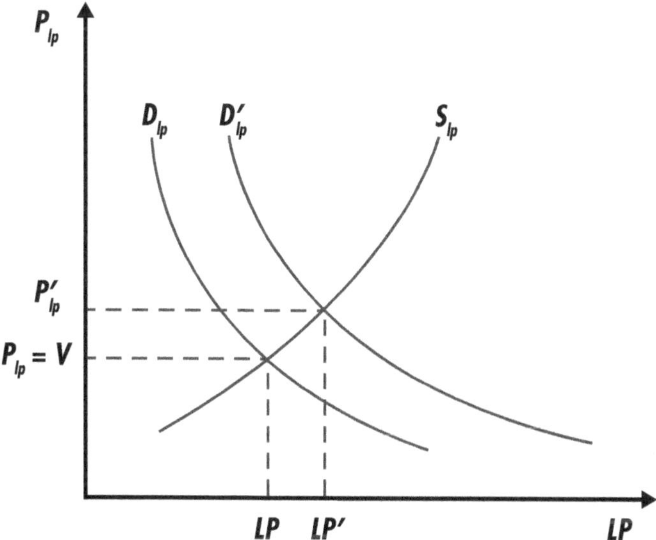

Figure 6.6 Market for labor power: increases in demand outstrip supply

(as capitalists compete for the available sellers of labor power).[17] Since the customary value of labor power hasn't changed, capitalists are forced to distribute a portion of the surplus-value to their workers (the difference between the value of labor power, *v*, and the higher price of labor power, P'_{lp}) – and that cuts into capitalists' profits.

The question is, are there any mechanisms within capitalism that keep this situation in check, to prevent the price of labor from rising to the point where it eliminates all capitalist profits?

Generalized Crisis

At this point in Marx's critique, we have clearly moved beyond another restrictive assumption – that the price of labor power has to be equal to the value of labor power. It need not (just as the market price of any commodity need not equal its exchange-value or value). What the capitalists have to pay to get access to the commodity labor power is its price, which may be above, below, or equal to the value of labor power (and, eventually, if the price of labor power continues to rise, it begins to approach the value of labor).

[17] This, of course, is the scenario imagined by liberal, Keynesian mainstream economists, who argue that workers will benefit when capitalist growth is rapid and the economy begins to approach full employment. What they forget, of course, is that workers continue to be exploited and to be forced to sell their labor power to their capitalist employers even if the price of labor power rises above the value of labor power.

So, what happens if the rising price of labor power cuts into the profits realized by capitalists? That may happen precisely because capitalist competition takes place without regard to the supply of labor power. In other words, there is no way of controlling competition to avoid reaching the limit of the supply of labor power (short of creating a cartel that regulates the wages paid to workers or calling on the state to put into place wage controls or to repress workers' wage demands). The consequence is that the survival of marginal firms (the less efficient firms in any given industry, with lower profit margins) is made more difficult. These firms will then lay off workers, cut their orders for means of production and raw materials, outsource production to areas where the price of labor power is cheaper, and so on.

One possible outcome, of course, is that the business of those firms is absorbed by others, which decide to expand their operations. Then, it's business as usual. The accumulation of capital continues in an uninterrupted fashion.

But business failures may become widespread and negatively affect other firms – if nothing else, because efficient firms depend on purchases from inefficient firms in other industries, and it takes time to create new supply chains. Moreover, the price of labor power may continue to rise, negatively affecting capitalists that had not been in a particularly marginal position before. Then, Marx argues, a generalized crisis may occur, in which negative economic conditions are imposed, against their individual wills, on all capitalists. Such a crisis represents an interruption in the self-expansion of value. Then, the accumulation of capital becomes paralyzed, as firms slow down or stop investing altogether in new constant and variable capital. Unemployment rises and firms declare bankruptcy. And, when banks are involved, credit becomes frozen.

What then? One result is that the demand for labor power will fall, thus leading to a decrease in the price of labor power. If such a situation lasts long enough (say, during a long recession or depression), the value of labor power, workers' customary standard of living, may eventually fall to a level equal to the lower price of labor power. On one hand, that may restore capitalists' profits, since they now have to pay less to get access to the commodity labor power. On the other hand, capitalists who produce and sell wage goods may be in trouble, since they will have a difficult time realizing the value of their commodities.

Concentration and Centralization

Another result of the generalized crisis is a decline in the price of constant capital, as new machinery and raw materials are left unsold and existing stocks of both are put up for sale by failed capitalists. This is what Marx refers to as the "slaughtering of capital values," a fall in the price of the elements of constant capital, which may then be purchased by other capitalists who manage to survive the generalized crisis. The decline in capital values leads, in turn, to the concentration and centralization of capital (KI, 776–7). Surviving firms grow larger (thus concentrating capital in larger and larger units) and increase their market share (thereby centralizing the capital in fewer and fewer hands). Then, of course, the accumulation of capital may proceed apace, especially if the state steps in to bail out firms that are "too big to fail" and surviving firms are allowed to engage in mergers and acquisitions, even at the expense of the degree of competition in the economy.

Marx's idea that the concentration and centralization of capital occur during the "normal" course of capitalist development is itself a direct rebuke to mainstream economics. One of the key assumptions of mainstream economic theory is the idea that (a) the economy is characterized by perfect competition and (b) perfect competition continues over time, since any super-profits capitalist enterprises make are competed away.[18] That's why most of the models used by mainstream economists, as well as much of their policy advice, are predicated on perfect competition.[19]

Marx arrives at a very different result. In his approach, even if the economy starts out in a situation that might be characterized by perfect competition (thus, once again, allowing mainstream economists their best-case scenario), the capitalist firms that survive a crisis can use a portion of their profits to purchase the assets of other firms (either directly through mergers and acquisitions, or indirectly by buying up their now-cheaper constant capital and hiring unemployed workers). The

[18] The usual theory of perfect competition within mainstream economics proceeds in the following manner: First, in equilibrium, the market price is such that total revenue equals total costs for identical firms in an industry. Second, an exogenous increase in demand increases the market price above the old equilibrium, thus leading in the short term to extra-normal or super-profits for firms in that industry. Finally, in the long run, firms enter the industry to attempt to capture some of those super-profits, thus increasing market supply, lowering the market price, and eliminating the super-profits. Much the same story is told when, in the opposite scenario, a decrease in demand leads to losses and firms exit the industry, thus restoring perfect competition with no super-profits.

[19] There is another reason why this model of the competing away of super-profits is so important for mainstream economics. Let's remember that "normal profits" are embedded in the cost curves – and, like all factor payments that make up the cost curves, they are equal to marginal productivity. So, in aggregate, all incomes are accounted for. But what about super-profits or what mainstream economists refer to as "economic profits"? They aren't a return to anything. They depend not on productivity but, instead, on something else. Chance or entrepreneurship. And that simply can't be allowed. Fortuna does not create value, and entrepreneurship (whether conceived as human capital or a separate factor of production) doesn't simply stop if and when residual profits disappear. That's why the "long run," which permits free entry and exit, is a key part of the definition of perfect competition within mainstream economics.

resulting concentration and centralization of capital thus undermine the conditions of perfect competition enshrined in the basic theory and textbooks of mainstream economists.[20]

In Marx's view, these processes of concentration and centralization – what today is often called a "winner-take-all" economy – mean that the large capitalist enterprises are able to beat the smaller capitalists because they have both the interest and means to win the competitive battle. They can produce commodities more cheaply, offer better pay and working conditions to prospective workers, augment or replace workers with new machinery and technologies, eventually charge higher prices for the commodities they sell, engage in lobbying and other measures to tailor government policies to their ends, and so on. The result? "It always ends in the ruin of many small capitalists" (KI, 777).

The emergence of giant oligopolies and monopolies also brings into existence a new feature of capitalism: the credit system. The formation of joint-stock companies (or publicly traded corporations) is made possible by the concentration and centralization of capital, because these large companies can use credit to merge with and acquire the assets of other enterprises, thereby growing even larger. They are also able to attract the "money resources, which lie scattered in larger or smaller amounts over the surface of society" (KI, 778) – whether through bank loans, initial public offerings of stock, or, increasingly these days, through venture-capital and private-equity financing.

And the result? Not only do individual enterprises grow in absolute size and increase their dominance within markets. Those same enterprises tend to leave the workers behind:

> On the one hand, ... the additional capital formed in the course of further accumulation attracts fewer and fewer workers in proportion to its magnitude. On the other hand, the old capital periodically reproduced with a new composition repels more and more of the workers formerly employed by it. (KI, 780–1)

Reserve Army

According to the classical political economists, such as Malthus, capitalism is no different from any other form of economic organization: it is characterized by a natural law of excess population. In good times (e.g., with

[20] It is true, mainstream economists do have models of imperfect competition. But they are introduced and taught only after all the basic propositions of their theory have been proved, and only because certain exogenous conditions create exceptions to perfect competition. Hence, the idea of "natural monopolies." What they distinctly rule out is the endogenous movement or transition from perfect to imperfect competition.

higher levels of food production), population grows exponentially and eventually outstrips the supply of food; then, as a result of starvation, the population tends to decline.

Marx challenged Malthus's theory of population and proposed an alternative explanation: capitalism itself is both the cause and consequence of an excess supply of workers, which he called the Industrial Reserve Army (KI, 781–94). Today, we might refer to it as the reserve army of unemployed and underemployed workers. The size of that potential workforce changes, and is distributed unevenly throughout society.

In Marx's view, the accumulation of capital gives rise to at least four different layers of the reserve army (KI, 794–802):

1. "Floating" – workers who are frictionally unemployed, because they are in transition between jobs.
2. "Latent" – workers who are unemployed for longer periods of time, for example, because of a decline in a sector or industry (such as the transition from agriculture to industry or traditional manufacturing to high-tech).
3. "Stagnant" – workers who are subject to irregular employment or discouraged from looking for a job (because of the negative physical and/or psychological effects of capitalist employment).
4. "Lumpenproletariat" – workers who regularly operate outside the official market for labor power (e.g., because they are engaged in other economic activities, often informal or illegal).

What Marx is referring to, then, is an endlessly changing but often massive army of workers who cannot be considered regularly employed at full-time capitalist jobs – and therefore suffer from various degrees of precarity. They may be between jobs or are forced out of declining sectors or industries or are able to work only intermittently or who move back and forth between the formal market for labor power and other activities. They often confront lower wages, changing work schedules, the need to work at various part-time jobs, forms of employment that require skills less than they received through education or on-the-job training, and debilitating social, psychological, and physical conditions.

The members of this reserve army are missing from both mainstream economic models and official unemployment statistics, which tend to focus on a simple binary between employed and unemployed workers. Such a perspective leads to an endless debate back and forth between cyclical versus structural unemployment – of workers who would benefit from stimulus measures (because of an insufficient demand for labor power) or additional jobs training (because of an underproductive supply of labor power). But that debate avoids exactly the questions Marx suggests need to be asked: How long have these workers been unemployed or underemployed? What kinds of jobs are available to them? What are the wages, benefits, and working conditions they face? And, perhaps most important, why under capitalism are there so many workers whose only choice is to successfully sell their labor power to someone else or to face the dire consequences of being unable to do so?

In Marx's view, the critique of the reserve army is a critique of capitalism itself. That's because it is the reserve army of unemployed and underemployed workers that regulates the price of labor power.

> The relative surplus population is therefore the background against which the law of the demand and supply of labour does its work. It confines the field of action of this law to the limits absolutely convenient to capital's drive to exploit and dominate the workers. (KI, 792)

Within mainstream economics, however, excess wages are responsible for creating unemployment. The mainstream argument, illustrated in figure 6.7, is that there is full employment when the price of labor power is in equilibrium (P^*_{lp}), such that the quantity supplied of labor power by workers is equal to the quantity demanded of labor power by employers (at LP^*). Unemployment can therefore only occur when the price of labor power is above the equilibrium ($\underline{P}_{lp}$) – say, because of a wage floor, such as a minimum wage or collective-bargaining agreements; that's when the quantity supplied of labor power (LP^s) is greater than the quantity demanded of labor power (LP^d). In other words, within mainstream economics, wages determine the level of unemployment (and employment):

6.2 $$\Delta P_{lp} \rightarrow \text{unemployment}$$

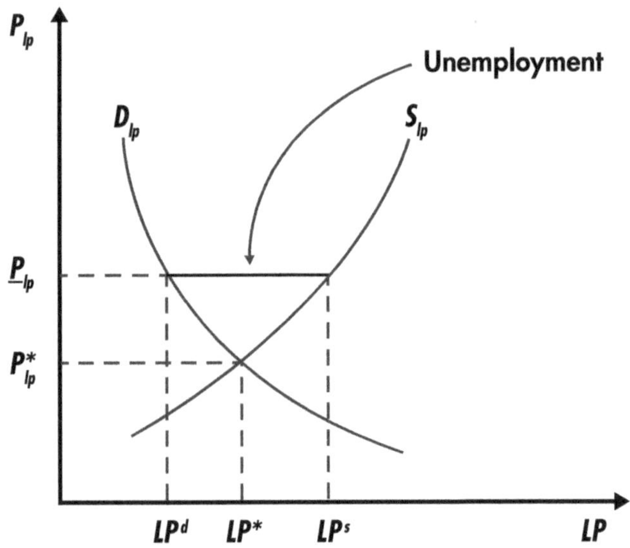

Figure 6.7 Unemployment in mainstream economics

This theory is the basis of the oft-repeated mainstream attack on minimum wages – that they may be well intentioned but, in the end, their only effect is to hurt workers, by killing jobs and creating unemployment.[21]

The Marxian critique goes in a radically different direction. What Marx does is reverse the causality, arguing (as we saw above) that it is the accumulation of capital that affects both the demand for and supply of labor power. And it is the resulting reserve army that regulates the level of workers' wages. The larger the army of unemployed and unemployed workers, which is created by the accumulation of capital, the more downward pressure there is on the wages of employed workers (as well as for the workers who eventually manage to sell their ability to work). Therefore, for Marx, the argument runs in the opposite direction:

6.3 $$\Delta K \rightarrow \text{unemployment} \rightarrow \Delta P_{lp}$$

The difference between the two theories could not be starker. In Marx's view, it is the normal workings of capitalism, not natural population growth (as Malthus argued) or misguided attempts by policymakers to intervene in markets (as contemporary neoclassical economists maintain), that causes both unemployment and low wages for workers. In other words, the attempt to maintain the conditions for capitalist exploitation, and to appropriate larger and larger quantities of surplus-value, has the effect of keeping wages in check and leaving workers further and further behind the small group at the top that captures the resulting surplus-value. Or, as Marx wrote,

> Accumulation of wealth at one pole is, therefore, at the same time accumulation of misery, the torment of labour, slavery, ignorance, brutalization and more degradation at the opposite pole, i.e., on the side of the class that produces its own product as capital. (KI, 799)

Production of Commodities by Means of Capital

Once again, we can see that Marx's focus is on movement and change, not on any kind of static equilibrium. This methodological aspect of his critique is carried over to his discussion of the movement of capital as self-valorizing value – in the often-overlooked discussion of the circulation of capital in volume 2, as well as in the much-debated chapters on the rate of profit in volume 3 of *Capital*.

[21] Even if their argument that minimum wages cause unemployment were valid (and much recent research, beginning with the work of mainstream economist and Nobel laureate David Card, casts doubt on that conclusion), mainstream economists always forget to mention the possibility of expanding the demand for labor power (shifting D_{lp} to the right in figure 6.7), which readers can verify would mean both increased wages for workers and no increase in unemployment.

We have already seen, in chapter 5, how over time capitalism is characterized by a tendency for the rate of profit ($\rho = s/[c + v]$) to fall. The classical political economists worried that external factors, such as the scarcity of land or labor (leading to higher land rents or wages), would diminish capitalists' profits, leading to a slowdown in the accumulation of capital and eventually causing capitalism to grind to a halt. Marx's response was that, if capitalism exhibited such a tendency, it was capitalist competition over super-profits, and therefore a factor *internal* to capitalism, that would lead capitalists to invest in constant capital and create the conditions for the rate of profit to fall.

Marx, it should be noted, also recognized a series of "counter-tendencies," which would lead to an increase in the rate of profit. Thus, as we have seen, the same capitalist investments might decrease the value of the items in the wage basket, thus leading to a lowering of the value of labor power and an increase in relative surplus-value. Similarly, an increase in the supply of labor power would lower its price and, after a period of time, perhaps even its value, thus increasing the rate of exploitation. The cheapening of the elements of constant capital – due to new sources of raw materials (especially abroad, as capital expanded into other areas of the globe), new methods of producing machinery, or the "slaughtering of capital values" – would also bolster capitalist profits. All of these, alone or together, would lead to an increase in the rate of profit.

The distinction between tendency and counter-tendency (in chapters 13 and 14 of volume 3 of *Capital*) is actually arbitrary. It could just as easily be the case that the conditions leading to increases in the rate of profit were treated as the tendency and the falling rate of profit as the counter-tendency. The reason Marx focuses on the tendency of the rate of profit to fall is because that is the issue that haunted classical political economy. What Marx does is show that, if such a tendency exists, it's because of factors intrinsic to a capitalist economy.

It is precisely that combination of tendency and counter-tendencies that leaves the actual path of the rate of profit indeterminate. Or perhaps better: it means the movement over time of the rate of profit – up, down, or unchanged – depends on the concrete, changing conditions within which capitalists' decisions are made and capitalism as a system operates.

Some Marxian economists argue, in contrast, that capitalism is characterized by "long waves" of growth and decline, determined by movements in the rate of profit.[22] In their view, capitalist accumulation is charac-

[22] See, e.g., the work of Anwar Shaikh ("The Falling Rate of Profit as the Cause of Long Waves: Theory and Empirical Evidence," in *New Findings in Long Wave Research*, ed. Alfred Kleinknecht, Ernest Mandel, and Immanuel Wallerstein, pp. 174–202 [London: Macmillan Press, 1992]); Fred Moseley ("The Rate of Profit and the Future of Capitalism," *Review of Radical Political Economics* 29/4 [1997]: 23–41); and Gérard Duménil and Dominique Lévy, "The Historical Trends of Technology and Distribution in the

terized by fluctuations around a long-term or "basic" curve – and the inevitable result is for that basic rate of profit, apart from cyclical movements, to fall over time. The idea is that, when, during the course of capitalist investment, the limits of existing knowledge and technology are reached, profits will have decreased to the point that a generalized crisis ensues, initiating a period of stagnation, a situation that lasts until profitability can be restored (even as the basic rate of profit may continue to fall) and the accumulation of capital and economic growth will once again resume.

While the movement of the rate of profit tends to generate significant attention in debates about the Marxian critique of political economy, Marx himself was equally concerned with the various ways the mythical conception of capitalism within mainstream economics – outside of time, instantaneously adjusting, always in full-employment equilibrium – was replete with problems.

For example, Marx argued, the movement of money capital, from an initial sum of money as capital to a greater amount of money, has a temporal dimension.[23] Capitalists are under pressure to sell the commodities they produce, in order to realize the value and surplus-value embodied in them. And that takes time. Therefore, they are forced to wait or to share a portion of the surplus-value they appropriate from their workers with merchants, whose task it is to make sure the commodities' values are fully realized as quickly as possible in the form of money.

By the same token, capital is always a mixture of circulating and fixed capital. It is circulating capital when it takes the form of money but, when it is invested in buildings, machinery, and raw materials, it is considered fixed. In the language of contemporary mainstream economics, capital is both putty and clay, both mobile and rigid. What this means is that any model (such as is often found with mainstream economics) that presumes instantaneous adjustments of capital from one putty form to another overlooks the rigidities involved in fixed, clay-like capital. Thus, for example, the capital involved in the steel industry cannot be easily or instantaneously transformed into the capital of another industry, such as agriculture or healthcare (which, of course, affects workers, when they are told to simply move from being unemployed in one sector to obtaining jobs in another). The distinction between circulating and fixed capital also

U.S. Economy Since 1869: Data and Figures" (September 2016) http://www.cepremap.fr/membres/dlevy/dle2016e.pdf.

[23] What Marx is referring to is $M - C \ldots P \ldots C' - M'$, where all terms are defined as before (M is the original amount of money capital, C is the value of the commodities purchased, P is the process of production, C' is the value of the commodities produced, and M' is the amount of money the capitalist ends up with after the commodities are sold, with M' being greater than M).

means the return on money (the interest rate) won't generally be equal to the profit rate (especially when, as mainstream economists assume, the profit rate or price of capital is presumed equal to the marginal product of capital).

Finally, capitalism always faces a problem of effective demand. That's generally not the case within mainstream economics. In a typical mainstream macroeconomic model (such as the aggregate supply–aggregate demand model we saw in chapter 2), the economy is in equilibrium – except for short periods of adjustment between equilibrium points. In the neoclassical version, the equilibrium is characterized by full employment, where all goods and services that are produced are sold and all factors of production (including labor) are fully employed.

Mainstream Keynesian macroeconomics is, of course, different. In the Keynesian model, the economy can and often will reach an equilibrium point at less than full employment – creating a recessionary gap – because of a shortfall on the demand side of the economy. A problem may arise if any one of the components of aggregate demand (consumption, investment, government expenditures, and net exports) decreases because of some external or unexpected event (such as a rise in taxes, a drop in business confidence, a reduction in government spending, or a decrease in foreign demand).

Not so in Marx's critique. The problem of effective demand is internal to capitalism, and arises from the class dynamics of a capitalist economy. We have already seen that, if the price of labor power falls, there may not be enough demand to purchase the wage goods that capitalists either have produced or expect to produce. That is a fundamental problem within capitalism: each capitalist wants to pay their own workers as little as possible, to boost their profits, but they want other capitalists to pay their workers as much as possible, in order to purchase all the consumer goods available on the market.

What about surplus-value? What happens in a capitalist economy depends crucially on whether or not and how the surplus-value that is appropriated from wage-laborers is actually spent. One portion of the surplus-value may, but need not, be used for the accumulation of capital – for purchases of additional elements of constant and variable capital. Other portions, as we have seen, may be distributed, depending on the circumstances, to other industrial capitalist enterprises, financial capitalists, merchant capitalists, landlords, advertising agencies, the state, and stockholders as well as internal management and corporate accounting, sales, purchasing, and research and development departments. So, for example, the distributions of surplus-value may fuel financial markets but not the so-called real economy – Wall Street but not Main Street. And, even if they do raise the rate of growth on Main Street, they lead to more exploitation of the working-class and thus more surplus appropriated by their employers.

In the terminology of mainstream macroeconomics, aggregate demand in a capitalist economy is the initial amount of capital ($K = c + v$) while the aggregate supply is the value of the goods that are produced ($W = c + v + s$) on the basis of that capital. Moreover, there is no necessary balance between them – between aggregate demand and aggregate supply – whether ex ante or ex post, in the short run or the long run.

6.4 $$\text{aggregate demand} = K < W = \text{aggregate supply}$$

This, readers may recognize, is the Keynesian problem of effective demand. But here it is formulated in the class terms of the Marxian critique of political economy – and decades before Keynes used it to criticize the mainstream economics of his day (without, however, any references to Marx).

Not only is there a necessary and persistent gap between aggregate demand and aggregate supply, the overall trajectory of a capitalist economy can be expected to be fundamentally unstable. That's because, while workers will generally spend all they have on the commodities they need to reproduce their labor power, expenditures of surplus-value will be much more volatile. The reason is, those expenditures depend on the expectations and spending patterns of the recipients of the surplus-value – and therefore on the various and changing decisions of industrial capitalists, financial capitalists, merchant capitalists, members of the top 1 percent, public officials, and so on and so forth. Those decisions are capricious and fundamentally unpredictable precisely because there is no underlying necessity to spend the surplus-value in any particular fashion, no matter how much or how little a capitalist economy is regulated by the state. Moreover, any rational calculations that may go into those decisions are subject to considerable uncertainty about the present state and future trajectory of a capitalist economy.

Once again, we can see that Say's Law cannot hold – not in a system of monetary exchange, and not now in a specifically capitalist context that involves the production of commodities by means of capital.

Looking Ahead

We have now completed our introduction to the basic elements of Marx's critique of political economy as presented in the three volumes of *Capital*. What remains is to see how these concepts and methods can be used to tackle some of the concrete issues that have emerged within mainstream economic theory and contemporary capitalism.

We turn to that task in the next chapter.

Suggested Readings

David M. Brennan, "The Capitalist Firm," in *Routledge Handbook of Marxian Economics*, ed. David M. Brennan, David Kristjanson-Gural, Catherine P. Mulder, and Erik M. Olson, pp. 171–9 (New York: Routledge, 2017).

Stephen Cullenberg, *The Falling Rate of Profit: Recasting the Marxian Debate* (London: Pluto Press, 1994).

Andrew Kliman, "Tendency of the Rate of Profit to Fall," in *Routledge Handbook of Marxian Economics*, ed. David M. Brennan, David Kristjanson-Gural, Catherine P. Mulder, and Erik M. Olson, pp. 225–33 (New York: Routledge, 2017).

Bruce Norton, "Accumulation," in *Routledge Handbook of Marxian Economics*, ed. David M. Brennan, David Kristjanson-Gural, Catherine P. Mulder, and Erik M. Olson, pp. 198–214 (New York: Routledge, 2017).

Thomas Piketty, *Capital in the Twenty-First Century* (Cambridge, MA: Harvard University Press, 2014).

Stephen A. Resnick and Richard D. Wolff, *Knowledge and Class: A Marxian Critique of Political Economy* (Chicago: University of Chicago Press, 1987).

Bruce Roberts, "What Is Profit?" *Rethinking Marxism* 1, 1 (1988): 136–51.

PART III

APPLICATIONS, DEBATES, AND CONSEQUENCES

Chapter 7

APPLICATIONS OF MARXIAN ECONOMICS

We have now worked our way through many of the basic concepts and methods of Marx's critique of political economy.

We started, in chapter 4, with Marx's analysis of the commodity, commodity exchange, money, and commodity fetishism. Then, in chapter 5, we saw how Marx produced his theory of capitalist exploitation, the value of specifically capitalist commodities, and the different ways capitalists are able to extract surplus-value from their workers. Finally, in chapter 6, we looked at how Marx defined wages and profits, analyzed the distributions of surplus-value, and then discussed the implications of those distributions for the reproduction of capitalism and capitalist growth.

In each case, we saw how Marx's approach – the new concepts he formulated and the novel methods he utilized – gave rise to a two-fold critique. He developed a ruthless criticism both of mainstream economic theory (of his day and, by extension, of our own times) and of capitalism (as it existed then, in the middle of the nineteenth century, and today). I also offered a variety of concrete examples to illustrate those conceptions and concerns.

But, of course, there are many other issues in mainstream economics and the history of capitalism that invite further discussion and elaboration – a variety of specific topics that Marxist economists have grappled with in the century and a half since Marx first formulated his critique of political economy. In some cases, the application of Marx's critique to these issues is straightforward, since Marx himself had already analyzed them. However, in many other cases, a great deal of additional work has been done to update and extend Marx's critique.

That's the goal of this chapter – to see where the Marxian critique of political economy might lead in terms of analyzing problems that have plagued both mainstream economics and the capitalist system throughout their histories.

Crises

Let's start where we left off at the end of the last chapter – the idea that crises are an ever-present possibility within capitalism. But, according to Marx, they are neither inevitable nor predictable. And they don't all stem from the same causes or have the same consequences.

The possibility of crises created by tendencies internal to capitalism is one of the hallmarks of Marx's critique, a view that separates it from the entire history of mainstream economics. Within the mainstream approach (especially, the relatively new branch, dating from the 1930s, called macroeconomics), economic downturns may in fact occur but they are always caused by something outside of capitalist markets. Capitalism, when left to its own devices, is always in balance and hums along at a steady pace – creating more wealth, more employment, more prosperity for everyone.

If problems do emerge, it's always because of an outside factor, some kind of external "shock" (as we saw in chapter 2). In fact, the debate about the nature of that external cause sets the narrow limits of the discussion that takes place among mainstream economists. For some, on the more conservative, free-market (neoclassical or neoliberal) end of the theoretical spectrum, problems can emerge on the supply side of the economy – from, say, a natural disaster or an unwarranted government intervention in markets. Thus, for example, in examining the causes of the Second Great Depression, neoclassical macroeconomists (such as John B. Taylor) blame not capitalism itself, but the shift away from rules-based monetary, fiscal, and regulatory policies toward more discretionary policies.[1] On the other end, more liberal (Keynesian) economists argue that economic downturns may occur based on complications on the demand side of the economy – from, say, an exogenous or external shift in expectations or a government decision to "tighten" economic policy (often referred to as "austerity," as, for example, when the monetary authority increases interest rates or policymakers attempt to decrease fiscal deficits). For Keynesian economists (like Paul Krugman), the Second Great Depression was caused by the housing bust – the dramatic decline in housing prices, which in turn led to a dramatic drop in residential investment as well as a decline in consumption spending (because of the destruction of household wealth).[2]

That debate about external causes among mainstream economists leads, in turn, to a lack of agreement about appropriate policy responses:

[1] J. B. Taylor, "The Role of Policy in the Great Recession and the Weak Recovery," *American Economic Review* 104 (May 2014): 61–6.

[2] "Botching the Great Recession," *New York Times* (12 September 2018), available at https://www.nytimes.com/2018/09/12/opinion/botching-the-great-recession.html.

conservatives are adamant that markets should be allowed to operate freely to move the economy back to full employment (which often involves focusing on a fall in workers' wages, without, however, ever mentioning capitalists' profits), while liberals are in favor of running budgetary deficits (so that the conditions can be created for private capitalists to increase investment, thus creating more growth and jobs).

What neither side of the mainstream debate allows for is the possibility that capitalism itself, not some external factor, creates economic downturns (and, for that matter, upturns), that crises and boom-and-bust cycles are intrinsic to an economy based on private capitalist decisions in markets. They are inherent in capitalism because it is characterized by generalized commodity exchange and because there is no mechanism that regulates what is done with the surplus-value that is appropriated and distributed.

Precisely because of that, capitalism is subject to regular fluctuations: the United States, for example, has experienced 34 recessions since the mid-nineteenth century, 13 since World War II. Many of those economic downturns have been relatively short-lived but, just in the last hundred years, three of them – the Great Depression of the 1930s, the Second Great Depression starting in 2007, and the Pandemic Depression – have been severe, widespread, and long-lasting. In all cases, in both recessions and depressions, the effects have been fundamentally unequal, born much more by workers at the bottom of the economic pyramid than capitalists and the recipients of distributed surplus-value at the top. That's the fundamental inequality inherent in capitalism. And, in all those cases, the transformations capitalism has undergone to attempt to emerge from one crisis have created the conditions for another one at some point down the line.

Now, to be clear, Marx does not suggest there is anything predictable about either the sequence or causes of capitalism's crises. They are always a possibility, expected and even inevitable, given the contradictions of capitalism, but when and how they occur are not governed by any kind of general law. Thus, each crisis needs to be analyzed in terms of its concrete characteristics – both its conditions and its consequences.

For example, the trigger for the first Great Depression was the series of stock-market crashes that occurred in the United States in 1929, starting in late September and culminating on Black Tuesday in October. Billions of dollars were lost, wiping out thousands of US investors; then it spilled over into the rest of the economic system, in the United States and around the world. The spark that set off the Second Great Depression was different: it was the failure of large investment banks (which either went bankrupt, such as Lehman Brothers, or were sold at fire-sale prices to other banks, including Bear Stearns and Merrill Lynch) that set off a run on the so-called shadow banking system, which spread through and then beyond the global financial system.[3] The Pandemic Depression was occasioned in still a third manner: it was instigated by the economic slowdowns and shutdowns provoked by successive waves of the novel coronavirus, as governments initiated a series of "stay-at-home" restrictions and businesses furloughed and laid off masses of workers.

Not only were the immediate triggers of the three economic depressions different; so were the larger sets of causes or conditions. In the case of the Great Depression of the 1930s, much of the US agricultural sector was already in a precarious state, as farmers faced falling prices for the commodities they were producing and were taking on increasing amounts of debt to pay for new land and machinery. In industry, a fundamental restructuring was taking place, as assets were shifted from individual ownership to private corporate holdings; meanwhile, leading corporations, financial firms, and the New York Stock Exchange promoted the idea of shareholder democracy – universal ownership of corporate stock – as part of a larger effort to shape public opinion. The 1920s also witnessed a "consumer revolution" (with purchases of everything from radios and washing machines to refrigerators and automobiles) based on an expansion of advertising and consumer credit ("Buy now, pay later"). Meanwhile, Wall Street became a financial bubble, based on mass marketing, the possibility of buying on margin, and a variety of techniques of stock manipulation (including "painting the tape").[4] It should come as no surprise that the stock market bubble would eventually burst and, once it did, that its effects would spread throughout both the US and world economies – leading to bank runs, business failures, and soaring unemployment that would last until World War II.

We have to look elsewhere to understand the background of the Second Great Depression. A central feature was the shift, at least in the United States, from industry to finance, which reflected the growing gap between stagnant wages and growing profits. Workers needed credit in order to maintain their customary standard of living, and the financial sector was only too willing to recycle corporate profits to expand their lending, especially for housing. Those loans were, in turn, carved up and sold as financial derivatives (thus further boosting bank profits) and

[3] The shadow banking system comprises financial intermediaries whose members are not subject to regulatory oversight, as well as unregulated activities by regulated financial institutions. Examples of intermediaries not subject to regulation include hedge funds and unlisted derivatives, while examples of unregulated activities by regulated institutions include credit default swaps.

[4] Painting the tape is a form of market manipulation whereby investors attempt to influence the price of a security by buying and selling it among themselves to create the appearance of substantial trading activity. The goal is to create the illusion of an increased interest in a stock to trick other investors into buying shares, which would drive the price even higher.

became the object of insurance bets (since it was likely that, at some point, the derivatives would decrease in value, when housing prices began to fall).[5] The possibility of a severe crisis turns out to have been decades in the making, but once the upward trajectory of the real-estate sector was reversed, the financial "house of cards" began to fall apart – and not only the US economy, but global capitalism itself, was brought to the brink of disaster.

And the third major set of crises of capitalism, the Pandemic Depression? The corporate and financial sectors (and with them the wealthiest individuals) had been bailed out during the previous depression, but the vast majority of people were still attempting to recover what they lost while their burdens increased (especially, again to take the example of the United States, the financial burden of paying for their children's postsecondary education and healthcare). Governments attempted to stem the spread of COVID-19 by closing schools and some businesses, thus forcing workers around the world to face a cruel choice: to continue to work in conditions that were hazardous to their health (e.g., in nursing homes, meatpacking plants, and public transportation) or to join the reserve army of the unemployed and underemployed (and thus to attempt to support themselves and their families on, in the best of circumstances, unemployment benefits or furlough pay).[6] Moreover, even during the subsequent recovery, capitalism created a whole series of shortages in its global supply chains, thus causing commodity prices to rise, especially the prices set by large corporations, even while workers' wages remained low. Once again, even with massive government assistance programs, capitalism was unable to contain either the pandemic or its economic fallout.[7] Meanwhile, the disastrous economic and social effects on the working-classes will likely be felt for years, if not decades.

Much more, of course, can be identified and analyzed in terms of the immediate triggers, larger causes, and economic and social consequences of these particular depressions, as also in the scores of other minor and

[5] A derivative is a financial security with a value that is reliant upon or derived from an underlying asset or group of assets (such as housing mortgages). The derivative itself is a contract between two or more parties, and the contract derives its price from fluctuations in the underlying asset (such as housing prices).

[6] The pandemic itself was caused at least in part by capitalism (e.g., through the razing of forests, increased trade in wildlife, and the proliferation of industrial farm herds), even before issues of health system preparedness, containment, and vaccinations became relevant. There is, however, no World Health Organization equivalent for the problems created by the intersection of capitalism and nature.

[7] Even the vaccines that were eventually created by various pharmaceutical companies (such as Pfizer, Moderna, and AstraZeneca) were only developed, produced, and distributed after governments entered into massive purchase contracts and thus guaranteed corporate profits.

major crises in the history of capitalism. From the perspective of the Marxian critique of political economy, two general points can be made: First, capitalism is always-everywhere on the verge of crisis; there's nothing settled or secure about its present state or future trajectory. It is constantly being unsettled and then stitched together – or, perhaps, superseded. Second, these disruptions, both large and small, are not accidents, but instead systemic and thus intrinsic to capitalism. Precisely because it is characterized by monetary exchange and the extraction and distribution of surplus-value, capitalism contains within itself both the possibility of falling apart and, given the divergent class interests and economic theories involved, determined efforts to put the pieces back together again, albeit in a different manner.

Class Structure

Another question readers will probably have in mind after working their way through the previous three chapters is: who exactly are the capitalists Marx keeps referring to? And, along with that: who are the workers, and what is the class structure of capitalism?

The issue of class doesn't even arise within contemporary mainstream economics. There are no classes, whether as the entry point or the conclusion of the analyses based on the theories and models developed and utilized by mainstream economists today. They literally don't see classes – only individuals (or, within mainstream macroeconomics, groups of individual behaviors).[8] The classical economists, in contrast, did refer to classes – but only as different groups of owners of things (labor, land, and capital) that went into the production process, which in turn gave them access to flows of income (wages, rent, and profits).

Marx, in contrast, put class at the center of his critique of political economy. Moreover, he defined class in a particular way: in terms of the production, appropriation, and distribution of surplus labor. So, Marx's analysis is distinctive in two ways: (1) he focuses on class (as against approaches that overlook or deny the existence of class), and (2) his analyses are based on a conception of class defined in a specific manner

[8] To be clear, it is not that mainstream economists can't see classes, as the work of John Roemer (*Free to Lose*, Cambridge, MA: Harvard University Press, 1988) and Samuel Bowles and Herbert Gintis ("Power and Wealth in a Competitive Market Economy," *Philosophy and Public Affairs*, 21 [Fall 1992]: 324–53) has shown. Roemer, Bowles and Gintis, and others have utilized all the basic concepts of contemporary mainstream economics to analyze the existence of classes and class exploitation within capitalism. What their work demonstrates is that mainstream economics, as it is generally understood on both the micro and macro levels, represents a *choice* not to acknowledge or develop a class analysis of capitalism.

(versus theories in which class is conceived in terms of something else, like power, status, or income, and not surplus labor).

In the most abstract terms, as we saw in chapter 5, capitalists (or, more specifically, industrial capitalists) are the ones who appropriate the surplus-value for literally doing nothing. They thus exploit their workers, and (at the same time or subsequently) distribute various portions of the surplus-value to themselves and to others.

The more concrete question is: who within contemporary capitalism actually occupies the position of industrial capitalist? Well, for starters, they are not the "top 1 percent" or the "billionaire class" – although many capitalists are in fact members of both groups. Those categories, which have become part of the contemporary lexicon after Occupy Wall Street and various left-wing political campaigns (such as that of Bernie Sanders in the United States and Jeremy Corbyn in the United Kingdom), are defined by how large their incomes are. They are clearly at the top of the pile in terms of the size of their incomes (and, even more, their wealth) but they are able to capture (and, via low tax rates, to keep) that money not by virtue of being capitalists, but by other means. They own private businesses (alone or with others) as well as stocks, bonds, and property (and receive dividends, capital gains, interest, and rent) and they are often chief executives of large corporations (and receive equity shares in addition to very high salaries). The various releases of enormous troves of hitherto-hidden financial documents – including the Panama Papers (2016), the Paradise Papers (2017), and the Pandora Papers (2021) – attest to their ability to capture and then hide in offshore tax havens their enormous wealth. They clearly benefit from capitalism but they are not necessarily the industrial capitalists Marx referred to.

To put it differently, those who belong to the "top 1 percent" or the "billionaire class" receive large shares of the surplus created within capitalism but they do not necessarily appropriate the surplus. They don't engage in class exploitation as capitalists; instead, a portion of the surplus is distributed to them by the group of people who are the real capitalists. So, stockholders are not capitalists. They buy (or receive as compensation) shares in capitalist enterprises, and receive a part of the surplus in the form of dividends and capital gains. Nor are CEOs (or, for that matter, chief information officers, chief financial officers, and other top executives). They are hired to run the corporations on a daily basis, and often receive a cut of the surplus in the form of exorbitant salaries, benefits, stocks, and, when they are let go, golden parachutes.

Who, then, personifies capital? It has to be the ones who – culturally, politically, and economically – are ultimately responsible for appropriating and distributing the surplus-value. Within modern corporations, capitalists are therefore the members of the boards of directors. They are elected by the shareholders, choose the management team, decide on the long-range objectives and strategies of the firm, and are the ones who directly appropriate and distribute the surplus-value.[9]

It is therefore a tiny group. Given that corporate boards are generally made up of 10–15 members, we are talking about (for the S&P 500 companies, in the United States) only 6,250 individuals. The number is even smaller (closer to 4,500), if we subtract interlocking directorates, that is, individuals who sit on more than one board. For all kinds of reasons, capitalists are also members of the top 1 percent, the billionaire class, stock owners, and CEOs. But, as capitalists – as appropriators and distributors of the surplus, and thus the personification of capital – they are a much smaller group.[10]

It is also the case that, in smaller corporations and noncorporate enterprises, those who perform the role of capitalists also often occupy many other positions and engage in other activities: they may devise new commodities and new ways of producing those commodities, invest their own money, perform both productive and unproductive labor, engage in public relations, support politicians and finance political campaigns, and so on. They also may go to church, participate in families and households, vote in elections, pay taxes, and play myriad other roles in society. But, for them and for those who sit on the boards of directors of large corporations, they occupy the position of industrial capitalists only insofar as they appropriate and distribute the surplus-value extracted from their workers.

As we have seen (especially in chapter 6), capitalism also includes non-industrial capitalists who are also able to make profits from money capital – in merchanting, finance, real estate, and insurance – as well as noncapitalists – inside and outside corporations, such as shareholders, internal management, the state, landowners, and so on. The one thing they have in common is they find themselves in the position of being able to capture distributions of the surplus-value created by productive laborers.

What, then, of the working-class? Again, at an abstract level, workers or wage-laborers are those who are forced to have the freedom to sell their labor power to someone else. In a more concrete sense, we have already

[9] Other Marxian scholars define the capitalist class differently – not in terms of surplus labor, but in relation to property and power. Thus, for example, Erik Olin Wright (*Understanding Class* [London: Verso, 2015]) and Gérard Duménil and Dominique Lévy (*The Crisis of Neoliberalism* [Cambridge, MA: Harvard University Press, 2011]) define capitalists as those who own and control capital assets (such as stocks, bonds, and other financial assets) and exercise power, over both workers and other, smaller capitalists.

[10] The total number of publicly traded companies in the United States (which has about half of the world's stock-market value) has declined dramatically since the mid-1990s (from more than 7,000 to fewer than 4,000). This is because of the rise in (a) mergers and acquisitions and (b) venture-capital and private-equity businesses, both of which have changed the composition of the boards of directors of private corporations.

seen how Marx makes a distinction between productive laborers, who create surplus-value, and unproductive laborers, who don't. All of them sell their ability to work to someone else but not all of them create surplus-value. Only those laborers who are involved in the production of capitalist commodities (whether goods or services) are, in Marxian terms, productive laborers. Unproductive laborers may also be exploited (in the sense that they perform surplus labor, which is appropriated by someone else) but their surplus labor does not take the form of surplus-value. They exchange their labor power not for capital, but for an expenditure of distributed surplus-value.

That's the key difference between, for example, autoworkers and public-school teachers. Both groups of workers perform necessary and surplus labor, labor that is equivalent to the value of their customary standard of living and additional labor that is appropriated by their employers. But the former (the autoworkers) perform labor that creates value and surplus-value that are embodied in commodities, which are, in turn, sold by capitalists; the latter (the teachers) perform labor and surplus labor that are not embodied in capitalist commodities or realized as capitalist value and profits. The fact that public education is not sold as a capitalist commodity distinguishes public-school teachers (and their coworkers) from those who work in private education, which *is* sold as a capitalist commodity (even when the schools in which they work have nonprofit status). Still, what both groups of workers have in common is (a) they sell their labor power to someone else for a wage or salary and (b) they are exploited by their employers.

Real-world capitalism therefore comprises a dense class structure based on a complex and changing pattern of flows of appropriated and distributed surplus labor. Together, workers make up something on the order of 80–90 percent of the population of a country like the United States. The rest are either capitalists (a tiny portion) or recipients of the surplus (a somewhat larger group).

Class Consciousness and Class Struggle

Now we have a sense of the various positions that comprise the class structure of capitalism. But nothing can be automatically or necessarily read off those class positions in terms of what people think, do, or say. That's the case for at least three reasons.

First, a person's ideology or consciousness does not necessarily reflect, and cannot simply be derived from, the class position(s) they may occupy. There are lots of different ways people make sense of and respond to their class positions. For example, some productive laborers may think they are exploited by their employers and others may not (a lesson that many organizers for political parties and labor unions have learned the hard way). How workers make sense of whether or not they are exploited depends on many things, including the economic theories they use to understand their class position.[11]

Second, any individual may and probably does occupy more than one class position during the course of a day, a year, or a lifetime. They may, for example, occupy the position of exploited productive laborer (when they are engaged in the production of capitalist commodities), recipient of distributed surplus-value (if they receive dividends from the ownership of stocks, in the corporation they work for or other corporations), and appropriator of surplus labor (if they own a business with employees or in their own household).

Third, any country, whether or not it is generally referred to as capitalist, probably also includes a variety of other, noncapitalist class processes. Whether we are analyzing the economies of France, India, or China, we are likely to find many different class economies – capitalism, feudalism, slavery, communal, independent or Ancient, and so on – in households, enterprises, and farms, in both urban and rural areas, formal and informal sectors, and so on.

We return to this issue, of capitalism's others, below. What is important right now is that, from a Marxian perspective, there is no one-to-one correspondence between how people think or act and the class (and, for that matter, nonclass) positions they occupy.

While there may be no single or correct consciousness of class, capitalism is such that it regularly produces class struggles. That's because class struggles are defined by what people are struggling over, not by who's doing the struggling or what people think they are doing when they struggle over class. Class struggles are therefore defined in terms of scraps, scuffles, and skirmishes – individually and collectively, culturally, politically, and economically – over the class dimensions of society. What this means is that capitalist class struggles take as their object the class dimensions of capitalism. And, as we have seen, there are plenty of opportunities to struggle over surplus labor within capitalism – over the quantitative and qualitative dimensions of the appropriation of surplus labor, as well as over the distributions of surplus labor. It couldn't be otherwise, given the conflictual nature of class exploitation.

Absolute and relative surplus-value, as we saw in chapter 5, are struggles over capitalist class exploitation – between industrial capitalists and their workers. So, are attempts to eliminate the extraction of surplus-value

[11] The economic theories people use to make sense of their lives are not limited to those that are produced within and disseminated from the discipline of economics. They also include economic theories from other disciplines (from anthropology to cultural studies) and from outside the academy, in everyday life.

altogether, especially when people either challenge the existence of capitalism directly or when they attempt to enact noncapitalist class arrangements (an issue we return to in some detail in chapter 9). Similarly, based on the analysis in chapter 6, there are many different claimants on distributions of surplus-value, and therefore struggles that regularly take place over who gets how much of that surplus – between industrial capitalists and others (from finance capitalists to the state). Those struggles often rebound back on the production and appropriation of surplus-value, thereby engendering new class struggles.

There are, of course, famous examples of class struggles: the Spartacist Uprising in Germany in 1919; the Battle of Blair Mountain in 1921, the Flint sit-down strike of 1936, and President Ronald Reagan's mass firing of air traffic controllers in 1981 in the United States; the protests by nineteenth-century Luddites in England and the battle between Prime Minister Margaret Thatcher and British miners in 1984; the Paris Commune of 1871 and French General Strike of 1968; and the Indian General Strike of 2020. But there are many, many other examples, throughout the world – of negotiations, campaigns, attacks, strikes, and uprisings, both large and small – concerning the quantitative and qualitative dimensions of the production, appropriation, and distribution of surplus labor.

The long history of capitalism is therefore also a chronicle of such class struggles.

Patriarchy

The history of capitalism is, of course, about more than class and class struggles. People have identities other than those associated with their class positions, and capitalism has been intertwined with other structures of inequality and oppression from the very beginning. One such identity is gender, which is related in turn to the system of patriarchy. What then is the relationship among gender, patriarchy, and capitalism?

Once again, such a question does not arise within mainstream economics. In most mainstream economic models and texts, the issue of gender is barely mentioned – and, when it is, the discussion is mostly focused on whether or not discrimination based on gender is present in the labor market (in order to make sense of the longstanding and persistent inequality in the wages and salaries paid to men and women). That's it.

Within Marxism, in contrast, there is an established (albeit historically changing and uneven) critique of women's oppression and a tradition of thinking through the relationship between Marxism and feminism. That should come as no surprise because, as Barbara Ehrenreich explained in the mid-1970s,

> Marxism and feminism have an important thing in common: they are critical ways of looking at the world. Both rip away popular mythology and "common sense" wisdom and force us to look at experience in a new way.[12]

The combination of the two critiques is known as Marxist or socialist feminism.

As we have seen, Marxism, by itself, is a critique of both mainstream economic theory and capitalism, especially a critique of the class exploitation that is both intrinsic to capitalism and mostly overlooked within mainstream economics. What feminism adds is a critique of the inequalities and oppressions inherent in capitalist patriarchy. However, socialist feminism is not just an adding-together of the two, but a combination of Marxist and feminist approaches and concerns that critically interrogates the structures that lead to both class exploitation and gender oppression.

Now, it is true, neither class exploitation nor patriarchy started with capitalism. Both systems predate capitalist ways of organizing economies and societies – as both Marxists and feminists, alone and together, have investigated and made clear. Feudal lords in medieval Europe, for example, appropriated surplus labor in the form of rent from serfs. And that, according to Marx, makes capitalism no different from feudalism: both are based on the exploitation of the direct producers by another, much smaller group at the top of the economic and social pyramid. Feminists, for their part, have examined and criticized the ways women have been subjugated – by various means, from violence and sanction to custom and law – from ancient times, around the world. This was particularly the case with the advent of private property (including property in women) and the sexual division of labor (both inside and outside households).

Of particular interest is Engels's *The Origin of the Family, Private Property and the State* (based on Marx's notes on North American anthropologist Lewis Henry Morgan's *Ancient Society* and his own investigations into the history of Greece, Rome, Old Ireland, and the Ancient Germans), which first appeared in 1884 (ME, 734–59).[13] Primitive communism, according to both Morgan and Engels, was based not on the patriarchal nuclear family, but often on matrilineal descent – within societies in which there was no state, property was owned in common, and both men and women enjoyed relatively equal status. According to Morgan, the rise of alienable property disempowered women by triggering a switch to patrilocal residence

[12] Barbara Ehrenreich, "What is Socialist Feminism?" *WIN Magazine* (1976). Ehrenreich's article was republished, with a new introduction, by *Jacobin Magazine* in 2018 (https://jacobinmag.com/2018/07/socialist-feminism-barbara-ehrenreich).

[13] Marx had planned to write a study based on Morgan's research. His notes were transcribed and edited by Lawrence Krader in *The Ethnological Notebooks of Karl Marx* (2nd ed., Assen, The Netherlands: Van Gorcum, 1974).

and patrilineal descent. Engels expanded on this idea, describing the "overthrow of mother right" as "the *world-historic defeat of the female sex*" (ME, 736, emphasis in original) and the "first class antagonism" (ME, 739), which historically coincides with the struggle between men and women in monogamous marriage. Thus, Engels argued, the modern family was based on property rights (including strict rules of inheritance) and forced monogamy, which led to the enslavement of women, the proliferation of immorality, and prostitution – ruled and regulated by a state that favored the exploiting classes. Engels therefore concluded that, in his time, only by eliminating the class antagonisms of capitalism would the "full freedom of marriage" (ME, 750), based not on property but mutual attraction, be possible.

Building on and extending the work of Marx and Engels, as well as later generations of socialist feminists, the focus today is on capitalist patriarchy, which represents a particular way – in many different economic and social contexts – that class exploitation is reinforced by patriarchy, and vice versa. It is the focus on that combination that separates socialist feminism from both mainstream economics and liberal feminism (and thus the concern with, at most, analyzing gender discrimination within markets).

Thus, for example, real-world capitalism is not just a vast accumulation of commodities. It also involves significant amounts of labor that is not involved in the production of commodities, often within households. And much of that labor, including surplus labor, is performed by women. What this means is that the value of labor power (as we initially discussed in chapter 5) needs to be redefined: it is sufficient to reproduce the customary standard of living of the owners of labor power only to the extent that workers rely on production (of many things, from meal preparation and clothes-laundering to child-rearing and emotional care) that takes place within households.

Under capitalism, women have also been responsible for much of the "caring" labor that takes place outside their own households. Historically, they (especially poor, single women) have worked as domestic laborers, nannies, and cooks in other people's households, as well as in schools, healthcare facilities, and offices. They also form the backbone of many parts of the new – precarious and low-paying – service industries, working to produce commodities – such as food preparation, childcare, nursing, and so on – that were once created, in non-commodity form, within households.

Starting in the 1930s, many more women (including nonpoor, married women) were forced to have the freedom to sell their labor power to employers in factories and offices, often in addition to continuing their household labor. In many instances, they have earned less than their male counterparts – either in segregated jobs, which keeps their own pay lower than it might otherwise be, or, when they are in direct competition with male workers, weakening the wage demands of all workers. The result in both cases is increased exploitation of the working-class.

That's one tendency. Another is that, as the labor-force participation rate of women has risen, and women have increasingly earned their "own" wages and salaries outside households, they have been able to challenge traditional forms of patriarchy within households – for example, by challenging male-exclusive property rights and otherwise demanding nonexploitative ways of organizing the economic and social life of their households. One of the consequences is that the kind of nuclear family that has long been taken as "natural" (and historically contextualized by Morgan and Engels, consisting of a married couple and their children) now makes up less one third of the total number of households in the United States. Increasing numbers of women now live in married-couple households without children, their own households (with or without children), and with others not in relations of marriage.

However consequential, those changes have not eliminated patriarchy, class exploitation, or the nexus between them. For example, women's bodies continue to be regulated – commodified, disciplined, and punished – by both private corporations and the states that attempt to keep capitalism in place. They are often called on and configured in specific ways to sell commodities (to both men and women), through a wide variety of economic and social practices: corporate advertising campaigns; characters depicted in films and television shows; norms learned in households, churches, and schools; and so on. Women have also been transformed to do more work, both inside and outside households, in order to boost the levels of production and productivity promised by capitalism. In general, women are subject to such pressures when capitalism is operating smoothly, and then required to pick up the pieces when it is not.

It is therefore necessary, now as in the past, to focus on the particular ways the reproduction of patriarchy is intertwined with capitalism – both reinforced by the continued existence of capitalism and, at the same time, serving as a means whereby capitalist class exploitation is able to rely on the subjugation of women.

Racial Capitalism

It is impossible to analyze the history of capitalism without also examining the ways it is fundamentally intertwined with various forms of racial hierarchy and oppression (including racist institutions such as slavery). Much the same is true of contemporary capitalism, which reproduces (and is reproduced by) changing sets of racist ideologies and practices. That's why some scholars, such as Cedric J. Robinson, have added the adjective racial as a necessary supplement to capitalism.

Robinson's notion of racial capitalism is both a critique of and an extension of Marx's theory of capitalism. It is critical because, in Robinson's view, Marx failed to adequately account for the racial nature of capitalism. In other words, he exaggerated the extent to which capitalism represented a fundamental break from feudalism and served to homogenize the identities of workers. Instead, capitalism took on and then reinforced the racial orderings and practices – including slavery, violence, imperialism, and genocide – of the old order. Racialism thus served to encode and legitimate differentiated groups of workers who were subject to capitalist exploitation. By the same token, Robinson succeeded in extending Marx's idea that capitalism did not eliminate the class antagonisms of feudalism, but "established new classes, new conditions of oppression, new forms of struggle in place of the old ones" (ME, 474). Thus, from a Marxian perspective, racial capitalism can be seen to have established and relied upon new racially defined classes, new conditions of race-class oppression, and new forms of race-class struggle in place of the old ones.

Mainstream economists, for their part, generally downplay or overlook the nexus between capitalism and racism. Much as in the case of gender, the topic of race and racism within mainstream economics gets little treatment; and, when it is mentioned, it is limited to a problem of racial discrimination within labor markets. Even then, the presumption is that, over time, discrimination on the basis of race will disappear.[14]

The Marxist critique of political economy moves in the opposite direction. Racism played an important role in the origins of capitalism; it has continued to be constitutive of class exploitation over the course of the history of capitalism; and today, while racism has in fact changed (in terms of both ideologies and institutions, including legal bans on racial discrimination), it continues to define the hierarchies and differentiations that are central to capitalism.

This is particularly true when capitalism undergoes crises and is otherwise challenged (which, as we have seen, has happened many times throughout its history). Then, the development of racist ideologies and practices appears as a natural "solution" (a solution which, indeed, essentially aggravates the crisis). The Pandemic Depression is a good example. In the United States and in many other places around the world, the combination of health and economic crises exposed the already-existing inequalities based on race (and, with it, ethnicity). It also exacerbated

[14] That's because, contemporary mainstream economists argue, rational employers that compete with one another will take advantage of arbitrage opportunities and relinquish any racist "tastes" they may have. That still leaves open the possibility of "statistical discrimination" – the use of race as a surrogate for the unobservable characteristics that cause productivity differences among workers – but then the problem is not racism but those "real" underlying differences. In both cases, according to mainstream economists, markets succeed in eliminating racial discrimination over time.

those inequalities, as members of racial and ethnic minorities both found themselves in precarious frontline or essential jobs, were more vulnerable to the damaging effects of the novel coronavirus, and received considerably less medical attention as the virus spread in waves within and across countries.

Racial hierarchies are also often invoked when it comes to the issue of government entitlements and the dignity of work (which we initially discussed in chapter 6). It's an old argument, that markets function only on the promise of reward and mobility (and presumably will not work without the threat of poverty and immiseration). It then becomes possible to tell a story of undeserving takers and welfare cheats, economic and social parasites who undermine "hard-working people" who are forced to put up with high taxes to finance government programs. Within racial capitalism, such distinctions are inextricably tied up in a racial hierarchy – such that to be white is to be a hard worker and overburdened taxpayer, while nonwhite (Black, Hispanic, or otherwise) means choosing not to work and accepting dependence on government "handouts." In fact, many such dualities – the deserving and undeserving poor, makers and takers, industrious and lazy – have been regularly encoded in and through the categories of race.

But the origins of racial capitalism appear much earlier – when racism was invented and, where it already existed, was harnessed to justify the slave trade, slave production, and colonial domination. In each case, the workforce ripped out of Africa, put to work on slave plantations in the West, and forced to work for the colonizers, was deemed racially inferior and thus made readily available for commodification, forced labor, and expropriation. The same practices have been used to justify mass movements of people within and across nations – including Europe and North America – to be put to work and, when they resisted, subjected to violent reprisals and even genocide.

One consequence was that the profits from those activities were utilized to accumulate vast amounts of capital, thus giving impulse to the emergence and development of capitalism. During the late-sixteenth to early-nineteenth centuries, the Triangular Trade system (illustrated in figure 7.1) that operated from Bristol, London, and Liverpool carried manufactured goods to West Africa, slaves to the Caribbean and North American colonies, and sugar, rum, and other commodities to the European colonial powers.[15] The resulting wealth was invested into both existing factories (in England) and new factories (in North America), thus promoting capitalist growth in the North.

[15] According to ongoing research on the trans-Atlantic and intra-American slave trade (https://slavevoyages.org/), an estimated 12.5 million slaves were transported from Africa to colonies in North and South America.

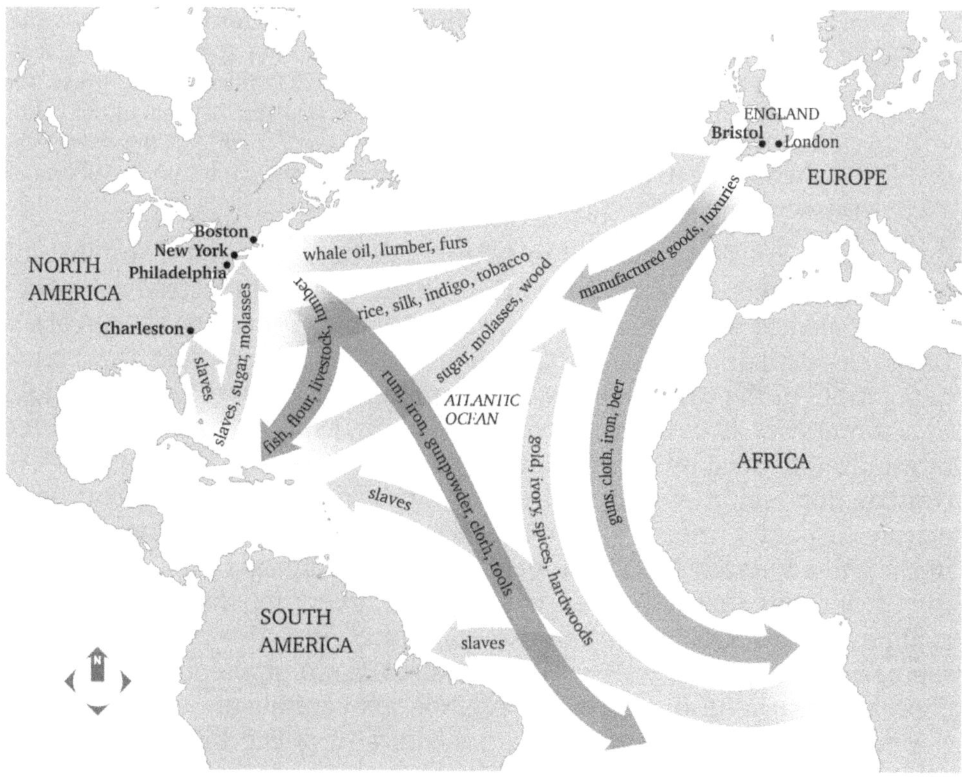

Figure 7.1 Triangular trade

Another outcome was the perpetuation of racist ideologies – spread through culture, codified in law, and reinforced by science – as "natural" differentiations that have persisted through the various forms and types of capitalism. They are always there, on or below the surface, to create and justify the inequalities created by capitalism. Racism has been invoked to explain why one group is at the top of the capitalist pyramid, and why there is such a hierarchy in the first place. It has also served to divide groups of workers from one another – different groups of native-born workers, one wave of immigrant workers as against earlier ones, workers predominant in one sector and denied entry to jobs in other sectors, the working-class of one country versus that of others, and so on. In fact, looking at the tensions between Irish and English workers, with a link to the US situation between Black and white workers, Marx wrote:

> Every industrial and commercial centre in England now possesses a working class divided into two *hostile* camps, English proletarians and Irish proletarians. The ordinary English worker hates the Irish worker as a competitor who lowers his standard of life. In relation to the Irish worker, he regards himself as a member of the *ruling* nation and consequently he becomes a tool of the English aristocrats and capitalists against Ireland, thus strengthening their domination *over himself*. He cherishes religious, social, and national prejudices

> against the Irish worker. His attitude towards him is much the same as that of the "poor whites" to the Negroes in the former slave states of the U.S.A. ...
>
> This antagonism is artificially kept alive and intensified by the press, the pulpit, the comic papers, in short by all the means at the disposal of the ruling classes. This *antagonism* is the secret of the *impotence of the English working class*, despite its organisation. It is the secret by which the capitalist maintains its power. And that class is fully aware of it.[16]

In recent decades, racial capitalism has been expanded to include other institutions and practices, including the "prison-industrial complex," police violence, and the commodification of racial identity. As Angela Y. Davis has explained, the spectacular growth of prisons and the prison population (in the United States, for example) reflects both the loss of jobs in communities abandoned by corporate flight, especially those populated by ethnic and racial minorities, and new possibilities for capitalist profit, in construction and provisioning, the use of prison labor, and the creation of private corporate prisons and contracts to run detention facilities.[17] Today, in the United States, Blacks are held in state prisons at a rate that is more than five times that of whites, while the incarceration rate for Hispanics is almost 50 percent more than that for whites. It is also the case that, by segregating people labeled as criminals, prisons simultaneously fortify and conceal the structural racism of contemporary capitalism.

Much the same holds for racist policing and police brutality. Initially created as slave patrols – to chase down, apprehend, and return to their owners runaway slaves and to provide a form of organized terror to deter slave revolts – police forces were subsequently involved in enforcing the racist Black Code, the Convict-Lease System, and Jim Crow segregation. Later, during the War on Drugs and the mass-incarceration movement of the 1980s, police surveillance and violence disproportionately affected Black and Hispanic, both native-born and immigrant, people. Thus, racial capitalism serves to identify the nexus between the racial ordering of society and the ongoing violence of capitalism.

A third example of contemporary racial capitalism stems from the legal and social preoccupation with the notion of diversity. As Nancy Leong has explained, predominantly white institutions are able to derive value from commodifying nonwhite racial identities, "thereby degrading that identity by reducing it to another thing to be bought and sold."[18] For example, a capitalist enterprise (say, a law firm) might seek to promote diversity, by increasing the nonwhite presence in the ranks of its employees. The result is, first, that the racial identity of the workers is commodified and, second, that the firm is able to extract more surplus-value because it is

---

[16] Marx to Sigfrid Meyer and August Vogt in New York (April 9, 1870), in Karl Marx and Friedrich Engels, *Selected Correspondence* (Moscow: Progress Publishers, 1975), p. 221.

[17] Angela Y. Davis, *Are Prisons Obsolete?* (Seven Stories Press: New York, 2003).

[18] Nancy Leong, "Racial Capitalism," *Harvard Law Review* 126 (June 2013): 2153–226.

able both to sell a racially diverse commodity and to expand the pool of potential employees and customers. On this view, racial capitalism and the commodification of racial identity are inextricably linked and mutually reinforcing. Racial capitalism has the effect of harming nonwhite people, since it creates pressure for them to engage in particular identity performances, thereby reinforcing inequality, and harming society as a whole, by impoverishing discourses around race, fostering racial resentment, and displacing potentially more effective measures to eliminate racism from society.

Today, the notion of intersectionality is a way of identifying and analyzing the ways class and race (as well as gender and other socially differentiated identities and experiences) overlap and constitute one another within capitalism. It serves both to unmask and to denaturalize the hierarchies of differentiation that make capitalist exploitation possible. It therefore occupies an important place in the Marxian critique of political economy.

Capitalism's Others

The existence of capitalism presumes the presence of other, noncapitalist ways of organizing economic and social life. That's because capitalism, according to Marx's critique of political economy, didn't always exist. Therefore, its various elements had to emerge within a noncapitalist setting. In Britain and Western Europe, that "primary accumulation of capital," as we will see in more detail in chapter 9, took place within feudalism.

What about today? While capitalism has been growing and spreading around the globe for the last two centuries, it certainly doesn't exist in isolation. Not even within countries – such as the United States or China or Brazil – that are generally referred to as capitalist. In fact, some have argued that capitalism is just the tip of the metaphorical iceberg, that below the water line many forms of noncapitalism exist and shape economic and social life (figure 7.2).

Those two issues – the origins of capitalism within noncapitalism, and the existence today of various forms of noncapitalism – simply don't arise within mainstream economics. In their theories and models, mainstream economists presume both that capitalism has always existed and that it is the only way most economies (save, perhaps, for "socialist" countries) are organized today.

One reason for this is that mainstream economists pay little if any attention to economic history in formulating their theories and models. They start with what they consider to be the "economic problem" of limited means and unlimited desires – which they assume is both transcultural and transhistorical – and then attempt to demonstrate that capitalism is the best, more efficient way of solving that problem. So, for

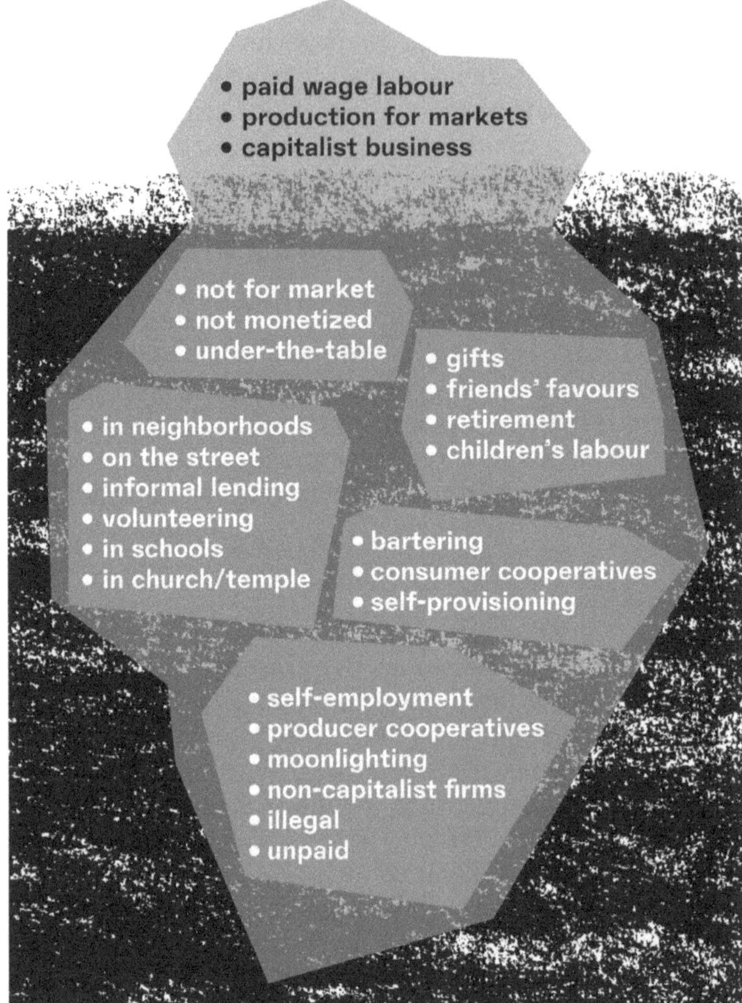

Figure 7.2 Capitalist and noncapitalist iceberg

Source: Diverse Economies Iceberg by Community Economies Collective

example, in the United States, no mention is made of the Native American economies that existed prior to colonization. Much the same is the case in the treatment of noncapitalist economies that preceded capitalism in Australia, France, Peru, and so on; they are all simply overlooked and play no substantive role in mainstream economic analysis.

Mainstream economists also forget about noncapitalist economies in analyses of contemporary economic and social life. They start with markets – characterized by supply and demand based on rational individual decisions and private property – without even a passing reference to other, noncapitalist economic behaviors and institutions. The only exception is government intervention in markets (such as rent-control measures and minimum wages), which neoclassical economists generally treat as both unwarranted and inimical to the desired policy objectives.[19]

The Marxian critique of political economy proceeds in a very different manner. First, Marx acknowledged – even more, he actively sought to analyze (in a famous section of the *Grundrisse*) – forms of economic and social life that preceded the emergence of capitalism.[20] There, his aim was to show how different capitalism was from noncapitalist forms of economic and social life (in their different approaches to property, labor, community, and so on), such that the emergence of capitalism, if and when it comes about, means that "pre-capitalist economic formations" had to have been disrupted and dissolved. In other words, the "relationship of labor to capital" is a relatively recent invention, a product of economic and social history, not its origin. Second, the Marxian approach is not – indeed, cannot be – based on the idea that capitalism today exhausts all the various ways economies and societies are or can be organized. Even if capitalism exhibits a tendency (one might describe it as a conceit or arrogance) to attempt to transform the entire world in its image, there are many different forms of property, labor, and community that do not follow the rules or logic of capitalism.

We have already seen some of them in this and previous chapters. For example, most households (whether of nuclear or extended families, constituted on the basis of marriages or comprising "unrelated" individuals) are not organized as capitalist enterprises or institutions. Yet, a great deal of labor and production does in fact take place within households. So, they represent an "economy," or a variety of different kinds of economy. But, for the most part, as illustrated in the economic iceberg of figure 7.2, they aren't organized on the basis of monetary exchange, wage-labor, or capitalist exploitation.

So, how do we make sense of those households? Marx and Marxian economists have developed a specific language to analyze the kinds of noncapitalist economies that are present within different households. Thus, for example, both historically and today, we would expect to find feudal households (in which the lord extracts surplus labor from the serfs who perform much of the labor), slave households (in which slave producers are owned, as human

---

[19] They are unwarranted because free markets, if left alone, produce better, more efficient outcomes. They are also inimical to well-intentioned attempts to create more just economic outcomes, because in the terms of mainstream economics they do exactly the opposite: rent control ends up limiting the supply of housing, while minimum wages destroy jobs.

[20] The section on "Forms Which Precede Capitalist Production" comprises pages 471–514 of the *Grundrisse*. It was published separately in 1952, as a pamphlet called *Formen die der kapitalistischen Produktion vorhergehen*, and then in English (supplemented by some extracts from *The German Ideology* and from the correspondence of Marx and Engels), in 1965, with an introduction by Hobsbawm. After the publication of *Capital*, Marx continued to conduct research on noncapitalist economies and societies, especially those associated with "primitive communism."

chattel, by the slaveowners), Ancient households (in which self-sufficient individuals carry out the necessary tasks), and communal households (in which the members of the household constitute a "commune" and collectively organize production activities). Even more, we would expect to see changes in the way households are organized over time – perhaps even "revolutionary" changes. Thus, for example, households that are organized in a feudal manner – in which the (often-male) lords extract feudal rent in the form of labor from (often-female) serfs – have come under intense pressure, emanating from both inside and outside those households. Over time, members of some of those households have created a different kind of economy – where there are neither lords nor serfs but, instead, a communal way of appropriating and distributing surplus labor.

But, of course, households are not the only domain of noncapitalist economy, even in places where we look through a conventional lens and see (only above that water line) capitalism taking place. Examples include barter exchanges (e.g., between neighbors), gift exchanges (as is often the case between friends and family members), slavery (especially in illegal activities, such as sex work), self-employment (in many artisanal trades), worker-owned cooperatives (the most famous example being the Mondragón Corporation in the Basque region of Spain), feudalism (where indentured workers are involved), retirement programs (like Social Security, where workers from older generations share in the surplus created by younger generations of workers), and so on.

These and many other examples of capitalism's others are of interest to Marxian economists for two reasons: First, they serve to challenge the idea that mainstream economics and capitalism, despite their ambitions, have colonized the entire world of ideas and institutions. Second, they are a reminder that the emergence of noncapitalist economies is, indeed, possible – especially as capitalism lurches from crisis to crisis and leaves masses of workers behind.

Globalization

Globalization is not a recent invention. It did not emerge in the 1970s or, for that matter, in the 1870s. Capitalism was marked by a globalizing tendency from the very beginning.

That was certainly the view expressed by Marx and Engels in one of the most famous passages of the *Communist Manifesto*:

> The need of a constantly expanding market for its products chases the bourgeoisie over the whole surface of the globe. It must nestle everywhere, settle everywhere, establish connexions everywhere.
>
> The bourgeoisie has through its exploitation of the world-market given a cosmopolitan character to production and consumption in every country …

> All old-established national industries have been destroyed or are daily being destroyed. They are dislodged by new industries, whose introduction becomes a life and death question for all civilised nations, by industries that no longer work up indigenous raw material, but raw material drawn from the remotest zones; industries whose products are consumed, not only at home, but in every quarter of the globe. (ME, 476)

While on the surface the conception of capitalist globalization in the Marxian critique of political economy appears to coincide with the views of mainstream economists, the differences could not be starker.

Within mainstream economics, globalization is analyzed in terms of efficiency. The classic case is international trade in goods and services (but much the same argument is made about flows of finance across national boundaries). According to mainstream economists, in models that date back to the work of Ricardo and continuing through the present, international trade allows countries to specialize in the production of commodities for which they have a relative cost advantage, and then to trade with countries that have other relative advantages.[21] The result is increased production and consumption, thus expanding global output and growth. That's why mainstream economists (and politicians and policymakers who have been persuaded by the arguments of mainstream economics) celebrate free international trade and support new free trade agreements (like GATT, the General Agreement on Tariffs and Trade, and NAFTA, the North American Free Trade Agreement) and institutions (such as the European Union and the World Trade Organization).[22]

How is the Marxian approach different? While they hold no nostalgia for national industries or modes of consumption, Marx and later Marxian economists start where mainstream economists leave off – with the issue of class. For them, it is not just globalization, but capitalist globalization. It is not nations pursuing global trade, but the bourgeoisie or capitalist class.

From a Marxian perspective, what mainstream economists overlook or refuse to understand is that, when international trade takes place, it has nothing to do with an individual in one country (say, the United States) buying a commodity (a scarf perhaps) from an individual in another country (say, China) as if they were just equal neighbors engaging in a mutually beneficial transaction. There are other economic processes involved. The consumers in the United States sell their ability to work to capitalist enterprises, and then use their wage or salary to purchase goods

---

[21] The key is that the benefits of international trade stem from relative or comparative, not absolute, advantages. Even a country that has an absolute advantage (or, for that matter, disadvantage) in the production of goods and services will benefit from specializing in the production of some commodities and then trading them for commodities produced in other countries.

[22] There are also liberal critics of free trade agreements within mainstream economics, who sometimes support domestic industries and argue in favor of protectionist policies.

and services, some of which are produced in other countries. Many of those same corporations have decided to produce goods in other countries, and thus to export jobs (in a process called outsourcing), while other corporations have decided to purchase the goods and services they sell either from their own subsidiaries in other countries or from corporations located in other countries. In those other countries, the workers are not deciding to sell their goods to consumers in the United States; the corporations they work for are making those decisions.

Simply put, international trade doesn't take place either between individual consumers and producers or between countries. International trade takes place between, and increasingly within, corporations located within different nations.[23] Capitalists therefore make the decisions about where and how commodities will (and will not) be produced, and where and how workers will (and will not) be employed. They also decide who benefits.

Both sets of decisions occur in a larger context, of course. Government regulations – for example, trade tariffs, tax regimes, laws governing labor unions, and so on – affect where corporate activities are located, how production is carried out, the level of wages, and the manner of distribution of the surplus. But the capitalists are the ones who, within those parameters, have the right to make those decisions – and, in addition, to affect the policies that are actually adopted by national governments and within international agreements.

Global capitalism has, of course, changed over the course of its history. At one time (especially in the nineteenth century), it meant industrialization in the Global North and deindustrialization in the mostly noncapitalist Global South (which was, in turn, transformed into a provider of raw materials, which became cheap commodity inputs into northern capitalist production). Later, especially after decolonization (following World War II), we saw the beginnings of capitalist development in the South (under the aegis of the state, with a set of policies economists often refer to as import-substitution industrialization); this involved a reindustrialization of the South (producing consumer goods that were previously imported) and a change in the kinds of industry prevalent in the North (which both exported consumer goods to the rest of the world, since, after the first Great Depression and World War II, they were once again growing, and often provided inputs into the production of consumer goods elsewhere). Later (especially from the 1970s onward), with the accumulation of capital in India, China, Brazil, and elsewhere, noncapitalist economies were

[23] International trade increasingly takes place inside giant multinational corporations, which move goods and services among their subsidiaries. Therefore, international trade is actually planned; it does not match the mainstream image of arm's-length transactions in free markets.

disrupted and millions of peasants and rural workers (and their children) were forced to have the freedom to sell their ability to work in urban factories and offices. As a result, their monetary incomes rose (which is not to say their conditions of life necessarily improved), which is reflected in the growing elephant-body of the global distribution of income (as seen with the hump representing the bottom 50 percent of the global population in the lower left of figure 7.3).

But global capitalism continues to be arranged and reconfigured both within and across countries to the benefit of a tiny group at the top. Thus, the top 1 percent across the globe continues to find itself in the position of capturing the surplus created by the world's workers, just as they did when capitalist globalization began. The only changes that have taken place are the following: (a) the number of workers who are involved in producing surplus-value (which has dramatically increased, especially in the Global South); (b) the geographical location of the members of the 1 percent (with many more now in India, China, Brazil, and elsewhere); and (c) the way the surplus is captured (either directly, from the production of capitalist commodities within the North and South, or indirectly, especially in the North, through finance, insurance, and other services).

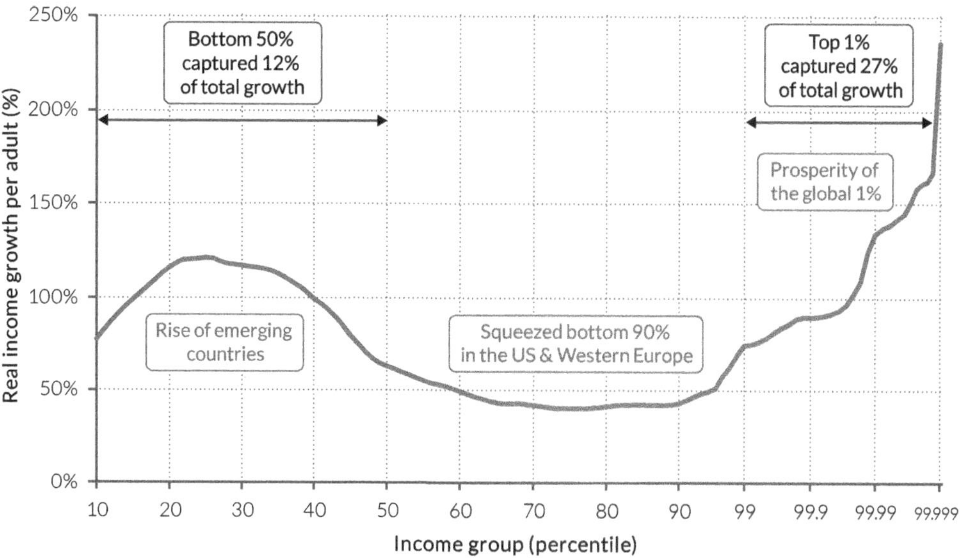

Source: WID.world (2017). See wir2018.wid.world for more details.

On the horizontal axis, the world population is divided into a hundred groups of equal population size and sorted in ascending order from left to right, according to each group's income level. The Top 1% group is divided into ten groups, the richest of these groups is also divided into ten groups, and the very top group is again divided into ten groups of equal population size. The vertical axis shows the total income growth of an average individual in each group between 1980 and 2016. For percentile group p99p99.1 (the poorest 10% among the world's richest 1%), growth was 74% between 1980 and 2016. The Top 1% captured 27% of total growth over this period. Income estimates account for differences in the cost offliving between countriesl Values are net offinflationl

Figure 7.3 Elephant curve of global inequality, 1980–2016

Source: WID.world (2017); see wir2018.wid.world for more details

According to the Marxian critique of political economy, the alternative is not, as some critics maintain, to protect or support certain national industries, which often privileges one nation's workers and pits them against workers in other countries. Instead, the goal is to imagine and create a different kind of globalization, one that is not governed by interests of the small group that is already at the top of the world's distribution of income and wealth.

Capitalocene

The debate about the world's ecological predicament is heating up and, as it turns out, the Marxian critique of political economy is at the center of that debate.

That's because capitalism, from the very beginning, has both relied on and altered the natural environment. Early on, it transformed both the way people live, crowding workers into large unsanitary urban centers, characterized by polluted air and inadequate water, with the result that people's health actually declined. Later, the extraction of enormous quantities of raw materials and the transition to industrialization based on fossil fuels led to further polluting of the natural environment around the world and a rise in carbon dioxide emissions that has set off a cascade of catastrophic effects we now recognize as global warming.

The other reason that the Marxian critique of political economy is relevant to the current debate about the natural environment is that it serves to challenge the particular bias that is built into mainstream economics – that institutions (such as corporations and markets) can be taken as given and the despoiling of the natural environment and the climate crisis can be solved by a go-slow path for cutting carbon dioxide. Hence, mainstream economists tend to focus on cap-and-trade markets (based on the idea that we should delay necessary transformations to create a low-carbon economy to avoid hurting the current high-carbon economy) and not fundamental changes in the institutions that have caused capitalism's environmental problems in the first place.

Both of those arguments have persuaded Marxian economists to insist that the proper name for the current geological age is not the Anthropocene, but rather the Capitalocene.

The term Capitalocene has two major advantages. First, it points to the ways capitalism – the particular tendencies and dynamics associated with the appropriation and distribution of surplus-value, the accumulation of capital, and much else – has made the despoiling of the natural environment central to the production and distribution of commodities and, at the same time, shifted its effects onto workers and poor people, who suffer from higher levels of air, water, and other kinds of pollution and the effects of global warming than anyone else. It therefore shifts the discussion from individuals or humanity in general to history and society, and therefore to the particular ways capitalism has transformed the way human beings affect (and, of course, are affected by) their natural environment. Second, it serves to recognize a longstanding literature criticizing the relationship between capitalism and the remaking of the natural environment – the rich tradition of attempts, sometimes referred to as green-red alliances or eco-socialism, to develop a relevant economic analysis and effective response to urban and rural pollution, the practices and paradigms of capitalist industry and agriculture, and the current climate crisis.[24]

And mainstream economists? When a small number of them first directed their attention to environmental issues, their work represented a challenge to the presumption of unlimited growth in mainstream economics. Now, however, as the threats posed by changes in the natural environment have actually become more ominous, mainstream economists have pushed back against prescriptive regulatory approaches in favor of more market-oriented policies. The idea behind tradable permits (which set a specific target or cap on total emissions and allocates or auctions the necessary number of pollution permits to polluters to meet that goal) and emission taxes (which provide incentives for polluters to find cost-effective solutions to emissions control) is to encourage corporations to choose to control greenhouse gas emissions.

From a Marxian perspective, one problem with the mainstream approach is that it ignores distributional issues, such as the effects of regressive carbon taxes, because carbon consumption increases less than in proportion to income.[25] Moreover, attempts to curb carbon use via the price mechanism leaves the control over the surplus in corporate hands. Therefore, capitalist corporations still have both the interest and the means to either tailor the permits and taxes or to avoid the policies altogether in order to maintain their ability to appropriate and keep as much of the surplus as possible. A third problem is that mainstream economists tend to cast the environment as scarce, as immutable or given. There are, they believe, only so many

[24] There is, in fact, a long line of eco-socialists, from William Morris in the late-nineteenth century and the members of the Proletkul't movement during the Soviet Revolution to Rudolf Bahro (the East German dissident), James O'Connor (who founded the journal *Capitalism, Nature, Socialism*), Joel Kovel (who cowrote with Michael Löwy *An Ecosocialist Manifesto* [2001] and the next year his famous book, *The Enemy of Nature: The End of Capitalism or the End of the World?* [2002]), Vandana Shiva (who writes about and fights for changes in agriculture and the production of food, in India, Bhutan, and elsewhere), John Bellamy Foster, Jason Moore, and many, many others.

[25] This is illustrated by the response of France's yellow-vest protestors in response to the proposal for an increase in gasoline taxes – that the government talked more about the end of the world and less about the end of the month.

resources. And there are immutable biological, chemical, and physical processes that govern nature. Therefore, we need to take them all as given, and protect them from society's growing needs, the very essence of scarcity.

What mainstream economists (and not a few of their liberal critics) do not want to think about is that each society – each way of organizing the economic dimensions of our lives, each way of arranging the production, consumption, and distribution of goods and services – has its own laws of resources, both human and nonhuman. Of workers and oil, of population as well as water. What that means is that changing institutions leads to a change in scarcity – of what is scarce, how it is scarce, what scarcity means, and so on. It is not a question of acknowledging and adapting to scarcity, as mainstream economists suggest we do, but of undoing existing forms of scarcity by changing the institutions whereby we treat resources – again, both human and nonhuman – as scarce. Instead of what? Instead of abundant, overflowing, unproductive, and so on.

A concrete example is the ongoing dispute over Monsanto's seed patents. Monsanto is creating a particular kind of scarcity, which is useful to its bottom line: a limited quantity of patented seeds and intellectual property. This stands opposed to the farmers who want to save and share seeds, and thus to treat nature as not scarce but abundant – as providing an ample supply of seeds and a proliferating variety of foods, and as the basis of livelihood for millions of farmers. Another example is the scarcity of land as private property for cattle ranchers in the Amazon rainforest, which is being created in a searing wave of fires and deforestation. The alternative is the abundance of forest products – such as latex, traditionally gathered through carefully scored rubber trees by communities of Brazilian rubber-tappers.[26] A third example is healthcare: in the United States, for example, it has been produced as a scarce good – created by a mostly private system of medical care, health insurance, and prescription drugs. The result is that many people, especially those at the bottom of the economic pyramid, are unable to enjoy decent, affordable healthcare, thus creating an accumulation of additional health problems, including reduced lifespans, for a large portion of the population.

Recognizing those historically and socially created scarcities is the start of a fundamentally different analysis of both the causes of pollution and global warming and of possible alternatives. It allows us to see capitalist corporations (and not individual consumers) as the source of environmental problems, and then envision new ways (alongside and outside the control

[26] *The Burning Season*, a 1994 film directed by John Frankenheimer, chronicles the fight by Chico Mendes (played by Raul Julia) – a member of a community of rubber-tappers, union organizer, and environmental activist – to oppose the despoiling of the Amazon rainforest by private corporations aided by the Brazilian government.

of those corporations) of organizing the production and consumption of goods and services.

Looking Ahead

These are just a few of the examples of ways the Marxian critique of political economy has been and can be used to analyze concrete problems in capitalist development. They serve to illustrate both the ways Marxian economic theory challenges the limits of mainstream economic theory and capitalism and provides a way of imagining and implementing alternative policies and institutions.

In the next chapter, we will see how many aspects of that Marxian critique have been discussed, debated, and further developed by the generations of economists and other thinkers that have worked in the tradition first established by Marx and Engels.

Suggested Readings

Drucilla Barker and Suzanne Bergeron, "Marxism, Feminism, and the Household," in *Routledge Handbook of Marxian Economics*, ed. David M. Brennan, David Kristjanson-Gural, Catherine P. Mulder, and Erik M. Olson, pp. 390–8 (New York: Routledge, 2017).

Brett Clark and Stefano B. Longo, "Marxism and Ecology," in *Routledge Handbook of Marxian Economics*, ed. David M. Brennan, David Kristjanson-Gural, Catherine P. Mulder, and Erik M. Olson, pp. 399–408 (New York: Routledge, 2017).

Zillah R. Eisenstein, *Capitalist Patriarchy and the Case for Socialist Feminism* (New York: Monthly Review Press, 1978).

Sut Jhally, *Capitalism Hits the Fan: Richard Wolff on the Economic Meltdown* (Northampton, MA: Media Education Foundation, 2009) [DVD].

Naomi Klein, *This Changes Everything: Capitalism vs. The Climate* (New York: Simon & Schuster, 2014).

Karl Marx, *Grundrisse*, trans. Martin Nicolaus (London: Penguin Books, 1973).

Jason W. Moore, ed., *Anthropocene or Capitalocene: Nature, History, and the Crisis of Capitalism* (Oakland, CA: PM Press, 2016).

Erik K. Olsen, "Production and Unproductive Labor," in *Routledge Handbook of Marxian Economics*, ed. David M. Brennan, David Kristjanson-Gural, Catherine P. Mulder, and Erik M. Olson, pp. 122–34 (New York: Routledge, 2017).

Cedric J. Robinson, *Black Marxism: The Making of the Black Radical Tradition* (Chapel Hill: University of North Carolina Press, 2000).

Eric Williams, *Capitalism and Slavery*, 3rd ed., intro. Colin A. Palmer, Foreword by William A. Darity (Chapel Hill: University of North Carolina Press, 2021).

Richard D. Wolff, "Marxian Class Analysis," in *Routledge Handbook of Marxian Economics*, ed. David M. Brennan, David Kristjanson-Gural, Catherine P. Mulder, and Erik M. Olson, pp. 29–41 (New York: Routledge, 2017).

Chapter 8

DEBATES IN AND AROUND MARXIAN ECONOMICS

We now have a good sense of the Marxian critique of political economy – where it came from, what its basic concepts and conclusions are, and how it can be put to use to analyze a series of important concrete issues. However, like all economic theories, Marxian economics also has a long tradition of discussions and debates. That's because the Marxian approach has been criticized by mainstream economists, forced to confront new questions and circumstances, and interpreted in different ways by successive generations of Marxian scholars.

In this chapter, we examine some of the key criticisms of Marxian economics by mainstream economists, focusing in particular on their rejection of the labor theory of value. We also look at some of the significant debates within the Marxian tradition, both inside and outside economics, and assess their contributions to contemporary Marxian economics. Along the way, we briefly explore the writings of some of the key historical figures (from Rudolf Hilferding, Rosa Luxemburg, and Vladimir Lenin to Maurice Dobb, Paul Baran, and André Gunder Frank) and some of the contemporary individuals and schools of thought (including Samir Amin, Richard Wolff and Stephen Resnick, and David Harvey and Monthly Review, Dependency Theory, and Analytical Marxism approaches).

Labor Theory of Value

The most appropriate place to start this chapter is with the key object of criticism by mainstream economists: the Marxian labor theory of value.

Let's remember that Marx adopted the labor theory of value because it was the basis of classical political economy, the mainstream economic theory of his time. That was his starting point, which he then criticized, revised, and extended in order to produce a particularly Marxian critique of political economy. The Marxian version of the labor theory of value then became the centerpiece of much of the theoretical and analytical work carried out by Marxian thinkers from then until now.

What has the Marxian theory of value made possible? As we have seen, it has served as the basis for a ruthless critique of both mainstream economic theory and capitalism – in terms of general theory, ethical implications, and concrete analysis. Thus, for example, Marx demonstrated that (a) the production of capitalist commodities is based on the appropriation of surplus-value, and thus the exploitation of workers; (b) capitalist exploitation violates the norms, summarized as "just deserts," of both mainstream economics and capitalism; and (c) the Marxian theory of value can be used to analyze a wide variety of specific issues, from capitalist crises to climate change, in a manner quite different from classical and contemporary mainstream economics.

It should come as no surprise, then, that mainstream economists have argued against and rejected the Marxian labor theory of value from the very beginning. Through the lens of their own theory of value, which we discussed at length in chapter 2, they don't see either the usefulness or validity of a Marxian class-based treatment of value. They have also been joined, for different reasons, by some nonmainstream economists from outside the Marxian tradition.

In the history of economic thought, there are two major criticisms of the Marxian labor theory of value. The first is that the Marxian approach is theoretically and empirically wrong, because the market prices of commodities do not correspond to labor values. Instead, according to mainstream (especially neoclassical) economists, the prices that are determined by supply and demand in markets do not, and cannot, reflect the amount of labor embodied in commodities during the course of production. The second criticism is that Marxian labor values are "redundant," and therefore not necessary to analyze capitalist commodity production and exchange. This is a view articulated by a group of nonmainstream, neo-Ricardian economists mostly associated with the work of Piero Sraffa.[1] Their argument is that it is possible to proceed directly from the "technical coefficients" of production to calculate commodity prices without ever referring to labor values. So, Marxian labor values are not so much wrong as, in their view, unnecessary.

Together, the two criticisms have been utilized to keep the Marxian critique of political economy out of most economics textbooks and courses, relegating it either to the history of economic thought (which,

[1] Piero Sraffa was a University of Cambridge economist who is best known for editing (with the assistance of Maurice Dobb) Ricardo's collected works, developing important criticisms of mainstream economics (including the assumption of perfect competition and, in *Production of Commodities by Means of Commodities*, the neoclassical theory of value), and for being a close friend of the Italian Marxist Antonio Gramsci (whose work we discuss below).

unfortunately, is rarely studied or taught these days) or to disciplines other than economics (such as sociology, anthropology, and cultural studies).[2] Marx (and, with him, Engels) was forced to respond to such criticisms, as have generations of Marxian economists since then.

In terms of the first criticism, Marx never claims that capitalist commodities necessarily exchange at prices that are equal to their labor values. Rather, the idea that exchange-values equal values is, as we saw, a simplifying assumption utilized in volume 1 of *Capital* that Marx demonstrates simply cannot hold in the analysis contained in volume 3 of *Capital*, where commodity prices do not and cannot equal their values.

The simplifying assumption in volume 1 was introduced for two reasons: to give mainstream economists their best possible case (that capitalism is based on equal exchange) and to focus on the process of capitalist production (and defer, until the next two volumes, an investigation into the processes of and complications introduced by capitalist circulation). Then, in volume 3 of *Capital*, Marx shows that the prices of capitalist commodities generally won't be equal to the amount of value embodied in them during the course of production. That's because, in the later analysis, Marx introduces another aspect of mainstream economists' notion of capitalist production – that capital will flow to sectors with higher profits and, after all is said and done, the profit rate will be equalized across the economy as a whole. Once that happens, once the free mobility of capital is introduced and each capitalist receives surplus-value according to the average rate of profit, commodity prices cannot in general equal their production values. These are called prices of production, the form that exchange-value takes when capital is mobile and every capitalist receives the general rate of profit.

A simple numerical example shows this. Consider an economy that comprises two units of capital (or two capitalist industries), each with the following structure of values (where all the symbols – c, v, s, and W – are defined as before):

8.1

		PROFIT
K1	$30c + 5v + 10s = 45W$	10
K2	$40c + 5v + 10s = \underline{55}W$	$\underline{10}$
	$100W$	20

Capitalist one produces commodities that embody 30 units of constant capital (c), 5 units of variable capital (v), and 10 units of surplus-value

[2] A third criticism was later formulated by the members of the short-lived school of Analytical Marxism, which included G. A. Cohen, Jon Elster, and John Roemer. They considered the Marxian labor theory of value to be metaphysical, irrelevant, and inconsistent, and opted instead to use the tools of mainstream economics to analyze issues like exploitation (which they defined not in terms of surplus labor, but as an issue of property ownership, understood as the difference between the initial and final endowments of economic actors).

(*s*), while for the other capitalist the commodities embody 40 units of constant capital, 5 units of variable capital, and 10 units of surplus-value (all measured in hours of socially necessary abstract labor).

The rate of profit for the first capitalist is thus $\rho = s/(c + v) = 10/35 = 29\%$, while for the second capitalist it is $\rho = 10/45 = 22\%$. The average rate of profit is therefore $\rho = 20/80 = 25\%$.

The price of production, *PoP*, is such that each unit of capital receives the average rate of profit on their capital, or $PoP = (1 + \rho)(c + v)$.

8.2

		PROFIT
K1	(1.25) (30*c* + 5*v*) = 43.75*PoP*	8.75
K2	(1.25) (40*c* + 5*v*) = 56.25*PoP*	11.25
	100.00*PoP*	20.00

The first capitalist produces commodities that sell for 43.75 (which is less than their embodied value of 45), while the other capitalist has commodities that enter the market with a price of 56.25 (which is greater than the embodied value of 55). Thus, if commodities exchange at their prices of production, each capitalist will receive the average rate of profit and individual commodity prices will not equal their values. But two key aggregate equalities remain: the total amount of value (100*W*) continues to equal the sum of prices (100*PoP*) and the total surplus-value (20*s*) is equal to the sum of profits (20). Problem solved![3]

As for the second criticism, it is indeed possible to go from the technical coefficients of production (what are often referred to as input–output coefficients) to prices of production, without calculating the values of capitalist commodities. But then all of the analysis associated with those production values – the difference between labor and labor power, the appropriation of surplus-value and exploitation, the various distributions of surplus-value, and much else – would be overlooked or ignored.

In general terms, then, what we have are different accounting systems, which is what different theories of economic value are all about. The Marxian critique of political economy involves an accounting system in

[3] In a more advanced treatment, we would also have to transform the input values into prices of production. There is, in fact, a longstanding debate about the so-called Transformation Problem – the transformation of values into prices of production in Marx's critique of political economy – with many different definitions of and solutions to the problem. Participants in that debate include Anwar Shaikh ("Marx's Theory of Value and the 'Transformation Problem'," in *The Subtle Anatomy of Capitalism*, ed. Jesse Schwartz, pp. 106–37 [Santa Monica, CA: Goodyear, 1977]), Richard Wolff, Antonio Callari, and Bruce Roberts ("A Marxian Alternative to the Traditional 'Transformation Problem'," *Review of Radical Political Economics* 16 [1984]: 115–35), Alan Freeman ("The Logic of the Transformation Problem," in *Ricardo, Marx, Sraffa*, ed. Ernest Mandel and Alan Freeman, pp. 221–64 [London: Verso, 1984]), Fred Moseley "Recent Interpretations of the 'Transformation Problem'," *Rethinking Marxism* 23 [2011]: 186–97), and Andrew Kliman (*Reclaiming Marx's "Capital"* [New York: Lexington Books, 2007]).

which two numbers, not one, are attached to each and every capitalist commodity: value in production and the form of value in exchange. In volume 1 of *Capital*, Marx assumes that the amount of labor embodied in the commodity during the course of production is the amount for which the commodity is exchanged in markets. Then, in volume 3, Marx relinquishes that restrictive assumption and demonstrates that, with the free mobility of capital, the new form of exchange-value, the price of production, is such that individual commodity prices will *not* be equal to their values.

That's not an inconsistency or mistake but one of the hallmarks of the Marxian critique of political economy. The Marxian labor theory of value serves, at the different levels of abstraction captured in volumes 1 and 3 of *Capital*, to explain the source of the value and surplus-value that are realized through the sale of capitalist commodities. In both cases, the two aggregate quantities hold: the sum of values is equal to the sum of exchange-values and the total surplus-value is equal to total profits. Moreover, the two numbers attached to the commodity – value and exchange-value – reveal the different but interacting dynamics of production and exchange under capitalism.

Monopolistic Finance Capital and Imperialism

Karl Kautsky, Rudolf Hilferding, Rosa Luxemburg, Vladimir Lenin, Nikolai Bukharin, Leon Trotsky. Their names don't appear in mainstream economics textbooks, nor are their writings discussed in most economics courses. However, they are among the most important contributors to the discussions and debates that took place after Marx's death, in the late-nineteenth and early-twentieth centuries. They interpreted and endorsed the Marxian critique of political economy against those who sought to deny its validity and relevance, and then pushed that critique forward to analyze new developments within capitalism around the turn of the century. Their work was then further discussed and debated as the influence of Marxian ideas grew within the burgeoning socialist movements in Germany and Russia as well as in the rest of Western Europe.

Kautsky and Hilferding, in particular, defended the terms of Marx's theoretical work against its critics.[4] They also challenged the view promulgated by mainstream economists both that capitalism was characterized by perfect competition and free trade (domestically as well as internationally)

[4] Kautsky offered his interpretation and defense of Marx's critique of political economy, *The Economic Doctrines of Karl Marx*, in 1887; later (between 1905 and 1910) he published, at Engels's request, a first edited version of Marx's three-volume work *Theories of Surplus-Value*. Hilferding, who was one of Kautsky's closest friends and collaborators, wrote a review of one of the first full-scale mainstream attacks on Marx's critique of political economy, Eugen von Böhm-Bawerk's *Karl Marx and the Close of His System*, defending Marx's theory against Böhm-Bawerk's criticism.

and that more trade would result in social harmony and peace (again, domestically and internationally). They observed something quite different: a close connection among recurring capitalist crises, the concentration and centralization of capital, and aggressive overseas expansionism in a search for new markets and investment opportunities. The result was an extension of Marx's critique of political economy and the first steps toward the creation of a theory of what Kautsky and Hilferding considered to be a new form of capitalism: "monopolistic finance capital."

For mainstream economists, capitalism is a timeless system, characterized by the same laws in different times and places. The only exception is the extent to which capitalism operates with market imperfections or government intervention. Marxian economists generally take a different approach, looking for and analyzing changes in the forms or stages of capitalist development. For Kautsky and Hilferding, the main idea was that, beginning in the late-nineteenth century, industrial capitalists in the North were forming giant cartels, aided by the growth of banks and the expansion of bank credit, and that these large joint-stock companies endeavored to overcome capitalism's periodic crises and expand their profits by supporting protectionist measures at home and exporting capital to and searching for new markets in other countries. This new "dictatorship" of capitalists thus stood over and was opposed to the working-classes in their own countries (culminating in waves of trade union organizing and strikes) and to the interests of capitalists abroad (creating international rivalries and the possibility of all-out war). Hilferding's *Finance Capital: A Study of the Latest Phase of Capitalist Development* (published in 1910), in particular, was heralded at the time as the fourth volume of Marx's *Capital*, both the extension and completion of the project contained in the original volumes. Together with Kautsky's writings, it set the agenda for much theoretical and political discussion and further work in Marxian economics in the early decades of the twentieth century.

Rosa Luxemburg, for example, in her book *The Accumulation of Capital* (published in 1913), expressed the view that Marx (in his discussion of expanded reproduction) had downplayed the problem of "underconsumption": "the realisation of the surplus value for the purposes of accumulation is an impossible task for a society which consists solely of workers and capitalists" (p. 350). Therefore, she concluded, the accumulation of capital could only continue by capitalists' conquering new markets, outside of capitalism – selling both consumer goods and means of production to noncapitalist buyers both within Europe (such as peasants and small artisans within urban areas) and to countries where capitalism didn't yet exist (e.g., in India, the Americas, Africa, and so on). A key tool to open up such "external" markets was credit, which provided consumers in noncapitalist environments with purchasing power. However, these new markets would then be transformed into "internal" markets, which means the problem of capitalist underconsumption might be forestalled for a time but never finally eliminated. The result, according to Luxemburg, was the exact opposite of what mainstream economists at the time argued: an imperialist phase of capitalist accumulation that involved, among other things, the creation of commodity markets where they didn't already exist, a rise in capitalist industry that destroyed noncapitalist economies, and increasingly lawless and violent campaigns both against the noncapitalist world and among the competing capitalist countries.

The Russian Marxist Nikolai Bukharin also joined the debate, with his *Imperialism and World Economy* (written in 1915 but only published in 1917). As the title of his book suggests, Bukharin argued that capitalism had become a world economy, with the widening and deepening of markets in commodities (consumer goods, means of production, and raw materials) and money capital around the globe, characterized by an organized system of international banks, syndicates, cartels, and trusts allied at the same time to different national governments. The export of capital was not, as Luxemburg argued, a solution to the problem of underconsumption; instead, monopoly enterprises, backed by the state, exported capital in search of higher rates of profit in foreign countries. According to Bukharin, these different "national capitalisms," under the aegis of finance capital, would enter into imperialist rivalries in an attempt both to protect their own markets and to subjugate countries outside the industrialized North. His conclusion was that "Under such conditions there inevitably arises a conflict, which, given the existence of capitalism, is settled through extending the state frontiers in bloody struggles, a settlement which holds the prospect of new and more grandiose conflicts" (p. 106).

All these various elements were eventually assembled by the Russian Bolshevik leader Vladimir Lenin in his pamphlet, *Imperialism, the Highest State of Capitalism* (which was written in 1916 and also published in 1917).[5] His goal was to demonstrate that World War I was an imperialist war on the part of both sides – "a war for the division of the world, for the partition and repartition of colonies and spheres of influence of finance capital, etc." (p. 9) – and not merely an exception to otherwise peaceful capitalist development. Lenin noted, in particular, that non-Marxian economists' arguments that raw materials "could be" obtained in the open market, without "costly and dangerous" colonial policies, ignored the growth of monopolies and finance capital and their attempts to divide up the world.[6]

[5] Lenin also borrowed heavily from *Imperialism: A Study* (1902), by the English non-Marxian economist John A. Hobson. Lenin devoted considerable space to denouncing the changed views of both Kautsky and Hilferding (and other leaders of the so-called Second International, the organization of socialist and labor parties that was formed in 1889 and eventually dissolved in 1920), who argued that militarism and war were *not* in the interests of the capitalist class as a whole, but only of a small group of arms producers.

[6] Mainstream economists, pundits, and politicians make similar arguments denying the

Therefore, he concluded, "imperialism is the monopoly stage of capitalism" (p. 88). This in turn served to transform the nature of capitalism within the richest or most powerful nations: to allow them to "bribe" a section of the working-class with higher wages and to increase capitalists' reliance less on domestically produced surplus-value and more on flows of distributed surplus-value derived from capital exports.

Finally, Leon Trotsky (1879–1940), with his notion of "uneven and combined development," challenged both mainstream economists' presumption of a market-driven convergence of nations within global capitalism as well as some Marxists' notion that all nations would follow the same, linear scheme of capitalist development. Trotsky (as early as 1905, and then increasingly in the 1920s, with an eye on Russia) argued that, historically and perhaps especially with capitalist imperialism, nations would develop in a "planless, complex, combined" manner.[7] Thus, for example, with the spread of capitalism around the world, nations would not necessarily follow the path of England, Germany, and other nations where capitalism first developed; instead, they would develop unevenly (perhaps skipping over stages that other nations had followed) and in a way that combined different stages (leading to various permutations of capitalist and noncapitalist forms of economic and social life).

These diverse contributions to the project of interpreting, applying, and updating the Marxian critique of political economy were situated in the specific economic and political debates of their time. However, all of the elements were taken up – often utilized, sometimes challenged and discarded – by later generations of Marxist scholars.

We examine some of those later discussions below. But first, we need to look at another area of Marxian economics that was provoked by the spread of Marxian ideas within the flourishing left-wing European movements around the turn of the century and, then, the 1917 October Revolution in Russia: the economics of socialism.

Socialist Economics

The first third of the twentieth century witnessed two great debates concerning the possibilities and problems of creating a socialist economy. One took place in the new Soviet Union, in the midst of the Bolsheviks'

existence of imperialism every time a country is invaded by one of the great powers, such as was the case with oil and the US-led invasion of Iraq in 2003.

[7] Trotsky's theory of combined and uneven development was most consistently presented in his two-volume *The History of the Russian Revolution* (initially written while he was in exile in Turkey in 1929 and first published in Germany in 1930, translated and published in English in 1932, and, given his expulsion from the Soviet Union by Stalin, only published in Russia in 1997).

attempt to transform the existing tsarist economy into a socialist one. The other, the so-called Calculation Debate, was at first narrowly focused on the possibility of socialist planning but then took on wider significance, during the first Great Depression, when the participants were forced to consider the widespread failure of capitalist markets.

Socialism in Russia

The key to understanding the first debate is the idea, widely shared among Russian Marxists, that socialism represented not a separate economic system, but instead a transitional period, a way of moving from capitalism to communism. Moreover, as Lenin regularly chastised some of his fellow revolutionaries, neither Marx nor Engels had offered a blueprint for socialism and had written little about Russia. In fact, some European Marxists viewed Russia as the backward stepchild of Europe, and thus would be one of the last countries to have a socialist revolution. But Lenin and the Bolsheviks saw in Russia the desperate need, as well as the potential, for socialism. Moreover, as we saw in the previous section, Marxian economists argued the world had changed considerably since Marx's time, especially with the development of monopolistic finance capital and imperialism.

Lenin and the Bolsheviks thus faced a new question: how was this new socialist economy and society to be created? They inherited a mostly noncapitalist environment (with few capitalists and wage-laborers, most of the rest of the population being feudal landlords and various strata of peasants), an economy in shambles as a result of years of fighting during World War I, and determined opposition by large landowners and capitalists and an external invasion by the Allied powers. The initial plan was to nationalize most of the existing industries, to form a militarized army of workers, and to create collective farms in the countryside with the twin goals of boosting production and keeping the new "workers government" in power – a strategy that came to be referred to as "war communism."

While the Bolsheviks retained control and the imperialist intervention was eventually defeated, Russia remained in deep economic trouble and peasant opposition was increasing by late 1920. Lenin, the head of the Soviet government, formulated a new set of measures – the New Economic Policy – to stimulate agricultural and industrial production, yield more consumer goods, and revive the flagging trade between urban and rural areas. This involved supporting the formation of agricultural cooperatives and allowing peasants (after a "tax in kind") to keep a larger share of what they produced, encouraging more private trade, allowing a limited degree of foreign investment in joint ventures, and accepting the use of "bourgeois experts" (such as engineers and economists) in organizing and running the factories.

Along the way, the strategies and shifts in policy for constructing socialism in Russia were vigorously discussed and debated. Lenin, for example, went from focusing on what he considered to be the relatively simple project of taking over the "accounting and control" of the Russia economy (in 1917, in *The State and Revolution*) to accepting the existence of capitalism and attempting to channel it into state capitalism (in 1921, in *The Tax in Kind*). Bukharin, too, accepted that Soviet economic policy needed to respond to changed circumstances; while the long-term goal remained state ownership and the elimination of markets, he moved from a first model of direct state administration of the economy (as explained in his *The Economics of the Transformation Period*, in 1920) to a second model, which combined state industry and cooperative agriculture. While Bukharin viewed success in both cases as depending on the internally generated surplus of the state sector (and the maintenance of the class alliance, the *smychka*, between workers and capitalists), Evgeny Preobrazhensky argued for squeezing the noncapitalist peasant sector (as well as enforcing a strict state monopoly over foreign trade) to support a strategy of "primitive socialist accumulation."[8]

It should come as no surprise that Lenin's abrupt shift to an economic strategy that included "a free market and capitalism, both subject to state control," occasioned opposition from both the Left and the Right: Trotsky, for example, supported by radical members of the Communist Party, believed that socialism in Russia would only survive if the state controlled the allocation of all output. The other side, mostly socialists outside the Soviet Union (such as Eduard Bernstein, a leader of the Social Democratic Party of Germany), viewed the dire problems in Russia's economy as proving that creating socialism in Russia was premature; only after capitalism was fully developed, around the world, should socialism even be considered.

Finally, in 1928, in the wake of Lenin's death (in 1924) and after seven years' experience with the New Economic Policy, Lenin's successor, Josef Stalin, put an end to the debate about socialist economics. He and his allies brutally eliminated all opposition (including Preobrazhensky, Bukharin, and Trotsky) through purges and executions, and pushed to nationalize much of the economy, to forcibly collectivize agriculture, and introduce the first Soviet Five-Year Plan.

Socialist Calculation

In the meantime, haunted by the specter of the Soviet Union but distant from the actual problems of creating a socialist economy for the first time, a second debate broke out. The so-called socialist calculation debate took

[8] The next chapter includes an extensive discussion of Marx's analysis of the related idea of the emergence of capitalism in a noncapitalist context, the so-called "primitive accumulation of capital."

place mostly among mainstream economists – circumscribed by and, as time went on, testing the limits of their theory.

The general background of the debate was the break within mainstream economics in the last third of the nineteenth century, by neoclassical economists from classical political economy. The new mainstream economists (as we saw in chapter 2) redefined economics as a universal science that involved the study of the optimal allocation of scarce resources among alternative uses based on decisions made by rational, self-interested individuals. Their fundamental argument was that a capitalist economy, based on free markets and private property, is characterized by a self-regulating mechanism that guarantees an efficient allocation of resources.

However, starting in 1920, after the October Revolution and the German and Austrian revolutions of 1918–19, and the general rise in popularity of Marxist ideas, they turned their attention to a different issue: was socialist planning possible? What they meant was, could a nonmarket system guided by a central planning board replicate the presumed allocative efficiency of capitalism?

The Austrian economist Ludwig von Mises launched the first salvo in the debate, answering with an unqualified "no." Assuming that in capitalist markets economic agents are price-takers, von Mises emphasized the crucial role of prices in providing the information necessary in order to achieve a rational allocation of resources. Accordingly, it is only because of the existence of market prices that the law of supply and demand turns into a self-adjusting mechanism, spontaneously driving a market economy to an efficient equilibrium. A socialist economy, von Mises argued, was lacking private ownership of the factors of production and a free banking system, such that money prices would cease to play their informational role. Therefore, rational economic calculation was impossible, and any socialist system was necessarily inefficient.

Fred Taylor, the president of the American Economic Association, came up with a very different answer – that of market socialism. According to Taylor, a socialist economy in which the state guaranteed a certain minimum income to each citizen and authorized those citizens to spend their income as they saw fit, could, through a process of trial and error (changing prices to eliminate shortages and surpluses), replicate the results of von Mises's model of a capitalist economy.

With the outbreak of the first Great Depression in 1929, the socialist calculation debate assumed even more theoretical and political urgency – as capitalism across the world was on the brink of collapse and socialist ideas were spreading. While von Mises, and then Friedrich von Hayek and Lionel Robbins, continued to challenge the possibility of rational socialist planning – initially on theoretical grounds, then in terms of practical problems (such as collecting and processing all the necessary information) – other mainstream economists responded with a variety of models of market socialism.

Perhaps the most influential response and proposal within the terms of mainstream economics were formulated by Oskar Lange. His view was that the central planning board of a socialist economy could, at least in theory, perform "the functions of the market":

> It establishes the rules for combining factors of production and choosing the scale of output of a plant, for determining the output of an industry, for the allocation of resources, and for the parametric use of prices in accounting. Finally, it fixes the prices so as to balance the quantity supplied and demanded of each commodity. It follows that a substitution of planning for the functions of the market is quite possible and workable.[9]

Lange even turned the tables on the opponents of socialist calculation: not only could rational calculation work in a socialist economy; it would, or at least could, work "much better" than under capitalism. That's because a central planning board would be better able than markets alone to account for externalities (by setting the prices of natural resources), to preempt the negative effects of monopolies (by setting prices equal to marginal costs), and to avoid cyclical instability (because the state would control the level and rate of savings and investment).

The sprawling debate about socialist economic calculation took place mostly within the terms of neoclassical economics. The major exception was the contribution of the British Marxist economist Maurice Dobb, who argued that the participants in the existing debate made the mistake of ignoring the fundamental changes in institutions – such as a "change of property-rights and of class relationships" – under socialism.[10] In fact, Dobb argued, a free-market system was unable to regulate the production of consumer goods and capital goods, while socialist planners were capable both of deciding the appropriate rate of capital accumulation and of eliminating the kinds of recurring economic crises that are the products of private decision-making within capitalism. Therefore, it was the impossibility of *capitalist* economic calculation, not that of socialism, that should be of concern to economists – and attention should then be turned to analyzing the concrete challenges posed by the organization of a socialist economy.

Imperialism and Underdevelopment

After World War II (between 1945 and 1960), three dozen new states in Asia and Africa achieved autonomy or outright independence from their European colonial rulers, joining many Latin American countries that

[9] Oskar Lange, "On the Economic Theory of Socialism: Part One," *Review of Economic Studies* 4 (October 1936): 64.

[10] Maurice Dobb, "Economic Theory and the Problems of a Socialist Economy," *Economic Journal* 43 (December 1933): 588.

had achieved their independence in the early-nineteenth century. All of them confronted not only the economic and social legacies of colonial domination, but also the decline in world trade occasioned by the first Great Depression and World War II. In the midst of decolonization and the Allies' plan to restructure global capitalism, socialism and communism were attractive alternatives not only to Marxian economists and political activists in the North, but to many of the national liberation movements in the Global South.

Within mainstream economics, that period saw the beginning of modernization theory – a determined effort, on the part of academics (including, and perhaps especially, mainstream economists) and policymakers in the United States and Western Europe, to showcase capitalist development and make the economic and social changes necessary in the West's former colonies to initiate the transition to modern economic growth.[11] Reflecting the rise of Keynesian economics, the presumption was that government intervention was required to disrupt the economic and social institutions of so-called traditional societies, in order to chart a path through the necessary steps to shift the balance from agriculture to industry, create national markets, build the appropriate physical and social infrastructure, generate a domestic capitalist class, and eventually raise the level of investment to increase productivity in both rural and urban areas.[12]

Marxian economists saw the problem in a radically different manner. They engaged in extensive discussions and debates about the lingering effects of colonialism, the ongoing consequences of new forms of imperialism, and the prospects for development in the Third World. Previous generations of Marxists had presumed that colonialism and imperialism would destroy the existing noncapitalist economies and ways of life and initiate, if only through violent means, a process of capitalist development that followed the pattern that had already taken place in the North. What was new in the postwar debate was the idea that, as a result of colonialism and imperialism, the economies and societies of the South had been distorted and deformed to meet the needs of capitalist development elsewhere. The result was the "development of underdevelopment" in the vast periphery of global capitalism.

---

[11] At the same time, the Western powers attempted to reconstruct the global institutions of capitalism, through the triumvirate of the World Bank, the International Monetary Fund, and the General Agreement on Tariffs and Trade (predecessor to the World Trade Organization) that was initially hammered out in 1944 in the Bretton-Woods Agreement.

[12] That was the time of the big push, unbalanced growth, and import-substitution industrialization. Only later, during the 1980s, was development economics transformed by a successful pushback from the neoclassical wing of mainstream economics and free-market policymakers. The new orthodoxy, often referred to as the Washington Consensus, focused on privatizing public enterprises, eliminating government regulations, and the freeing-up of trade and capital flows.

Paul Baran was one of the first to challenge the traditional Marxian theories of imperialism, arguing that development outside the metropolitan capitalist countries (such as Western Europe, the United States, and Japan) had been rendered impossible.[13] Therefore, it was necessary for postcolonial countries to break with capitalism and initiate a process of socialist development.[14] According to Baran's theory of underdevelopment (initially presented in "On the Political Economy of Backwardness," in 1952, and then further elaborated in *The Political Economy of Growth*, in 1957), while there may have been a few colonies and dependencies where the populations profited from the inflow of foreign capital, "exploitation and stagnation" were the rule for most of the world outside the capitalist center. In other words, poverty and inequality in the periphery were caused by external forces and not (as assumed by mainstream economists) the result of some original or internally generated condition of the "backward," less-developed or underdeveloped, areas of the globe.

In the first instance, according to Baran, colonialism and imperialism involved siphoning off the extra or surplus product from areas in the capitalist periphery (such as India) and transferring it to the center (e.g., England).[15] The effect was to promote development in countries where capitalism already existed, and to undermine the possibility of capitalist development elsewhere. Then, in the second instance (e.g., after independence), underdevelopment continued to be reproduced because the surplus that existed either continued to flow from the periphery to the capitalist core (e.g., as repatriated profits on foreign investments) or was channeled into wasteful expenditures within the periphery (in the form of luxury consumption of, and military protection for, the ruling-classes). The only possibility that remained open for the Third World was to break from global capitalism and harness the economic surplus for eliminating poverty and promoting more equitable growth through socialist development.

Three examples serve to illustrate key points of the wide-ranging debate initiated by Baran's theory of underdevelopment: Dependency Theory as

[13] Baran was one of the only Marxist academics to survive the anticommunist witch-hunts of the McCarthy period. He managed to keep his job at Stanford University (although he was forced to teach at odd times, such as very early in the morning, to make his courses less attractive to students) and, at the time of his death in 1964, he was the only tenured Marxian economist in the United States.

[14] Initially, Marxian economists (including Baran) praised the swift industrialization that took place in the Soviet Union following World War II. Later, after they criticized the Stalinist approach to socialist development, they took inspiration from other socialist revolutions (in China, Cuba, and elsewhere).

[15] Baran's notion of the "economic surplus" is defined as the amount of output or income above what is consumed by most people (e.g., in the form of food, clothing, housing, and education) and is captured by the ruling-classes. In other words, it is the amount of savings or income left over after basic consumption. It is therefore related to but different from Marx's concepts of surplus labor and surplus-value.

formulated by André Gunder Frank, the Modes of Production school, and the theory of "accumulation on a world scale" by Samir Amin.

Frank, who was originally trained as a mainstream economist (working with Milton Friedman at the University of Chicago) later rejected central points of the mainstream approach to development and formulated what came to be called Dependency Theory. The so-called developing nations, Frank suggested, should be considered as *under*developed rather than *un*developed in order to distinguish stages of development historically produced from those that can be considered "original" conditions. The underdeveloped nations participated in a relation of dependency with the various countries of the developed world. Historically, the relationship was between a colony and the imperial power that conquered it. Later, it was more a matter of an underdeveloped country and those developed countries with which it had primary economic relations. Various names were given to the parties to these relationships, such as metropolis/satellite and center/periphery.

The metropolis/satellite relationship, to use the terms preferred by Frank, is one of dependency because of two features. First, the development of the satellite is dependent on the metropolis, that is, on forces external to the satellite's economy and society. This is an asymmetrical relationship, with the development of the metropolis being for the most part independent, that is, determined by factors largely internal to the metropolitan economy and society. The loss for the underdeveloped nation is twofold. Not only is it not in control of its own development; it does not materially benefit from the relation of dependency.[16] According to Frank, dependency relations in general and metropolis/satellite relations within global capitalism in particular are best characterized as monopolistic and extractive. The metropolis exerts monopolistic control over economic relations in the periphery. This position of power allows the metropolis to extract an economic surplus from the satellite. The appropriation of this surplus and its accumulation under the control of the metropolis was the central factor that deprived the underdeveloped nation of the ability to control its own growth, which leaves it dependent. In other words, where mainstream economists saw free markets and mutual advantage in international economic relations, Frank and other dependency theorists saw a structure of monopolistic relations and surplus transfer.

The debate concerning Dependency Theory entered a new stage with the emergence of the Modes of Production school.[17] The focus of the

[16] It is worth pointing out that the object of benefit or harm for Frank is the nation-state as such, rather than, for instance, classes within nations. Frank does discuss the fact that certain classes, local ruling-classes, can and do benefit, in the short term at least, from underdevelopment, but this benefit is understood against the backdrop of the harm done to the nation as a whole.

[17] The Modes of Production approach comprises the contributions of many different

explanation of the persistence of underdevelopment is shifted by the Modes of Production theorists away from what they understood to be the excessive emphasis in traditional Dependency Theory on a global scheme that exaggerates the role of external relations and markets. Instead, while not denying the importance of global phenomena, relations between nations, and flows of commodities and capital, they focused on developing and utilizing the concept of modes of production to construct an alternative understanding of underdevelopment.

The various efforts to construct a theory of modes of production grew out of a reaction against Frank's seeing "capitalism everywhere," that is, that commodity flows or markets were present and such markets were sufficient to characterize the economies in question as capitalist. (It also represented a rejection of the then-standard, traditional Marxist idea of a unilinear path of economic and social development, from noncapitalism to capitalism.) Instead, they used the concept of modes of production (which they defined as a combination of four factors – the pattern of ownership of the means of production, the form of appropriation of the economic surplus, the degree of the division of labor, and the level of development of the technologies of production) to analyze the "articulations" among and between the various capitalist and noncapitalist modes of production. The central focus was the system of relations between the capitalist mode of production and the set of noncapitalist modes of production in the countries of the Global South.

In their view, it was important to distinguish three distinct and successive stages of articulation. In the first stage, the capitalist mode of production is "imported" into the noncapitalist peripheral society and proceeds to *reinforce* and, in some instances, to *create* noncapitalist modes of production – such as when capitalists are able to rely on raw materials produced in noncapitalist (e.g., slave or feudal) modes of production. Second, capitalism "takes root" and *uses*, from its dominant position, the noncapitalist modes of production – a good example of which is the widespread production of inexpensive wage goods through individual or Ancient modes of production, in what is often referred to as the informal sector. Finally, at some point not yet reached by most developing countries at the time, the capitalist mode of production *supplants* all noncapitalist modes of production – and is reproduced (via a market for labor power and the capitalist production of wage goods, means of production, and raw materials) on the basis of capitalism itself. The general conclusion of the articulation of modes of production theorists was that the development of

scholars, including Ernesto Laclau, Pierre-Philippe Rey, Maurice Godelier, and Barbara Bradby. See Aidan Foster-Carter, "The Modes of Production Controversy," *New Left Review* 1/107 (January–February 1978): 47–77 for a summary and critical discussion of the Modes of Production debate.

capitalism on a world scale involves, first, the creation and maintenance and, only later, the breakdown and dissolution of noncapitalist modes of production.[18]

The various conceptualizations of dependency and underdevelopment, from Baran to Modes of Production, were synthesized and recast as a distinct version of Dependency Theory in the work of Egyptian Marxian economist Samir Amin. Basically, Amin combined notions of the world capitalist system and the articulation of modes of production with the internationalization of capital and a theory of unequal exchange. The central element of Amin's model of the world economy is the relationship between the two groups of core and periphery countries as complementary opposites. These two poles are created by the history of capitalist expansion from the core. According to Amin, a core and periphery exist during all three of the stages of capitalist development: mercantilist, competitive, and monopoly-imperialist capitalism. However, the dichotomy becomes "hardened" in the third, imperialist stage: from that point on, no country of the periphery is capable of joining the core.

The reason for this hardening of the core and periphery is that Amin considers these two parts of the world economy to be governed by fundamentally different laws of development. The contrast is between *autocentric* and *extraverted* accumulation. The nature of development in the core is such that it determines its own development as well as that of the periphery. The key relation making for a pattern of autocentric accumulation in the center is the balance between increases in productivity and wages.[19] It results in an expansion of the internal market and the balanced development of both producer and consumer goods industries. This balance is also supported by surplus transfers from the periphery on the basis of unequal exchange. The periphery, on the other hand, is barred from achieving such a balance. Its pattern of accumulation is characterized as extraverted, deformed, and dependent. The coexistence of capitalist and noncapitalist modes of production in the periphery means that there is no necessary relation between the levels of productivity and wages.

The key mechanism in Amin's model whereby the two patterns of autocentric and dependent development are reproduced is the process of unequal exchange between core and periphery. Amin argues that the

---

[18] Thus, underdevelopment and dependency have somewhat different meanings in this framework compared to what we have seen in the case of Frank. For the articulation of Modes of Production theorists, underdevelopment is caused by the persistence of precapitalist modes of production (and their associated ruling-classes) as they are reproduced in their articulation with the dominant capitalist mode of production.

[19] Amin presented this model of autocentric and extraverted development in summary form in 1974 ("Accumulation and Development: A Theoretical Model," *Review of African Political Economy*, no. 1, 9–26 [1974]) and explored it at length in 1975 (*Accumulation on a World Scale*, 2 vols, New York: Monthly Review Press).

essential condition for unequal exchange is that real wage differences are larger than productivity differences in the periphery than in the core. The prices (of production) at which the goods of the center and periphery exchange are such that a surplus is transferred to the former from the latter. This surplus transfer (Amin calls it an "imperialist rent") means that there is an external drain on internally generated investment funds and the reproduction of a limited internal market within the periphery.

The result is that, against the presumptions and pronouncements of mainstream economists (as well as previous generations of Marxists), capitalism in the peripheral countries (even where it is most advanced, such as in India, Brazil, and South Africa) remains an appendage to the imperialist world order and cannot lead to stable and equitable forms of economic and social development. The irony is that, in recent decades, development in the capitalist center has become increasingly like that of the periphery – with more instability, growing inequality, and expanding precarity for the working-class.

Outside Economics[20]

The Marxian critique of political economy emerged from a wide range of intellectual sources. Marx (as well as Engels) did not just consult economics texts, but read widely in philosophy and social theory (as well as in mathematics and the natural sciences).

Mainstream economics, especially today, is quite different. With few exceptions, mainstream economists tend to ignore – and, in many cases, to denigrate – work in other academic disciplines.[21] One reason is because, in their view, mainstream economics is a "science," and work in other areas falls short of that standard. The other reason is because many of the issues others consider to be relevant to economics – such as ethics, the state, noncapitalist economies, and the like – are treated by mainstream economists as either reducible to economic rationality or exogenous to capitalist markets.[22]

---

[20] There are many journals in disciplines other than economics that regularly publish articles related to the Marxian critique of political economy. English-language journals include the following: *Antipode: A Radical Journal of Geography*, *Dialectical Anthropology*, *Radical Philosophy Review*, *Historical Materialism*, *Critical Sociology*, *Radical History Review*, and *Socialist Register*.

[21] One exception is psychology, especially in behavioral economics, which is focused on the effects of psychological (as well as cognitive, emotional, cultural, and social) determinants of the decisions of individuals and institutions and how those decisions vary from those presumed within neoclassical economics.

[22] For example, mainstream economists explain the actions of states and state actors (politicians and administrators) in the same terms as economic actors: as the product of

In contrast, Marxian economics has drawn on ideas from outside economics from the very beginning, establishing a tradition that has been maintained by successive generations of Marxian economists. They, unlike their mainstream counterparts, consider the economy to be embedded within the larger society, both affecting and affected by everything else happening in the social world. Moreover, Marxists working in disciplines other than economics have been influenced by and have made their own contributions in turn to the Marxian critique of political economy. In this section, we look at some examples (which are suggestive but certainly not exhaustive) of contributions from outside economics that have influenced the work of Marxian economists.

Philosophy is one area that should come as no surprise, especially given the ways the Marxian critique of political economy has been influenced from the start by theories about knowledge, ontology, and much else that philosophers have traditionally discussed and debated. A relatively recent example is the work of the French Marxist philosopher Louis Althusser, who not only was active in articulating a specifically Marxist position in philosophy, but spent considerable time reading, teaching, and writing about Marx's *Capital*. One of his most famous (and controversial) arguments was that the critique of political economy outlined in *Capital* represented a fundamental break from notions of totality, causation, and much more than can be found in both classical political economy and Marx's earlier writings, thereby helping to disengage Marxian thought from the deterministic and mechanistic approaches inherited from the Stalinist period.[23]

A second example, which has become particularly influential in cultural studies and political theory, is the work of the Italian Marxist Antonio Gramsci. One of the important contributions developed in his *Prison Notebooks* (written while he was imprisoned by the fascist leader Benito Mussolini) was his theory of hegemony – the use of both force and consent whereby the rule of the capitalist class is secured within society. As we have seen, the class of industrial or productive capitalists is relatively small: the members of the boards of directors of the main capitalist enterprises comprise just a few thousand individuals in the United States. There is also the somewhat larger group which is beholden to the capitalists, who "share in the booty" and receive a cut of surplus-value for providing some of the conditions of existence of the continued extraction of surplus-value. While such numbers are not inconsequential (either in quantity or in public awareness, as scandals of escalating CEO pay and the accumulated wealth

self-interested rational calculations. By the same token, they treat resource endowments as irrelevant, except as given outside their models, to the explanation of capitalist markets.

[23] While often accused of creating a "structuralist" interpretation of Marxian theory, in later years, Althusser moved even further away from such views by formulating a "materialism of the encounter" or "aleatory materialism," which emphasized the role of contingency and chance.

of Fortune 500 members provoke concern and sometimes even outrage), it is still the case that the vast majority of the population do not appropriate, distribute, or receive the surplus. Then how, given the small number who benefit, do capitalist class projects get produced historically and continue to exist within society? Gramsci's answer was that particular configurations of force and consent, especially the common sense of an era, lead to the dominance of one class project over others. Therefore, it is necessary to challenge and to create an alternative to the prevailing common sense to form the basis of a different, noncapitalist class hegemony.

Geography is a third source outside economics that is relevant to the Marxian critique of political economy. To take but one example, British-born geographer David Harvey (who has written various companion books and produced a series of online lectures on Marx's *Capital*) has long been concerned about the relationship between capitalism and space. In recent years, he has focused on what he calls "accumulation by dispossession" – in addition to the accumulation of capital based on the exploitation of living labor in production. What this means is that, through various means (such as privatization, financialization, the management of crises, and state redistributions), public and private entities are dispossessed of their wealth, which becomes increasingly concentrated in the hands of the few at the top of the capitalist economic pyramid.

The fourth and final example is anthropology, the source of much of our knowledge of noncapitalist economies and societies. Anthropologists, of course, focus on the ways social behaviors and institutions, including economic ones, are constituted by culture. That is particularly the case when it comes to gift exchanges (starting with the work of French anthropologist Marcel Mauss), which presumes and reinforces social obligations between gift-givers and recipients (since giving gifts entails the creation of a social relationship). But the gift is also subject to power and inequality (since gift-giving can and often does entail imposing an obligation on the recipient) and involves considerable indeterminacy (since neither the timing nor the kind of return gift is at all certain).

However, Marxian economists have argued, the same lesson can be carried over to other forms of exchange: there is nothing at all certain about any act of exchange, and nothing less symbolic and/or laden with responsibility, meaning, and so forth. Likewise, there is something fundamentally constitutive about identities and subjectivities in every act of market exchange. Buying and selling are overloaded activities: trading partners not only may be of several different minds about transactions; they are also often uncertain as to what exactly such transactions mean in terms of their own and others' wealth and property, the effects on their well-being, who or what subject positions they occupy, and what exactly is being traded. And exchanges often constrain freedom, since one of the only ways to meet needs and desires within capitalism is to purchase commodities, which in turn means most people are forced to have the freedom to sell their ability to work to someone else and/or to go into debt (which means they are subject to exorbitant interest rates as well as credit checks and other invasions of privacy). To be clear, marking the impossibility of exchange is not intended to erase the real differences between gift and market exchange (or, for that matter, the range of other transactional activities). Nor is it a call to eliminate or move beyond all forms of exchange, whether through markets or some other means. It is merely a reminder that exchange, including capitalist commodity exchange, like the gift, is fragile, indeterminate, and incomplete, not to mention often times violent and unequal.

These are just four examples of the many theories and analyses from outside economics that are germane to the Marxian critique of political economy. They demonstrate, in different ways, how Marxian economics, in contrast to mainstream economics, both draws from and contributes to discussions and debates in a wide variety of other areas and academic disciplines.

Back to Economics[24]

Ethics

As it turns out, the gift also serves to bring us back to the issue of ethics. That's because the gift disrupts the "circle of value" that separates economy from non-economy (including, and perhaps especially, ethics): it creates a moment of undecidability within both economic discourse (because it undermines the idea that there is a single value principle, thus occasioning an ethical choice between different theories of value) and within the economic and social order (which, because the structures of calculable exchange are rendered impossible, suggests a constitutive role for ethics). In this sense, the gift offers something more than a set of practices oriented around generosity or sharing. It represents the very impossibility of a discourse of economics and an economic order devoid of and separate from ethics.

We have already seen how the Marxian critique of political economy challenges the ethical claims of mainstream economics, in at least two senses: First, it shows how all theories of economic value are necessarily informed by (and, in turn, contribute to) particular ethical claims. Mainstream economics is no exception. While mainstream economists may

[24] There are many journals, around the world, that have a tradition of publishing articles on or related to Marxian economics. Relevant English-language journals include the following: *New Left Review*, *Rethinking Marxism*, *Science and Society*, *Monthly Review*, *Capital and Class*, *Capitalism Nature Socialism*, and *Review of Radical Political Economics*.

presume or assert that what they are doing is "science," completely separate from values and ethics, they can't detach their theoretical and analytical work from the idea that private property and markets lead to outcomes characterized by "just deserts" – that everyone gets what they deserve.

That ethical claim has been disputed by Marx and later Marxian economists, who have demonstrated that capitalism can't but fail the test of "just deserts." The appropriation and distribution of surplus-value mean that some economic agents – capitalists and those who receive distributions of surplus-value – are able to capture portions of the surplus for doing nothing. In that sense, they get more than what they deserve; and the workers who produce the surplus get less. The existence of class exploitation thus points in the direction of a different ethical claim: that workers, the direct producers, not be excluded from participating in the appropriation and distribution of surplus-value.[25]

There's also a second ethical dimension of Marxian economics: the commitment to "ruthless criticism" implies a practice of always questioning the moral premises and political positions of both economists (including, of course, Marxian economists) and economic systems (not only capitalism, but also socialism and communism). In this sense, ethics is not about having or positing ready-made answers to regulate the practice of economists or the operation of economic institutions. Instead, the ethical embodied in the critique of political economy is the imperative to always sustain a critical position toward the existing state of affairs and, since there are no guarantees, the will to risk a different economic and social organization of the surplus.

Other Economic Theories

The Marxian critique of political economy does not and cannot stand on its own. Clearly (as we have seen throughout this book), it represents an ongoing critical engagement with mainstream economics. It also draws from and contributes to many fields and disciplines other than economics (as we saw in the previous section). There's also a third set of discussions and debates: with economic theories other than mainstream ones.

These nonmainstream theories are often referred to as heterodox economics. Throughout his life, Marx was engaged in an ongoing dialogue with the work of other economic theories (such as those of Pierre-Joseph Proudhon, the German Social Democrats, and Adolf Wagner) that also

[25] To be clear, this doesn't mean that workers – for example, in socialism or communism – should be allowed to capture or keep all the surplus they create. Class exploitation is eliminated when those who create the surplus participate in appropriating and distributing that surplus. This is an issue to which we return in the discussion of alternatives to capitalism in the next chapter.

represented criticisms of capitalism and mainstream economics. That tradition of discussion and debate with other heterodox theories carries down to the present. In recent years, two such theories stand out: rent-seeking and Modern Monetary Theory.

The obscene amounts of income captured by the top 1 percent or the billionaires, and the fact that much of that income is associated with what are widely seen as economically useless activities (such as the ownership and speculative trading of corporate equities, serving as CEOs of large corporations, and the risky behaviors of the financial sector), have called into question, once again, neoclassical marginal productivity theory. It has become increasingly difficult to square the concentration of income among those at the very top (and the stagnation of incomes for pretty much everyone else) with the idea that everybody gets what they deserve, according to their marginal contributions to production.

That's why some otherwise-mainstream economists (such as Nobel laureate Joseph Stiglitz) have turned their attention to the idea of rent-seeking behavior. In their view, large corporations, such as the leading "high-tech" firms (like Amazon, Microsoft, Apple, Alphabet, and Facebook), characterized by highly concentrated ownership, have managed to use a combination of technical innovations and access to credit to erect barriers to entry and, once created, to restrain competition. This rising monopoly power has increased corporate profits and boosted stock prices, which have produced gains that are enjoyed by a small population of stock-holders, corporate management, and lending banks, while the labor share of income has declined.

Marxian economists have, as we have seen, long recognized both the existence of and the problems associated with "monopoly capital."[26] But they are critical of the work of the new rent-seeking economists because of what is missing: a theory of where the rents come from in the first place. From a Marxian perspective, the surplus-profits or rents captured by monopolies and oligopolies represent distributions of the surplus that was originally appropriated by capitalists from their workers. In other words, rent-seeking economists ignore or overlook the idea that the incomes of the small group at the top can be explained by their capturing, via rent-seeking behavior, a larger and larger share of the surplus produced by those who labor at the bottom.

Another recent contribution to the debate within economics that has attracted the attention of Marxian economists is Modern Monetary Theory.

[26] In fact, in the postwar period, Paul Baran joined with Paul Sweezy and others associated with the *Monthly Review* journal (including Samir Amin) to create a particular school of thought within Marxian economics referred to by the title of Baran and Sweezy's most famous book, *Monopoly Capital*. They, however, are never referred to or credited in the contemporary writings of the rent-seeking economists.

From the perspective of the Marxian critique of political economy, two formulations that represent both criticisms of and alternatives to those of mainstream economics are particularly relevant: government deficits and bank money. Perhaps the best known (and, in many ways, most controversial) aspect of Modern Monetary Theory is the logic of running budget deficits. The mainstream view is that the government imposes taxes and then uses the revenues to pay for some portion of government programs. To finance the rest of its expenditures, the state then borrows money by issuing bonds that investors can purchase (and for which they receive interest payments). But, mainstream economists complain, such borrowing has a downside: budget deficits increase the demand for loans, because the government competes with all the loans that private individuals and businesses want to take on – thus leading, in the short run, to the so-called crowding-out effect and, in the long run, to an increase in government debt and the potential for a government default.[27] Advocates of Modern Monetary Theory dispute both of these conclusions: First, they argue, governments should never have to default so long as the country has a sovereign currency, that is, if they issue and control the kind of money they use to tax and spend (so, for example, the United States, with its dollars, but not Greece, which is in the euro zone). Second, taxes and bonds do not and indeed cannot directly pay for spending. Instead, the government creates money whenever it engages in spending.[28] Clearly, this is useful from a Marxian perspective, because it creates room for government spending on new social programs, especially those that benefit the working-class.

The second major contention between mainstream economics and Modern Monetary Theory concerns the role of banks – in particular, the relationship between bank lending and money. Mainstream economists consider banks to be institutions that take in deposits, which then provides them with the funds to lend at a profit. Accordingly, the ability of private banks to lend is considered to be constrained by the reserves they hold. In other words, banks are seen as financial intermediaries, funneling deposits and then (backed by reserves) allocating a multiple of such deposits to the best possible, most efficient uses. From the perspective of Modern Monetary Theory, private banks don't operate in this way. Instead, they

[27] The crowding-out effect is the idea that rising public sector spending drives down private sector spending, because government borrowing leads to substantial rises in interest rates, which has the effect of absorbing the economy's lending capacity and thus discouraging private businesses from making capital investments.

[28] So why, then, does the government need to tax at all in Modern Monetary Theory? There are two major reasons: First, taxation makes sure people in the country use the government-issued currency, because they have to pay taxes in that currency (and not, for example, in some kind of foreign, local, or digital currency). Second, taxes are one tool governments can use to control inflation. They can, for example, take an amount of money out of the economy, which keeps aggregate demand from putting upward pressure on prices.

create money, by making loans – and reserve balances play little if any role. This is therefore a valuable complement to the original Marxian theory of endogenous money.

The problem, from a Marxian perspective, arises in the terms of the major complaint registered by Modern Monetary economists – namely, that government stimulus plans have mostly been directed to the finance, insurance and real estate sectors, which are considered unproductive and extractive, and not to the "real" economy, which is not. Let's remember Marx's argument: the productive/unproductive distinction has to do not with what is produced, but rather with how it is produced. Within capitalism, labor is productive if it results in the creation of surplus-value, and, if it doesn't (such as is the case with managers and CEOs who supervise the production of goods and services, as well as all those involved in finance, insurance, and real estate), it is not. So, the Marxian distinction is focused on surplus-value and thus exploitation. That is the major point overlooked in much of Modern Monetary Theory. Finance, insurance, and real estate are extractive in the sense that they receive a cut of the surplus created elsewhere in the economy. But so are other industries, such as capitalist manufacturing and services, since the boards of directors of enterprises in those sectors extract or appropriate surplus-value from their own workers.

From a Marxian perspective, then, the crucial distinction – both theoretically and for public policy – is not that between banking and the so-called real economy, but between classes that appropriate and receive distributions of the surplus and the class that actually produces the surplus.

Looking Ahead

We have seen in this chapter that what keeps the Marxian critique of political economy alive is not any fidelity to what Marx (or Engels or any other particular Marxist) wrote, but its ongoing critical engagement with both transformations of capitalism and current theoretical and political debates. From the very beginning, Marxian economists assumed the task of revising and updating their theories and extending their analyses into new areas. In order to accomplish this, they have explored the richness of their own tradition and learned from (and contributed to) areas of thought other than economics. They have also reformulated their critique in the light of changes within mainstream economics as well as the emergence of new heterodox theories and approaches within economics.

But the question remains: where do we go from here? In Marxian economics, the answer can be found in the transition debates – the idea that capitalism had a beginning (it hasn't always existed) and it might have an end (so that a transition to a form of economic and social organization other than capitalism is both necessary and possible). That's the focus of the next, and final, chapter.

Suggested Readings

Louis Althusser and Étienne Balibar, *Reading Capital*, trans. Ben Brewster (New York: New Left Books, 1970).

Paul A. Baran, *The Political Economy of Growth* (New York: Monthly Review Press, 1957).

Paul A. Baran and Paul M. Sweezy, *Monopoly Capital* (New York: Monthly Review Press, 1966).

Peter Boettke, ed., *Socialism and the Market: The Socialist Calculation Debate Revisited*, 9 vols. (New York: Routledge, 2000).

Nikolai Bukharin, *Imperialism and World Economy* (London: Martin Lawrence, 1929).

Nikolai Bukharin and Evgenii Preobrazhensky, *The ABC of Communism* (London: Penguin Books, 1969 [1922]).

Anjan Chakrabarti and Anup Dhar, "Economic Development," in *Routledge Handbook of Marxian Economics*, ed. David M. Brennan, David Kristjanson-Gural, Catherine P. Mulder, and Erik M. Olson, pp. 310–22 (New York: Routledge, 2017).

Richard B. Day and Daniel Gaido, eds., *Responses to Marx's* Capital: *From Rudolf Hilferding to Isaak Illich Rubin* (Boston: Brill, 2018).

Antonio Gramsci, *Selections from the Prison Notebooks*, ed. Quintin Hoare and Geoffrey Nowell Smith (New York: International Publishers, 1971).

Andre Gunder Frank, *Capitalism and Underdevelopment in Latin America: Historical Studies of Chile and Brazil* (New York: Monthly Review Press, 1969).

Barry Hindess and Paul Q. Hirst, *Pre-Capitalist Modes of Production* (London: Routledge & Kegan Paul, 1975).

Lenin, *Imperialism: The Highest Stage of Capitalism* (New York: International Publishers, 1939).

Rosa Luxemburg, *The Accumulation of Capital*, trans. Agnes Schwarzschild (New York: Routledge, 2003 [1913]).

Walter Rodney, *How Europe Underdeveloped Africa* (Washington, DC: Howard University Press, 1981).

David F. Ruccio, *Development and Globalization: A Marxian Class Analysis* (New York: Routledge, 2010).

Ian Steedman and Paul Sweezy, eds., *The Value Controversy* (London: Verso, 1987).

Chapter 9

TRANSITIONS TO AND FROM CAPITALISM

In previous chapters, we explored the contemporary relevance and historical sources, and then the basic concepts and conclusions, of the Marxian critique of political economy. We also saw how that critique can be applied to a variety of important economic and social issues as well as some of the key debates it has provoked among later generations of Marxian economists.

Yes, we have covered a lot of ground. But we are still not finished. That's because everyone wants to know: where does it all lead? In particular, what are the *political* implications of the Marxian critique of political economy?

Political issues come up because the goal of the Marxian approach is to create the conditions whereby it ceases to be relevant. That makes it radically different from mainstream economics, which is based on the presumption that it will always be necessary. Mainstream economists start with the notion of scarcity, which they assume is universal – since, in their view, it is both transcultural and transhistorical. All societies, at all times, they argue, face the problem of scarcity – which can be solved through an economic system based on private property and markets. So, there cannot be a place or time when mainstream arguments about the efficacy and ethics of capitalism are not applicable.

Marxian economists approach the issue differently. Their critique first emerged within and was directed at capitalism (as well as the economic theory that, through various incarnations, has served to sing the praises of capitalism) – and it only remains relevant as long as capitalist class exploitation exists. Since their aim is to eliminate the causes and consequences of that class exploitation, in effect Marxists want to contribute to the task of creating the economic and social conditions whereby their critique is no longer germane. In short, they want to put themselves out of a job.

That's why the issue of transition is so important. As we will see in this chapter, it signifies the idea that capitalism has both a beginning and an end. Marxian economists have long focused on, analyzed, and debated two important transitions: the transition to capitalism (e.g., from feudalism), and the transition from capitalism (e.g., to socialism or communism).

But there's a rub: much to the surprise of many readers, Marx (and his frequent coauthor Engels) never presented a blueprint of socialism or communism, either in *Capital* or anywhere else. Try as they might, all readers and commentators have been able to find in Marx and Engels's enormous body of work are a few general phrases – but nothing in the way of specific designs of what a socialist or communist society should look like, much less a path to get there.

In fact, we can go so far as to say, there is no such thing as a Marxian political agenda, valid for all times and places. Again, that sets it apart from mainstream economics, which does have such an agenda: to foster private property and free markets where they exist, and to create them where and when they don't exist. The Marxian critique, on the other hand, doesn't – and, indeed, can't – offer such a political program.

If there is no all-purpose set of policies or strategies that can be derived from the Marxian critique of political economy, what can it offer? What we have is, at most, a general orientation – which involves a cautious imperative (to risk a different economic and social organization of the surplus, without any guarantees we'll get it right) based on a combination of a dire warning (that things cannot remain as they are) and a political opening (that things do not have to be the way they are). The rest depends on an analysis of the concrete circumstances and possibilities of transforming and moving beyond capitalism – in particular times and places. But the Marxian critique of political economy does not contain either a specific blueprint or a general formula for making a transition away from and beyond capitalism.

Transition to Capitalism

In the extensive Marxian literature on the topic, it's simply referred to as the "transition debate" – the transition to capitalism from a different, noncapitalist economy and society. Such a debate does not exist within mainstream economics. The reason is because, in their theory and models, mainstream economists simply assume that capitalism, in one form or another, has always existed.

That's certainly the case within contemporary mainstream economics. In classical political economy, there are references to an "early and rude state of society which precedes both the accumulation of stock and the appropriation of land."[1] But the presumption is that a "primitive accumu-

[1] Adam Smith, *The Wealth of Nations* (New York: Bantam Dell, 2003), p. 67.

lation" naturally takes place such that capitalism emerges and develops on its own basis. In point of fact, Marx remarks in *Capital*, "This primitive accumulation plays approximately the same role in political economy as original sin in theology. Adam bit the apple, and thereupon sin fell on the human race" (KI, 873). The quote is from chapter 26, "The Secret of Primitive Accumulation," which opens part 8, the last section of volume 1 of *Capital*. Marx's discussion of how, within England and elsewhere in Western Europe, the economic structures of capitalism grew out of the feudal economy – how "the dissolution of the latter sets free the elements of the former" – is the cornerstone of the ongoing debate about the transition to capitalism.[2]

Note that Marx's analysis of where capitalism came from is presented at the *end* of the first volume of *Capital*, not (as many readers might expect) at the beginning. That's because Marx had to produce, via the initial steps of his critique of political economy, the basic concepts of his theory of capitalism before using them to construct a history of the emergence of the conditions of existence of capitalism. So, he starts the first part of his critique with a deconstruction of the commodity and ends with a historical analysis of the primitive accumulation of capital.

Note also that the section on primitive accumulation is itself another part of Marx's critique of political economy. It is aimed at challenging three key propositions of mainstream economics: (a) that widespread poverty preceded the development of capitalism and that capitalism, if allowed to flourish, will eventually solve the problem of poverty; (b) that the emergence of capitalism was caused by exogenous factors (such as technology and population growth); and (c) that the birth of capitalism was peaceful and otherwise "idyllic" (and therefore is the result of individual initiative and voluntary contracts, free from any force or government intervention).

According to Marx's analysis, all three propositions can and should be challenged. First, the poverty of the great majority of people before and after the Industrial Revolution, who owned little except their ability to work, was itself a consequence of the emergence of capitalism. The existence of widespread poverty was not, as many mainstream economists

[2] The famous "transition debate" began with a symposium originally published in *Science and Society* in the early 1950s, which included such distinguished contributors as Maurice Dobb, Paul Sweezy, Kohachiro Takahshi, and Christopher Hill. (In 1985, Verso published the complete texts of the original debate, together with new materials produced by historians since then.) It resumed with a debate that originally appeared in the journal *Past & Present*, provoked by a 1976 article by Robert Brenner (the contributions to the so-called Brenner Debate were published by Cambridge University Press in 1985) and continued, in 1979, with an article by Stephen Resnick and Richard Wolff ("The Theory of Transitional Conjunctures and the Transition from Feudalism to Capitalism in Western Europe," *Review of Radical Political Economics* 11[3]: 3–22).

then as now have argued, a pre-existing problem that would inevitably be solved by fostering the development of more capitalism.[3] While refusing to romanticize the lives and living standards of the direct producers before capitalism, Marxian economists do point out the new forms of poverty that are created when workers are dispossessed and forced to have the freedom to sell their labor power to capitalist employers. Second, the transition to capitalism came about because of contradictions and the resulting changes within feudal society, not the effect of some external or exogenous cause, which led to the emergence of the elements of what eventually came to be constituted as capitalism. And third, the actual history of the development of capitalism, far from being idyllic, was a process in which, as Marx wrote, "conquest, enslavement, robbery, murder, in short, force, play the greatest part" (KI, 874).

One way to think about Marx's discussion of primitive accumulation is to return to the market for labor power, as in figure 9.1.[4] As we saw in chapter 5, the existence of labor power as a commodity – the buying and selling of workers' ability to expend mental and manual energy in the process of laboring – is one of the key conditions of capitalist exploitation. Workers are forced to have the freedom to sell their labor power, and

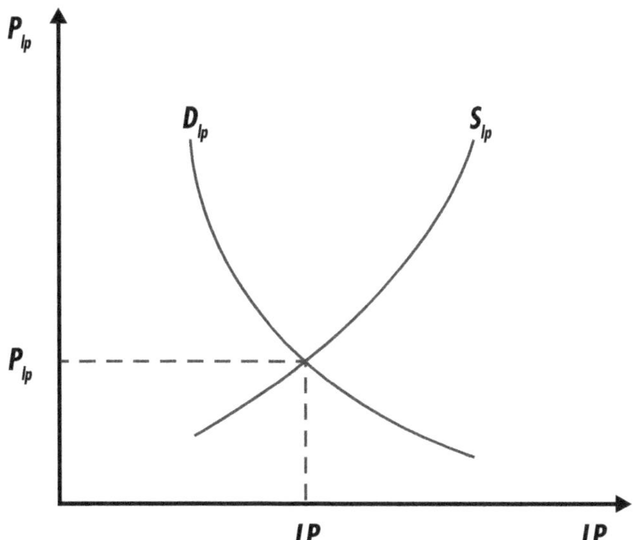

Figure 9.1 Market for labor power

[3] Mainstream economic historian Deirdre McCloskey never tires in scolding the critics of capitalism that "the Great Fact of modern life, the most surprising secular news since the domestication of plants and animals, is the rise of real income per head" ("The Rhetoric of the Economy and the Polity," *Annual Review of Political Science* 14 [2011]: 184).

[4] Where all the elements are defined as before: the quantity of labor power (*LP*), the price of labor power (P_{lp}), the supply of labor power (S_{lp}), and the demand for labor power (D_{lp}).

capitalists, once they've purchased that commodity, are in the position of extracting labor from labor power and of appropriating surplus-value during the course of production.

Mainstream economists simply assume a market for labor power (and therefore the existence of capitalism), and write down the equations and draw the supply and demand schedules on the chart as if they are natural and have always existed. This is not unlike many young people, who presume (or are certainly encouraged to think, by their parents and the larger society, not to mention the weight of their accumulated debts) that the unquestioned goal of their schooling is to acquire the necessary skills, establish the personal connections, and to otherwise prepare themselves for the job market.

Marx's analysis is quite different. Over the course of eight chapters, Marx describes the historical process whereby one particular freedom emerges: the freedom to buy and sell labor power as a commodity. Primitive accumulation is the birth of that specific freedom – and, of course, all its economic, political, and cultural conditions of existence (including, as we have seen, the freedom to buy and sell commodities). A successful primitive accumulation of capital thus represents a revolution in all spheres of economic and social life, the end result of which is the "age of capital."

In terms of the supply of labor power (S_{lp} in figure 9. 1), Marx shows how "a mass of 'free' and unattached proletarians was hurled onto the labour-market" (KI, 878) as a result of the process whereby the agricultural population – made up at the time of feudal serfs and peasant proprietors – was expropriated and otherwise forcibly driven off the land. This occurred through such means as the "enclosure of the commons," via government decrees by which the landlords granted themselves as private property the land the direct producers traditionally possessed and used in common. But early on, there weren't enough jobs for those workers. So, since many were turned into beggars, thieves, and vagabonds, "partly from inclination, in most cases under the force of circumstances" (KI, 896), they were forced to become wage-laborers – by a combination of legislation (which made vagrancy and the paying of "higher wages than those fixed by the statute" illegal) and then, over time, through education and habit (such that the conditions of capitalism appeared "as self-evident laws of Nature").

As for the demand for labor power (D_{lp} in figure 9. 1), part of it came from capitalist farmers, who managed to usurp the common lands (on which peasant farmers had been able to graze their herds and grow crops) and accumulate enough wealth to hire agricultural laborers. Another segment stemmed from merchants, who were able to convert their accumulated wealth from trade into capital; they became capitalist manufacturers, who took advantage both of the destruction of rural domestic industry and the growth of internal markets. Still a third portion of the capitalist demand for labor power was enabled by government force – through a combination of colonial policy, which secured foreign markets for the budding industrialists; protectionism, which endeavored to keep out foreign competition; and public debt, which fostered the ownership of safe public bonds and the growth of financial intermediaries and the modern credit system. Together, they created a class of employers, a "hot house" for domestic industry, and the demand for labor power.

Thus, Marx argues, the historical genesis of capital meant both "annihilation" of the feudal system – through the expropriation of the direct producers and the concentration of property in the hands of a separate class of capitalist employers – and the creation of a new economic and social system – "under the stimulus of the most infamous, the most sordid, the most petty and the most odious of passions" (KI, 928). The result of that long, uneven, often violent history was the market for labor power.

We need to pause on two caveats before moving on. First, the section on the primitive accumulation of capital can be (and often has been) read as a kind of teleology, as a historical process with a necessary endpoint. That's because it was written looking back, and therefore in an attempt to analyze the elements that needed to emerge in order for capitalism to exist. But, of course, actual history is not governed by any kind of inexorable or predetermined logic. Capitalism may have developed in this manner in England but there was nothing inevitable about it; and there are plenty of places where the emergence of capitalism followed a different pattern or where the transition to capitalism never happened at all. Still, it remains, capitalism simply cannot emerge without the historical development of the conditions whereby capitalists and workers meet one another as opposing classes, with different interests, in the market for labor power.

Second, a successful primitive accumulation of capital doesn't mean that capitalism stops developing and changing. As we have seen in previous chapters, capitalism continues to be transformed and to assume new forms and shapes (some Marxian economists refer to them as phases or stages) over time. These include the concentration and centralization of capital; the reproduction of the sellers of labor power and the creation of a reserve army of the unemployed and underemployed; the tendency and counter-tendencies of the rate of profit and the recurrent boom-and-bust cycles of the accumulation of capital; and the movement from individual private property to more social forms of property, such as joint-stock companies (what today we call corporations and stock markets) and interest-bearing capital (commercial banks, investment banks, and other financial institutions).

That's just what we find in Marx's *Capital*. We can add to those changes the following elements:

- the globalization of capital and the formation of giant multinational corporations, which expand and coordinate different production sites around the globe, as well as sources of raw materials and machinery and sales of finished commodities;
- an increasing role of the state in ensuring the reproduction of capital through infrastructure, support for education, research and development, and economic coordination (such as monetary and fiscal policies, to attempt to manage the contradictions between capital and labor and among different claimants on distributed surplus-value);
- new productivity-enhancing digital and robotic technologies, as well as the production and distribution of knowledge (and thus the incorporation of information and information-processing into more and more sectors of capitalist economies);
- the rise of shadow money, and private credit-money more generally (which involve growing corporate cash pools and their consolidation among asset managers, leading to the concentration of a large and growing share of savings by a small number of asset managers);
- and, finally, the growth of the working-class and the expansion of labor unions and other forms of working-class activism (on behalf of labor and in support of other social and political movements) around the globe.

In fact, one of the key questions posed by Marx and Engels, as well as successive generations of Marxian economists, is: do such changes in the development of capitalism create the conditions of existence for a transition beyond capitalism?

Transition

Transition, as is clear from the previous discussion, is another way of thinking about development. In mainstream economics, development is defined in terms of the accumulation of wealth in the form of commodities. In their view, the more commodities are produced in a country, the higher is its GDP and therefore the more developed it is. So, mainstream economists analyze development in terms of a ladder: countries are arrayed from less developed to more developed – poor, middle-income, and rich countries – according to their wealth or GDP (or, more specifically, GDP per capita).

Marxian economists reject the idea of a single ladder, from less to more developed according to the level of national income. Indeed, they criticize any and all notions of development in general, and focus instead on qualitatively distinct forms of capitalist and noncapitalist development – different ways of arranging the appropriation and distribution of surplus labor. More a bush or tree than a ladder. Therefore, transition is defined as the movement from one way of organizing the appropriation and distribution of surplus labor to a qualitatively different way of organizing society's class structure.

In the previous section, we examined the transition *to* capitalism – the historical movement from a feudal class structure to a capitalist one. Now, the question is: what might the transition *from* capitalism look like?

Transition from Capitalism

To be clear, the idea that there can be a transition beyond capitalism – say, to socialism or communism – is not a forecast or prediction. It is more a question, and a political project. Certainly, given their ruthless criticism of capitalism, it's a project Marx and Engels, as well as generations of Marxian economists (not to mention other Marxian scholars and activists), hoped their work would contribute to.

But, again, there is no blueprint. In fact, in one of the postfaces to *Capital*, Marx ridiculed the idea that he should set his sights on "writing recipes ... for the cook-shops of the future" (KI, 99). One way of thinking about the Marxian critique of political economy is therefore as a combination of arrogance and humility. The arrogance stems from the presumption that an alternative to capitalism is indeed both necessary and possible – against the mainstream economics idea (echoed by generations of anti-Marxist politicians, such as Conservative British prime minister Margaret Thatcher) that there is no alternative to capitalism. But the critique is also based on a certain humility – that the transition beyond capitalism cannot be designed by intellectuals, sitting in their proverbial armchairs, but can only be a product of struggles, by masses of people, to criticize and change the society in which they live and work.

The way the Marxian critique of political economy contributes to the project of moving beyond capitalism is illustrated in two key texts: the *Manifesto of the Communist Party* and the *Critique of the Gotha Program*.

Communist Manifesto

Marx and Engels were commissioned in 1848 to write the *Communist Manifesto* for the Communist League (which later became the International Workingmen's Association). The first section begins quite dramatically with the well-known (controversial and much-misinterpreted) opening sentence: "The history of all hitherto existing society is the history of class struggles" (ME, 473).

Is that all there is to history – class struggles? From a Marxian perspective, certainly not. But it does provide a different focus, a specifically Marxian entry point, for understanding history. First, it emphasizes struggles as a way of changing the world, instead of a simple unfolding (such as mainstream economists' notion of history as an expansion of the freedom to buy and sell commodities). Second, it attaches the adjective class to those struggles, based on the idea that classes and class struggles have not been eliminated by capitalism, no matter how much mobility there may be between different class positions.[5] Capitalism still comprises the appropriation of surplus labor by one class from another, as well as distributions of surplus-value to still other classes. What capitalism represents, then, is an array of new classes, new forms of class exploitation, and new types of class struggles.

What this means is that, from a Marxian perspective, capitalism is both radically different from and absolutely the same as other class societies. It is different in the sense that it is more dynamic, it generates more wealth, it tends to be more universalizing than any previous form of economic and social organization. But it is also the same, because it, too, is based on class exploitation, generates class antagonisms, and creates the conditions for an alternative way of organizing economic and social life.

By the same token, capitalists are both different from and the same as previous ruling-classes, such as feudal lords and slaveowners. They run gigantic corporations, decide if, how, and where new investments will take place, spend and borrow enormous quantities of money, and thus affect the lives of masses of people around the world – much more so than any feudal lords or slaveowners, now or in the past. At the same time, capitalists appropriate surplus labor, and thus engage in the process of class exploitation – just as much as their feudal and slave counterparts.

Much of the *Communist Manifesto* is dedicated to exploring those differences and similarities. In fact, in many passages, Marx and Engels appear to be celebrating capitalism at least as much as their mainstream counterparts. For example, capitalism, they write,

> has been the first to show what man's activity can bring about. It has accomplished wonders far surpassing Egyptian pyramids, Roman aqueducts, and Gothic cathedrals; it has conducted expeditions that put in the shade all former Exoduses of nations and crusades. (ME, 476)

However, at the same time,

> The modern bourgeois society that has sprouted from the ruins of feudal society has not done away with class antagonisms. It has but established new classes, new conditions of oppression, new forms of struggle in place of the old ones. (ME, 474)

[5] In fact, one of the key arguments mainstream economists make in favor of capitalism is that no one is stuck in the class positions of their birth; instead, with effort, capitalism makes it possible to go from the bottom to the top (and, of course, to fall out of the top toward the bottom). There are two problems with this argument: First, mobility between class positions still presumes there are classes. Second, class mobility has declined dramatically (in many countries, such as the United States) in recent decades.

So, capitalism opens up new possibilities but then attempts to subject everything and everyone to one rule, to highlight only one activity: to make more money, to accumulate more capital, to extract more surplus-value. And everyone is encouraged to think of themselves in the same fashion. The capitalist class thus gives itself a universalizing mission: for people and institutions everywhere to become bourgeois. Business people are supposed to follow one dictum, the bottom line. Governments are encouraged to subject all programs to a cost–benefit calculus. And employees (not to mention young people, as future workers) are held responsible for augmenting and making rational calculations concerning their "human capital."[6]

The other key passage in the *Communist Manifesto* is often overlooked:

> All that is solid melts into air, all that is holy is profaned, and man is at last compelled to face with sober senses his real conditions of life, and his relations with his kind. (ME, 476)

Here the attention shifts to a theme we mentioned earlier in this book. The characteristics of capitalist modernity are change, self-criticism, becoming something else. In other words, capitalist modernity is a tradition of no tradition, in which, they argue, "all fixed, fast-frozen relations, with their train of ancient and venerable prejudices and opinions, are swept away" (ME, 476).

Capitalism is thus responsible for creating great "solid" economies and societies – by concentrating the means of production in a few hands, drawing millions and millions of people into great urban centers, creating a world market, forming "too big to fail" banks and industrial corporations, amassing giant fortunes. But it also includes a tendency to make them all "melt away" – through its periodic crises and society's attempts to regulate its excesses and ameliorate its negative effects.

Hence the big question for Marxists: is it possible that capitalism will be melted away by its own heat?

According to Marx and Engels, capitalism creates a new social force – the modern working-class or proletariat – that can learn the lesson taught by capitalists and become a new universal class. In other words, they ask, can

---

[6] The idea of human capital was invented in the early 1960s by neoclassical economist Theodore Schultz ("Investment in Human Capital," *American Economic Review* 51 [March 1961]: 1–17) as part of a more general attack on Marxian-inspired notions of capital (capital that is connected to profits and therefore exploitation), an extension of Adam Smith's theory of the causes of the wealth of nations (which, Schultz argued, should include the accumulation of all prior investments in education, on-the-job training, health, migration, and other factors that increase individual productivity), and an attempt to depict all economic agents, including laborers, as capitalists (who "invest" in and "manage a portfolio" of skills and abilities). Human capital can thus be seen as, simultaneously, a blunting of the critical dimension of capital (broadening it to matters other than profits and thus a particular set of claims on the surplus) and a step in the creation of the neoliberal subject (who seeks a "return" on its "investments" in itself).

workers utilize the melting logic of capitalism to create changes in the economy and society that can save not only themselves, but the capitalists and everyone else too, from the ravages of capitalist exploitation?[7] What they mean by revolution, then, is the concentration of that heat, after which: "In place of the old bourgeois society, with its classes and class antagonisms, we shall have an association, in which the free development of each is the condition for the free development of all" (ME, 491). The transition from capitalism thus has the potential of both fulfilling an old promise of freedom and expanding its meaning.

The final surprise that greets readers of the *Communist Manifesto* is the list of demands at the end (ME, 490). It includes the following:

- A heavy progressive or graduated income tax.
- Abolition of all right of inheritance.
- Equal liability of all to labour.
- Free education for all children in public schools. Abolition of children's factory labour in its present form.

From our vantage point, in the twenty-first century, the list is not particularly radical. It certainly does not constitute a blueprint for socialism or communism, at least as they are conventionally understood. Instead, it's a program of specific policies that would change the lives of workers (as they were in 1848, in Western Europe) for the better.[8]

Critique of the Gotha Program

One of the last of Marx's major texts, the *Critique of the Gotha Program*, was his response (written in May 1875) to the proposed platform of the Social Democratic Workers' Party of Germany.[9] It offers Marx's most detailed

[7] To be clear, the working-class represents a universal class not because of some kind of inherent nobility, but because championing a program of eliminating class exploitation can benefit even those who are not members of the working-class, since they will no longer be forced to lose or undermine or otherwise forsake their humanity by engaging in unethical, self-serving behaviors. Thus, eliminating capitalist class exploitation can be seen as restoring humanity to everyone, both the performers and appropriators/recipients of surplus labor.

[8] A good question for consideration and discussion is: what would such a list of demands look like today?

[9] The Social Democratic Workers' Party of Germany was a Marxist socialist party, one of the first political organizations established among the nascent German labor unions of the nineteenth century. It officially existed under that name for only six years (from 1869 to 1875) but, through changing names and political alliances, its lineage can be traced to the present-day Social Democratic Party of Germany. The Gotha Program, a draft platform for a party congress, was heavily influenced by the ideas of Ferdinand Lasalle. Marx and Lasalle met and became friends during the revolutions of 1848 (when Lasalle was imprisoned and Marx forced to flee Germany) but, over time, their views on theoretical and political matters increasingly diverged.

analysis of the transition from capitalism to communism – and includes the famous phrase, "From each according to his ability, to each according to his needs!" (ME, 531).

The document utilizes many of the key concepts of the Marxian critique of political economy discussed in earlier chapters of this book: labor, surplus labor, private property, commodity fetishism, and so forth. Marx invokes them here to critically discuss what German Marxists at the time considered to be a pressing question: what would a "fair distribution" under communism look like?

What they were referring to is the distribution of the total social product of labor, which is equal to the total value produced in the new, communal society ("wherein the instruments of labor are common property and the total labor is co-operatively regulated"). They can be thought of as the communal equivalents of the capitalist concepts of total value (*W*), which is equal to the sum of constant capital (*c*), variable capital (*v*), and surplus-value (*s*). Should all the value produced (*W*) go to the workers? Marx's perhaps surprising answer is a resounding "no."

One reason workers should not get all of the total social product is because a portion (*c*) has to be set aside to replace the means of production that have been used up. Other portions (of *s*) have to be set aside for the expansion of production, a reserve fund for accidents and natural calamities, the general costs of administering the society, the "common satisfaction of needs," and for "those unable to work." Even under communism, then, workers would not keep their surplus labor.

That leaves the portion of the total social product required to reproduce the social existence of the direct producers (*v*). Does a fair distribution mean that it should be equally distributed among the workers? Again, Marx's answer is no – since "equal right" in the new society would turn out to be "an unequal right for unequal labor" (ME, 530). That's because workers have different capabilities, different amounts of effort and outcome, different size families and living circumstances, and so on. At least initially, then, a fair distribution would be an unequal distribution. Only later would it be replaced by a different notion of fair distribution: from each according to their ability, to each according to their needs.

What such a dictum accomplishes is to sever the idea of distribution within communism from the notion of fairness that is celebrated within mainstream economics and capitalism. "Just deserts," as we have seen, means that everyone gets what they deserve – that what people receive through markets (be they workers, landlords, or capitalists) corresponds to what they've contributed to production.

Separating those two moments – from each, to each – creates a different notion of class justice. It gives rise to two separate arenas of fairness: fairness in the allocation of work among society's members, and fairness in how the total social product is distributed to satisfy individual and social needs.[10] Distinguishing between the two serves, on one hand, to criticize the existing order – which promises in theory but cannot deliver in practice, through capitalist markets, that rewards are equal to contributions. On the other hand, it creates a different horizon, a way of imagining and enacting systems of contributions and rewards that are not determined by private property and markets, but rather by a radically different set of social standards and forms of deliberation.

One contemporary example, which has come up many different times during the history of capitalism, is a universal basic income. The idea is that everyone receives a cash allowance not connected to any kind of work requirement. The recipients are able to satisfy at least some of their needs without being forced to sell their ability to labor.

Whether or not such a program is feasible today (and many experiments with various kinds of guaranteed income are ongoing, and have had quite positive results), it does mean that at least three issues can be raised. First, it challenges the meaning of dependence. For example, why is selling one's ability to work for a wage or salary any less a form of dependence than receiving some form of government assistance (the much-decried government "handouts")? It certainly is a different kind of dependence – on employers rather than on one's fellow citizens – and probably a form of dependence that is more arbitrary and capricious – since capitalist employers have the freedom to hire people when and where they want, while government assistance is governed by clear, universal rules. Moreover, the dependence of capitalist employers on low-wage labor is diminished, since all workers now enjoy a higher income floor.

Second, mainstream economists and commentators often complain, "just giving people money" would disrupt the incentive to work and that "useful employment" gives people an "honorable and dignified role in society." What those opponents of basic-income schemes choose to overlook is that, in a world in which the majority of people are forced to have the freedom to sell their ability to work to someone else – in which, in short, labor power is a commodity – there is no necessary honor or dignity in work. It is a necessity, born of the fact that people need to earn an income to purchase commodities to sustain themselves and to pay off their debts. The most likely way to earn that income is to sell their labor power to a small number of other people, their employers, who in turn get to appropriate and do what they will with the surplus. It is precisely that

---

[10] George DeMartino (in "Realizing Class Justice," published in the January 2003 issue of *Rethinking Marxism* 5[1]: 1–31) refers to these as "productive class justice" and "distributive justice." He joins them to "appropriative class justice" (that is, "fairness in the processes by which some individuals and/or groups in society receive the social surplus produced by themselves or by others") to define a Marxian notion of class justice.

relationship that serves to reproduce and reinforce the separation between employees and their employers and to force the former to rely on the latter for their income.[11] The various universal basic income schemes being proposed don't eliminate the need to work, and therefore undermine the incentive to labor; but, like unemployment benefits, they certainly give workers more leverage against employers by making them less desperate to accept offers of low pay, few benefits, and harmful working conditions. They also help people feed, clothe, and shelter themselves while out of a job, without having to rely on emergency benefits that are only sometimes made available when a capitalist economy enters one of its downward spirals.

Third, where would the funding come from to support a universal basic income? The fact is, corporations throughout the world have been successful in shifting the financing of government assistance programs from their surpluses to workers' incomes. So, the solution to the pressure on workers' wages and standard of living is not to rule out new entitlements but to change how such programs are financed. One possibility is tapping into the enormous surplus that, under capitalism, is socially produced but privately appropriated. The other is for the government to create the necessary financing through its own expenditures.[12]

Ultimately, then, a universal basic income points toward a new realm of freedom, including freedom from the need to work for the benefit of someone else and from the need to hand over a growing portion of one's already-low individual income to finance a program that benefits the majority of people. Moreover, from a Marxian perspective, a guaranteed income would be even more successful if, instead of being instituted as a top-down initiative, it were tied to a class-conscious popular movement of poor people and workers.

---

[11] To be clear, a guaranteed basic income wouldn't, in and of itself, do away with that relationship or the need for most people to work for someone else. But it would certainly give those who work for a living other options – including the ability to find dignity away from and outside of work. Modern Monetary Theory economists, for their part, have argued that a government job guarantee (when the government steps in as the "employer of last resort" for unemployed workers) is preferable to a basic income guarantee because it enhances the capitalist macroeconomy (by providing a stable benchmark for the value of the domestic currency, stabilizing the business cycle, and enhancing price stability). See, for example, Pavlina R. Tcherneva, "Job or Income Guarantee?" Working Paper 29 (August 2003), Centre of Full Employment and Price Stability, University of Missouri, Kansas City.

[12] The same argument holds for financing a job guarantee: the government can directly hire workers, thereby eliminating the reserve army of unemployed and underemployed labor, by increasing taxes on the surplus or by creating the requisite funds through the government's own spending.

Marxian Economics and Utopia in the Twenty-First Century

The idea of a universal basic income is considered to be a utopian scheme – but one that is born out of the exigencies of twenty-first-century capitalism. It is utopian to the extent that it represents a distant horizon compared to the way most people within contemporary capitalism have to work to earn a living, and to scrimp and save (and go into debt) in order to even attempt to make ends meet. But it is increasingly being discussed and debated precisely because the situation is so dire: not only is inequality growing (from already obscene levels), with the working-class falling further and further behind the tiny group at the top, but recurrent crises (such as the Second Great Depression and the Pandemic Depression) have devastated workers, their families, and their communities. Moreover, looking forward, new technologies (such as robotics and artificial intelligence) threaten to deprive many blue-collar and white-collar workers of their jobs and livelihoods.

The problem right now is that any proposal to right the wrongs associated with capitalism are labeled utopian – naïve and unworkable – and then set aside. That's true even of the relatively modest global wealth tax proposed by mainstream economist Thomas Piketty in his best-selling book, *Capital in the Twenty-First Century*. Piketty is given credit for documenting the spectacular rise of income inequality from the mid-1970s onward, and then showing how wealth is even more unevenly distributed, which creates the specter of new inherited wealth dynasties, what he calls "patrimonial capitalism." And yet his proposal for a reasonable and moderate global wealth tax is considered a utopian dream and never seriously considered.

That's how much the level of our discourse – in the discipline of economics and in public debate – has fallen. The Marxian critique of political economy is different. It has included a utopian element from the very beginning, and fostered it through the work of generations of Marxian economists (not to mention scholars in other disciplines and activists who draw their inspiration from the Marxian tradition). But the relationship between utopia and Marxism is a contested, much-discussed and long-debated, aspect of Marxian economics.

There are, in fact, two common views concerning that relationship. One is that Marx (and Engels and other leading figures in the history of Marxian thought) presented a clear vision of an alternative, post-capitalist or communist society. On this score, it is enough to retrieve the elements of that vision from Marx's writings – akin to the utopias that have been described by countless authors, from Thomas More to Ursula Le Guin – and to chart a path or transition from the capitalist present to the clearly articulated communist future.[13] The other view is that Marxism repre-

[13] There are, of course, different interpretations of what that communism should look like, from state ownership to worker control. But there is general agreement, on this

sents a scientific, materialist analysis of capitalism – of the world as it is, without any need for a utopian vision. It is enough, from this perspective, to identify and analyze capitalism's "laws of motion," including the accumulation of mounting contradictions that will ultimately (perhaps inevitably) lead to its final crisis. Speculating about utopia can only distort and divert what is often referred to, borrowing Engels's nomenclature, as "scientific socialism."[14]

There are problems with both interpretations. The first view – that Marx left a well-specified conception of communism – is questionable because nowhere in his writings is there even an outline, let alone a complete specification, of what an alternative to capitalism might or should look like. It simply isn't there. It cannot be found in the early texts (such as the *Economic and Philosophic Manuscripts of 1844*) or in the *Communist Manifesto* or *Capital* (contrary to what readers expect when they first encounter them), or even in the later writings (such as the *Critique of the Gotha Program*). All readers encounter across the length and breadth of Marx's *oeuvre* are some general, albeit powerful, allusions and phrases: "abolition of private property"; a society that permits one "to hunt in the morning, fish in the afternoon, rear cattle in the evening, criticise after dinner"; "production by freely associated men"; "direct social appropriation"; and, of course, most famously "From each according to his ability, to each according to his needs!"

The only conclusion one can reasonably draw is Marx (and Engels) left behind some general, suggestive concepts and formulations (some of them, in fact, ironic or sarcastic) but certainly no detailed or worked-out conception of the economic and social institutions that might serve as the basis of a communist society. By the same token, we also have to recognize that *all* of Marx's major texts include such evocative phrases. That is, as against the second vision of a purely scientific, analytical Marxism, there *is* a utopian element in Marx's writings – a persistent idea that economic and social life can be different from (and certainly better than) what it is. That's true across the range of texts – from the more philosophical (such as the *1844 Manuscripts*) to the economic (such as the *Grundrisse* and *Capital*), from the political (such as the *Communist Manifesto*) to current events (such as *The Civil War in France*). In every single one of those texts, we find evidence that Marx was not only analyzing what is, but also suggesting what can and should be – informed by and pointing in a utopian direction.

Moreover, as we saw in chapter 3, Marx and Engels expressed their great appreciation for the work of the utopian socialists of the late-eighteenth

---

view, that Marx, Engels, and latter-day Marxian thinkers were inspired by and provided a detailed plan for a postcapitalist society.

[14] The term is from Engels's short book, *Socialism: Utopian and Scientific*, first published in 1880, which was mostly extracted from a longer polemic work, *Anti-Dühring*, published in 1876.

and early-nineteenth centuries. Indeed, Engels commented early on that, in his view, Fourier's project was not utopian enough:

> There is one inconsistency, however, in Fourierism, and a very important one too, and that is, his nonabolition of private property. In his *Phalanstères* or associative establishments, there are rich and poor, capitalists and working men … Thus, after all the beautiful theories of association and free labour; after a good deal of indignant declamation against commerce, selfishness, and competition, we have in practice the old competitive system upon an improved plan, a poor-law bastile [sic] on more liberal principles![15]

Even Engels's short book on "scientific socialism" contains what can only be considered effusive praise for the ideals and ideas of Saint-Simon, Fourier, and especially Owen:

> At this juncture, there came forward as a reformer a manufacturer 29-years-old – a man of almost sublime, childlike simplicity of character, and at the same time one of the few born leaders of men. Robert Owen … In the industrial revolution most of his class saw only chaos and confusion, and the opportunity of fishing in these troubled waters and making large fortunes quickly. He saw in it the opportunity of putting into practice his favorite theory, and so of bringing order out of chaos … Whilst his competitors worked their people 13 or 14 hours a day, in New Lanark the working-day was only 10 and a half hours. When a crisis in cotton stopped work for four months, his workers received their full wages all the time …
>
> In spite of all this, Owen was not content. The existence which he secured for his workers was, in his eyes, still far from being worthy of human beings. (ME, 691)

But we do know, of course, that Marx and Engels did in fact reject "utopian socialism" for their own time, in the middle of the nineteenth century. On what basis? Their criticism of utopian socialism (and Engels's defense of so-called scientific socialism) rests on two main pillars: the role of the working-class and the project of critique.

There should be no doubt, Marx and Engels envisioned the movement beyond capitalism not in terms of realizing some ideal scheme, no matter how well inspired and worked-out, but as the task of the growing working-class. In other words, the idea was that capitalism produces its own grave-diggers. The growth of capitalism – the widening and deepening of capital, in Britain and around the world – was accompanied by the growth of a class that had both the interest and the means to overturn the rule of capital. The working-class, in their view, was in the position of challenging the pretensions of capital to become a universal class, by posing its own universal aspirations – not for everyone to become a laborer but to abolish

[15] "Progress of Social Reform on the Continent," in Karl Marx and Friedrich Engels, *Collected Works*, vol. 3 (New York: International Publishers, 1975), p. 395.

the wages system itself and lay the basis for a different, noncapitalist way of organizing economic and social life.

Coupled with that, Marx and Engels developed a method of critique, which was first announced in Marx's letter to Ruge and then continued through their engagement with mainstream economics (as well as their own previous ideas). That notion of critique – a "ruthless criticism of everything existing" – not "the designing of the future and the proclamation of ready-made solutions for all time," is the utopian aspect of Marxian economics.

Really Existing Socialism

Of course, the Marxian critique of political economy today has to contend with the history of socialist and communist experiments that have been carried out in the name of Marxism. Both the good and the bad, the accomplishments as well as the failures. In the Soviet Union, Marxists have to take into account the radical transformation of the tsarist economy and the reconstruction of the economy after the devastation of World War II as well as the purges, executions, and forced collectivization of the peasantry under Stalin. In the People's Republic of China, they need to consider the elimination of rural poverty through the formation of large agricultural communes as well as the Great Famine caused by the Great Leap Forward. And in Cuba, they have witnessed the independence from US domination, the elimination of illiteracy, and the universal provisioning of high-quality healthcare but also the continued dependence on sugar production and the stumbles in creating more democratic political institutions.

That complicated legacy is a burden on the Marxian political economy. But it is also an opportunity to demonstrate what socialism or communism might mean today, at a different time and in different places.

It is a burden in the sense that contemporary Marxian economists have to accept the fact that such experiments were led and carried out by thinkers, political activists, and movements that both contributed to and were informed by the Marxian critique of political economy. And many aspects of those experiments are difficult, if not impossible, to defend today. Marxian economists also quickly add, however, so are many of the economic and social consequences of capitalism – from dreadful famines and deep economic crises to ongoing regional and world wars and fascist political movements and regimes.

Confronting that history is also an opportunity, in at least two senses: First, it is incumbent upon contemporary Marxian thinkers to utilize their theory to analyze what happened in the cases where socialism or communism has been tried. When they do so, they conclude that the changes that were made (e.g., in the Soviet Union, the People's Republic of

China, and Cuba, not to mention all the other examples) were the products of the particular histories of those countries – and therefore cannot be transferred directly to the world today. In other words, what socialism or communism might look like today – say, in the United States, France, or Chile – would differ radically from the examples we know of in the past. That's in part because the transition from capitalism would occur differently (more likely through social movements and elections than through violent revolutions), and in part because the participants today presume certain values and practices (such as those that make up, or are at least promised by, democratic political institutions) they are not inclined to give up.

Second, there has been a shift in thinking away from grand schemes, toward more partial (if still radical, transformational) changes. Thus, for example, few if any Marxian economists today articulate or defend the idea of an economy that is completely owned and planned by a single, central power. That's not what they mean by socialism or communism. Instead, they envision a plethora of forms of property ownership and economic coordination, which include, but are not limited to, instances of public ownership and planning. They are also interested in community projects, worker-owned cooperatives, local government enterprises, multinational agreements, and so on – ideas and initiatives that combine different kinds of ownership, markets, and planned coordination to lessen inequality and suffering and to create more economic justice (including new ways of producing, appropriating, and distributing the surplus).

Utopia and Critique Today

How, then, do Marxian economists think about utopia and the critique of political economy today? Less important than the alternative economic and social arrangements painstakingly devised by the utopian socialists or the scattered remarks Marx and Engels made about communism in their writings or the particular political demands of Marxist activists, movements, and parties in different places and times, including the history of really existing socialism – what is more important for *our times* is the utopian dimension of the critique of political economy.

The task handed down by the Marxian critique of political economy is to intervene in contemporary debates from the standpoint of a ruthless criticism. We, too, Marxian economists suggest, need to intervene in society's ongoing theoretical and political debates and engage in the process of "waking it from its dream about itself" (ME, 15). Thus, each time society faces the question of how to solve the economic and social problems it creates, the goal of the critique of political economy is to pose reasonable demands, which serve to demonstrate just how unreasonable the current common sense is.

Three examples demonstrate what this might mean.

First, consider the massive unemployment capitalist economies have regularly generated, especially in recent years. Yes, it is an enormous waste of human potential. But, from a Marxian perspective, we also need to see the reserve army of unemployed and underemployed workers as another way in which labor as a whole – employed, unemployed, and underemployed workers alike – is disciplined and punished so that it continues to be forced to have the freedom to sell its ability to work to their employers. Is there any alternative? One possibility, as Modern Monetary economists suggest, is to have governments capture and use a portion of the enormous surplus available in society to directly hire workers who are unemployed, underemployed, or employed in poorly paid or precarious jobs. Alternatively, local and national governments can make it easier for workers themselves to join together to provide jobs for themselves and for their fellow workers in the form of cooperatives and other worker-owned enterprises. In both cases, the goal is not just to provide the decent jobs private employers will not offer, but to change the way decisions are made about how jobs are created – and, ultimately, to decrease the number of hours worked by everyone.

A second example is Social Security. The average household in the United States and most other countries has managed to accumulate very little in the way of retirement savings. There simply isn't enough left over after paying their bills and helping their children get a start in life. That's why Social Security (or any one of a number of other retirement schemes around the world) is so important for them. Many countries thus have a system according to which the generations currently working support the generations that have retired. The schemes to cut future benefits (by lowering the amount paid out or raising the retirement age), or to privatize the entire system, threaten to sever that community relation in favor of reduced benefits and individual investment accounts. The fact is, contemporary society has the ability to *expand* benefits – by increasing payments and lowering the retirement age. All that is necessary to do this is raise the earnings limit on retirement taxes and to increase the share of the surplus corporations pay to make retirement systems like Social Security financially solvent for the foreseeable future.

Finally, a third example: there is much talk these days about inequality – a discussion that has certainly been galvanized by new research (within the academy and by nongovernmental organizations, like Oxfam) and movements (such as Occupy Wall Street). The problem is, the debate within mainstream economics (and political debate more generally) remains confined within narrow limits: between the idea that unequal outcomes are harmless and, in the end, justified by "the market"; and the view that existing inequalities can be ameliorated by more schooling, financial literacy, and tax reform. The debate is thus stuck between market distributions and after-market redistributions. It is not about the way the existing pattern of distributions and redistributions is based on the way the surplus itself is created, appropriated, and captured under capitalism. That, from the perspective of the Marxian critique of political economy, is the root of the problem.

As Marxian economists see the issue, people today need to be encouraged to imagine and enact different solutions to the problems of unemployment, retirement, inequality, and much else – without a predetermined path or ideal scheme. The goal, in other words, is to challenge and disrupt the existing common sense, and thus to open up radically new economic and social possibilities.

Suggested Readings

T. H. Aston and C. H. E. Philpin, eds., *The Brenner Debate: Agrarian Class Structure and Economic Development in Pre-Industrial Europe* (New York: Cambridge University Press, 1985).

Rajesh Bhattacharya and Ian J. Seda-Irizarry, "Primitive Accumulation," in *Routledge Handbook of Marxian Economics*, ed. David M. Brennan, David Kristjanson-Gural, Catherine P. Mulder, and Erik M. Olson, pp. 144–54 (New York: Routledge, 2017).

Anjan Chakrabarti and Anup Dhar, "Transition," in *Routledge Handbook of Marxian Economics*, ed. David M. Brennan, David Kristjanson-Gural, Catherine P. Mulder, and Erik M. Olson, pp. 323–35 (New York: Routledge, 2017).

Gregory Claeys and Lyman Tower Sargent, eds., *The Utopia Reader*, 2nd ed. (New York: New York University Press, 2017).

Maurice Dobb, *Studies in the Development of Capitalism* (New York: International Publishers, 1947).

Thomas Piketty, *Capital in the Twenty-First Century* (Cambridge, MA: Harvard University Press, 2014).

Beverly J. Silver, *Forces of Labor: Workers' Movements and Globalization Since 1870* (Cambridge: Cambridge University Press, 2003).

The Transition from Feudalism to Capitalism, intro. Rodney Hilton (London: Verso, 1985).

Philippe Van Parijs and Yannick Vanderborght, *Basic Income: A Radical Proposal for a Free Society and a Sane Economy* (Cambridge, MA: Harvard University Press, 2017).

Index